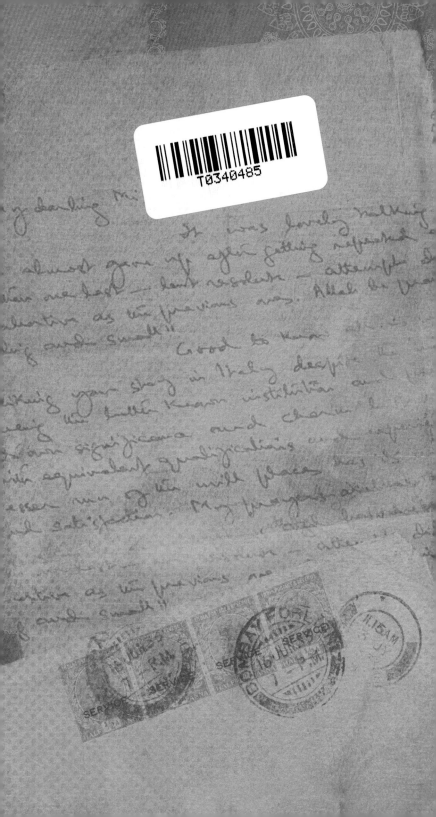

Broken Threads

Broken Threads

*My Family from Empire to
Independence*

MISHAL HUSAIN

4th ESTATE · *London*

An imprint of HarperCollins*Publishers*
1 London Bridge Street
London SE1 9GF

www.4thestate.co.uk

HarperCollins*Publishers*
Macken House,
39/40 Mayor Street Upper,
Dublin 1, DO1 C9W8, Ireland

First published in Great Britain in 2024 by 4th Estate

4

Book design by Richard Marston

A catalogue record for this book is available from the British Library

ISBN 978-0-00-853168-3 (Hardback)
ISBN 978-0-00-853169-0 (Trade Paperback)

Set in Garamond Premier

Printed and bound in the UK using 100% renewable electricity at
CPI Group (UK) Ltd

This book contains FSC™ certified paper and other controlled
sources to ensure responsible forest management.

For more information visit: www.harpercollins.co.uk/green

For my mother Shama, who kept the past alive

Freedom's Morning
August 1947

This stained daybreak, this morning after a pain-filled night
This is surely not the dawn for which we waited
For which we set out, with desire in our hearts
Convinced we would reach our destination

Somewhere in the heavens is the stars' final resting place
Somewhere is the place where the night tide washes in
An anchor for the ship of heartache

Faiz Ahmed Faiz (1911–84)
Part of the poem 'Subh-e-Azadi',
translated from the original Urdu

CONTENTS

The Family

Syed Shahid Hamid, born in Lucknow in 1911. Educated at Aligarh Muslim University and Sandhurst and commissioned into the Indian Army in 1934. Died in Rawalpindi in 1993.

Tahirah Butt, born in Aligarh in 1920. Educated at Lady Hardinge Medical College in Delhi and married Shahid in 1940. Died in Islamabad in 2011.

Mumtaz Husain, born in Multan in 1920. Educated at King Edward Medical College in Lahore and joined the Medical Service of the Indian Army in 1943. Died in Karachi in 2007.

Mary Quinn, born in Narsipatnam, in south India, in 1922. Trained as a nurse at Mayo Hospital, Lahore, before marrying Mumtaz in 1942. Died in London in 1984.

Shahid and Tahirah's children: Hassan, Shahnaz, **Shama** (my mother) and Ali.

Mumtaz and Mary's children: **Imtiaz** (my father, known as Tazi), Ejaz, Niaz, Saleem and Arshad.

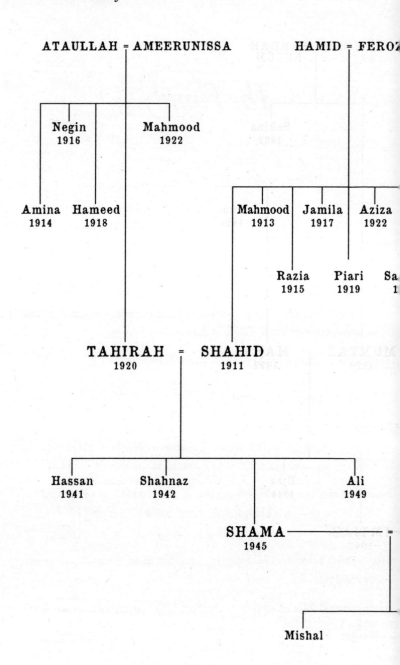

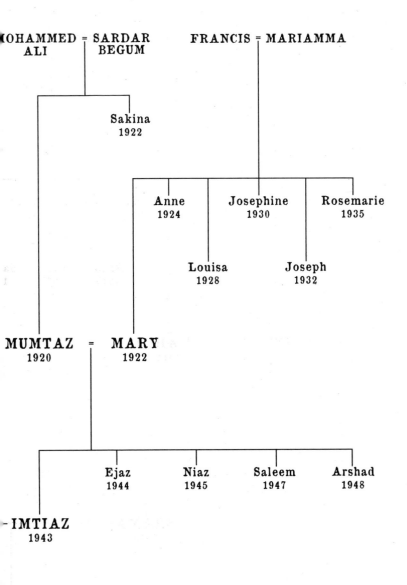

Other Characters

Syed Ahmad Khan, Muslim intellectual who lived through the 1857 Indian Mutiny and then founded a college at Aligarh, near Delhi, dedicating the rest of his life to improving his community's prospects through education. Knighted in 1888.

Syed Ross Masood, his grandson. Studied at Aligarh and Oxford and later led his grandfather's college after it became Aligarh Muslim University. Inspired E. M. Forster's *A Passage to India*.

Mohammed Iqbal, poet and philosopher, known in Pakistan as 'Allama' Iqbal, the great scholar. Regarded as a founding father because of a 1930 speech calling for the formation of a single 'North-West Indian Muslim State'. Died in 1938.

Mohammed Ali Jauhar and Shaukat Ali Jauhar, brothers who led the 'Khilafat' movement in India during and after the First World War, campaigning to preserve the authority of the Turkish Sultan as Caliph and leader of Muslims around the world.

Mohandas Karamchand Gandhi, Hindu lawyer turned activist who developed campaigns of non-violent resistance and civil disobedience in South Africa and then in India from 1915.

A leader of the Indian National Congress political party, he was assassinated by a Hindu extremist in 1948.

Mohammed Ali Jinnah, Muslim lawyer turned politician who was for a time involved with both Congress and the Muslim League party. Sought to secure rights for India's minority Muslims and then became the founder of Pakistan in 1947. Died in Karachi in 1948.

Fatima Jinnah, his sister and close companion. Worked to safeguard his legacy and ideals after his death and ran for President of Pakistan in 1965, two years before her death.

Liaquat Ali Khan, Muslim League politician and Pakistan's first Prime Minister. Assassinated in 1951.

Shaista Suhrawardy Ikramullah, member of the Muslim League from 1940. Became one of Pakistan's first female parliamentarians and represented the country at the United Nations.

Jawaharlal Nehru, Cambridge-educated son of a prominent Hindu lawyer. Joined Congress and became a key leader of the party during and after the Second World War. Independent India's first Prime Minister from 1947 until his death in 1964.

Abul Kalam Azad, prominent Muslim member of Congress and close associate of Gandhi. Became a minister in India after independence.

Stafford Cripps, member of the Churchill and Attlee governments who became involved in missions to India in 1942 and 1946, attempting to forge agreements on self-rule.

Claude Auchinleck, last Commander-in-Chief of the pre-independence Indian Army. Led Allied forces in North Africa in the Second World War, halting Rommel's advance in Egypt in 1942. Created a field marshal in 1946. Died in Morocco in 1981.

William Slim, British general who oversaw the retreat from Burma in 1942 and then led the forces which recaptured it from Japan in 1945.

Archibald Wavell, Commander-in-Chief, India, 1941–43 and then Viceroy. In 1945 he began the talks with Indian politicians which led to the formation of a pre-independence interim government. Sacked in favour of Mountbatten in 1947.

Louis Mountbatten, Viceroy from March 1947. Ten weeks later he announced the partition plan which was carried out that August. Became independent India's first Governor-General. Assassinated by the IRA in 1979.

Cyril Radcliffe, barrister, arrived in Delhi in July 1947 tasked with drawing the India–Pakistan border through the provinces of Punjab in the west and Bengal in the east.

Christopher Beaumont, former Indian Civil Service officer, appointed to assist Radcliffe. Lived as well as worked alongside him in Delhi in the summer of 1947.

Winston Churchill and **Clement Attlee**, British political leaders and prime ministers.

Names, Places and Language

Much of this story occurs before 1947, the year India gained independence and Pakistan was born, and place names have been left as they were at the time: Bombay rather than Mumbai, Calcutta rather than Kolkata, Allahabad rather than Prayagraj, and so on.

One shorthand reference remains the same: the area of north India where my mother's family came from continues to be known by the initials UP. In my grandparents' day it stood for 'United Provinces', whereas today it is the Indian state of Uttar Pradesh.

As far as people's names are concerned, Muslim families in South Asia would traditionally choose one or two given names for their child. Surnames did not exist and were not necessary in close-knit communities where everyone knew how people were related by blood or marriage. Thus my paternal grandfather was called 'Mumtaz Husain' because his parents liked these two names; amid the influence of British norms in the colonial era, 'Husain' then became the surname of his children and grandchildren.

My maternal grandfather was given the first name 'Shahid', which he used alongside 'Hamid', his father's first name. 'Hamid' then became the surname of my mother's family.

Many other sources of surnames were possible: 'Khan' signified descent from the Pathans (or Pashtuns) who came from the north-west and migrated to many parts of India. Clan names such as 'Chaudhry' might also be used, as could terms like 'Dehlvi', meaning a person from Delhi.

Girls were given first names, often used with the suffixes 'Bibi' or 'Begum', respectful terms for woman or lady.

'Syed' or 'Syeda' are prefixes for men and women who can trace their ancestry to the Prophet Muhammad. My grandfather Shahid was a Syed.

On language, I have often referred to Urdu words or phrases. Urdu developed in the north of India over many centuries and includes elements of Hindi, Persian, Arabic and Turkish. It was the native tongue of my maternal grandparents Shahid and Tahirah and is today the national language of Pakistan. Urdu and Hindi speakers can converse together with ease, given the many words common to both. On my father's side, my grandmother Mary grew up in the south of India speaking English and Telugu, while my grandfather Mumtaz's mother tongue was Multani (also known as Saraiki). He then acquired Urdu and English, and gained some proficiency in Punjabi after studying in Lahore.

The Wedding Present

When my mother's parents married in the north of India in May 1940 the bridegroom's five younger sisters were each given a sari to wear at the wedding, a gift from their own parents. It was a particularly happy family occasion, as they had all worried for some time that, at twenty-eight, my grandfather Shahid was pushing the boundaries of acceptable marriageable age. When the war began in 1939, they had a new reason to fret: as a serving soldier, he could be deployed abroad at any time. A wife and family of his own, they reasoned, would give him more to live for when faced with the perils of battle.

The saris were made of a heavy silk brocade in shades of beige and gold, embossed with repeating patterns and flecked with threads that shimmered when they caught the light. There is no photograph of the sisters, my great-aunts, wearing them but six decades later a fragment of one made its way to me in London, as a present for my own wedding. It had come from the sari given to Jamila, one of the five, and then inherited by her daughter Shahmeen. While most of the fabric had frayed badly over the years the embroidered border, the most robust part, was relatively intact, and Shahmeen had used it to edge a plain, woollen, sand-coloured shawl. This was her gift to me, a tangible link to a previous family wedding and to the people who connected us both.

I marvelled then – and now – that any part of the original sari had survived the disruption and dislocation of 1947, a seismic year in South Asia and one that forever changed the lives of my parents as young children. Our family story spans India, Pakistan and Britain, and the sari would have been in Lucknow, in India, when Shahid's family made a panicked departure for Pakistan. Shahmeen was then a six-year-old, in the care of her grandmother as her own mother had died a few months before, and I knew the entire household had packed and moved quickly at a time of insecurity. They took only the few possessions that could be easily transported by train and ship, but someone had thought to pack this particular sari and safeguard it for Shahmeen to have one day. Given the circumstances, she may have had little else that had once belonged to her mother.

Decades later I had the opportunity to visit India myself for the first time, to front a week of BBC News coverage from Delhi. The visa involved extra paperwork once I had ticked the box declaring I had relatives who had migrated to Pakistan, and the process was longer than for my colleagues. But the resulting trip was deeply resonant. I soaked up the atmosphere of a great city loved by my grandparents, and lost to them after 1947; I used my Urdu, was replied to in Hindi, and found common understandings as well as language everywhere I went.

After that my family story crept into the edges of my broadcast work on a few occasions: in 2007 when I reported from Pakistan on the sixtieth anniversary of independence; in 2009 when I travelled across India to make a BBC series on Mahatma Gandhi; and in 2020 for a piece about the Indian Army in the Second World War. I knew that the threads of our story lay far more in India than in present-day Pakistan because three of my four grandparents were born on that side of the border; the searing legacy of 1947 meant that for the rest of their lives they had little contact with the people and places of their youth.

I came at the story from a different perspective, born in England in the 1970s to a father who had come to train as a surgeon in the NHS and a mother who had joined him after their marriage. Both imagined they would return to Pakistan after a few years, but when I was two they moved to the Middle East and my brother Haider and I grew up in the United Arab Emirates and Saudi Arabia. At boarding school in the UK I became conscious of the deep roots all my English friends seemed to have, embedded into a network of similar families and closely attached to places and homes that went back generations. I had no such connection to the fabric of the land: I came and went from England, to parents who were themselves part of an expatriate community, almost as if I had no history of my own.

My one constant point of reference in those years was the home of my mother Shama's parents, in Rawalpindi in the north of Pakistan. Today, it is almost a suburb of the capital Islamabad, but my early memories date from the period before that city was built. The house had odd-shaped corners and split levels, both inside and in the garden, and an underground study where my grandfather Shahid would vanish to write books. Upstairs, one room had a floor-to-ceiling bookcase which swung out to reveal the secret cupboard where my grandmother Tahirah stored jewellery and silver. To be allowed to accompany her in and have a peek while she sorted things out was my great treat – and also a source of terror when it was followed by nightmares about the heavy door slamming shut, trapping me in the darkness, alone.

In truth, it was a house where people were rarely alone, which was part of its charm. There was a near-constant buzz of activity: uncles, aunts and cousins coming and going, gathering for the meals that happened strictly at set times, and each sharing bits of news and information about their day. Haider and I were only ever there in our summer holidays, when lunch would be followed by the afternoon siesta, a deep stillness descending on the house until the squeak of the tea-trolley wheels at 4. At night, Tahirah, whom we grandchildren called 'Achi Ammi' – the good mother – would place saucers of tiny white flowers by our bedsides, spindly blooms of star-shaped *motia*, a local jasmine, which would perfume the entire room. On those holidays there was always a moment of drama, when the sight of black clouds on the horizon signalled that the monsoon was rolling in. The rain would briefly cool the air before the heat resumed, this time humid rather than dry, but there was something soothing in the way the monsoon made the garden gleam with a suddenly fresher, almost neon, shade of green.

Both house and garden are long gone now, built over after they were sold in the 1990s. But even in the years when they seemed immovable and everlasting, I knew that the equivalent places of Shahid and Tahirah's own youth were lost to them, inaccessible across the India–Pakistan border. My grandmother was wistful about this at times. 'You never saw what we left behind,' she said to me on more than one occasion, and I knew she meant left behind in India. Shahid, though, was stoic. 'Guria,' he would say gently, using her nickname, which meant doll. 'No regrets.'

❧❧❧

My father's parents Mumtaz and Mary had a life of different complexities. They had married across ethnic and religious lines, as he was a Muslim from the province of Punjab, on the territory of present-day Pakistan, and she was a Catholic from the south-east of India. Knowing the importance of faith in both their lives, I asked him once how that worked. 'We understood each other perfectly,' he said, looking puzzled. 'It would have been much more difficult if one of us had had no religion.'

Still, I wondered about Mary. She died when I was eleven, so I never had the chance to ask for her version of their life together, but the key dates told their own story. When they married in 1942 their families were poles apart in language and culture as well as faith, but they did at least belong to the same country. Five years later, when independence took place, Mary had her life with husband and children on one side of the border while her mother and siblings lived more than a thousand miles away on the other. And, as a military wife, travelling to see them was a politically tricky undertaking as well as an expensive one.

One day, I thought, I will go to the places in India where Mary, Shahid and Tahirah grew up, walk the streets that they knew and try to understand more of the environments that shaped them. But when I dipped into this in 2014 while covering the Indian elections, I found that Tahirah's childhood home had just been demolished. I thought the same might well be true of key places in Shahid's and Mary's lives – assuming I could even find them, given how population growth and urbanisation have changed South Asia's landscapes and neighbourhoods.

I did have sources though, written ones as well as family memories, and as I thought about my grandparents' lives I realised that their generation were eyewitnesses to a great global shift, as the age of empire made way for the nation state. I knew some basic details: both couples had made the journey to Pakistan in difficult circumstances in 1947, and Shahid had observed the politics of pre-partition Delhi up close, as an aide to the last Chief of the British-era Indian Army. It was a time, he said, of some remarkable leadership and also of 'small men playing with the destiny of millions'. It was also a period in which women's lives were changing and thus my two grandmothers' experiences and opportunities were markedly different from those of their own mothers.

One photograph I found seemed to encapsulate that moment of transition and how it came amid a post-war camaraderie that was starting to cut across barriers of race, religion and rank. It was taken in the hill station of Simla in July 1947, where a group of family and friends had gathered for a child's party. It was the fifth birthday of my aunt Shahnaz, who is in the foreground of the picture with a white ribbon in her hair, looking up at my mother, in Tahirah's arms. I gazed at the scene in the knowledge that, within weeks, the group standing on the hilltop would be pulled in different directions: the British generals battling to contain outbreaks of devastating violence

and the young Hindu officer standing next to Tahirah shepherding her and the children to safety.

Shahid had written about this period, and I knew there was an account of my father's family's experiences too, because my other grandfather had spent time on his own, unpublished, memoir. When Mumtaz died, my uncle retrieved the text from his computer and shared it with us, but I had only ever skimmed through part of it. As I looked at it properly, I saw that it covered more than thirty years of his life, and I felt ashamed to see that, as he wrote, he wondered if any of us were even interested. 'There must be an inner hope that it will be worthwhile for anyone who comes across it, has the time to spare and the desire to – at least – glance over it,' he said. 'Otherwise why go through the exercise at all?'

He was writing in the years after he had lost Mary to cancer, when she was only sixty-two. It was partly because of her that he pressed on, concluding that this was a way 'to pay a small tribute to a person who stood by me through a turbulent life like a rock of stability and faith'. It would also, he thought, mitigate his 'abysmal loneliness', and he hoped that detailing his ancestry would be a resource for his children, grandchildren and future great-grandchildren, 'that they might know what made their existence possible'.

I knew then that my grandfathers had left me enough to get started, but comparable material on Tahirah and Mary would be more difficult, as is so often the case with records and sources on women. They had been first and foremost wives and mothers, and I remembered their letter-writing: the best hope had to be that some correspondence had survived. Of Mary I had only a few lines in a childhood birthday card and an inscription in a book given as a present, but Tahirah had written to me throughout my years at boarding school and university and I had bundles of these letters, tied up with string, stored in a cupboard. When I took them out and looked at them again, I remembered they were not always easy to decipher: her flowing handwriting was small, the Biro was sometimes smudged, and the lines were close together, covering every available inch of the lightweight airmail writing paper. There was, however, a familiar pattern, as each letter began with an expression of love, and how much she was looking forward to the next reunion, in England or Pakistan. Beyond that she wrote about the everyday: who was coming and going from the house and what was growing in the garden.

These letters would not give me what I sought, but within a separate cache preserved by my mother I discovered one sheet of paper that looked different. Here, rather than addressing a person, Tahirah had begun with a quotation. 'Reality is never new, but we are new to reality', she had written, ascribing the words to the architect Frank Lloyd Wright and following them with a paragraph about herself and what she saw as the contradictions of her life. There was her attachment to home, hearth and loved ones – 'one life seems too brief a span to enjoy them to my heart's content', she wrote. 'The other side of the picture is my mental involvement and suffering at the political turmoil around which my generation seems fated to live. Undoubtedly some nations that also achieved independence in the recent past have lived through much worse, and in comparison may consider this a Utopia, but that is poor consolation.'

There was no date, but from the events she went on to describe I could place her words in the late 1980s, as Pakistan moved from military dictatorship to an era when corruption and democratic politics went hand in hand. 'As a young army officer's wife I went through the Second World War,' she said. 'We had seen the emergence of Hitler, and it was nothing short of a miracle to witness his fall. The emergence of a personality like Gorbachev, endeavouring to put an end to Russian expansionism, is yet another miracle which may bring endless peace to mankind. And so one lives in the hope that to every action there is a reaction.'

It was, to my delight, intended to be the start of a memoir. 'For some years now I have felt the urge to put my reactions to so much that happens around me on paper,' Tahirah said. 'In years to come it may become a comprehensive and objective account of events that have shaped our destiny.' She planned to look right back, to periods she had lived through but whose significance she had been unable to appreciate at the time. 'Going back to when the concept of Pakistan had been accepted, a separate Muslim state to be carved out of India, I was politically not mature enough to realise the gravity of events taking place around me,' she wrote.

For several more paragraphs she continued, in longhand, with some crossings out as she rethought and reworked phrases before she copied out a neater version on a second sheet of paper. Then the account petered out: whether she was interrupted too often, lost heart or found it too emotional to look back, I will never know. But it meant that I was left with a tantalising fragment rather than the complete story I craved.

❦

It was my mother who came to the rescue when she told me she had found something else: two cassette tapes labelled 'Ama [Mother] talking' in her handwriting. She had a vague memory of recording

Tahirah, but at first we couldn't even check what was on the tapes: neither of us owned a cassette player anymore. Once we found one I was able to put in the first tape and press play and, sure enough, there was my grandmother's voice, heard for the first time in years.

She was speaking in 1993, I realised, not long after Shahid's death, and the content turned out to be an audio letter that I had carried back to my mother after a trip to Rawalpindi. 'Writing has been a bit tedious so I thought I would talk to you instead,' she said to Shama. 'Let me tell you the greatest thing that's happened to me in the last few months is your little daughter accompanying me to Pakistan. It's been such unmitigated and undiluted joy. I'm happy she's going back to you. Don't worry about me little one, I'm sure I'm going to be all right. I know I have your love, each one of you. I'm as well surrounded as one could possibly be, with your brothers and sister around me.'

It was, to my delight, a version of what she had intended in the fragment of written memoir I found. This time, as with my grandfather Mumtaz, the loss of a life partner was spurring her forward. 'I keep thinking to myself, what can I do to make him come to life again?' she said of Shahid. 'I know what it is: I have to pay a debt of honour and write something for him. Because that is what he wished me to do all the time. I can hear him say, "Writing comes so much easier to you than it does to me. You owe it to your children, you owe it to your country, to write." And now that he is not with us, I feel that maybe I can.'

She spoke mostly in English, interspersed with occasional bursts of Urdu, especially as she related her early years in the university town of Aligarh. 'I feel that before Pakistan came into being we had a complete life,' she said. 'Countries have their problems, whether they're ruled by others or by people that actually belong, and nothing is perfect. All I know is that the life I had before the partition of India was as beautiful and as rich as it was afterwards.'

Some of this she went on to detail, including her student days in Delhi, her wartime experience while Shahid was serving in Burma, and her post-1947 worries about the ageing parents who remained in India and the cross-border friendships that were impossible to maintain. 'In certain ways people of my generation were not complete for a long time,' she said. 'We were used to a pattern of life, friends that we had made and kept despite prejudices of life, like religion. But these things don't really matter, the human values do.'

It was, again, an incomplete record but I knew as I listened that I could fill in the gaps with my own journey into the past, putting what felt like a jigsaw of the family story together. 'We said goodbye to Delhi,' my grandfather Mumtaz wrote of August 1947. 'And, although I did not know it then, also to the parts of India where I had spent most of my service life and was not destined to return to, ever.' It was as though a crucial thread in all of their lives was broken that year, as freedom came alongside separation. The break was more definitive than they could imagine at the time, and its legacy continues today in the lack of contact between most citizens of India and Pakistan. But my grandparents' story is one of Britain, too, as their lives were directly affected by choices made in London about how to govern, and then cast off, the colonies. These were the threads I picked up, to set individual lives against the backdrop of their times.

PART ONE

Citizens of Empire

I

Mary

Mary was the only one of my four grandparents who was not a Muslim and whose existence was part of a very specific coming together of Europe and India: her mother Mariamma was born a Hindu and her father Francis Quinn was a Catholic Irishman.

The first Europeans arrived in India at the dawn of the sixteenth century, shortly before the establishment of the Mughals, a Muslim dynasty that would be the dominant power for the next two hundred years. The first of these emperors was Babur, a near contemporary of Henry VIII, and between them the Mughals were responsible for most of the best-known monuments of India and Pakistan, from the Taj Mahal to the Lahore Fort. Their reach spread through battle and alliance and it is because of them that we have the English word 'mogul', signifying a person of great power.

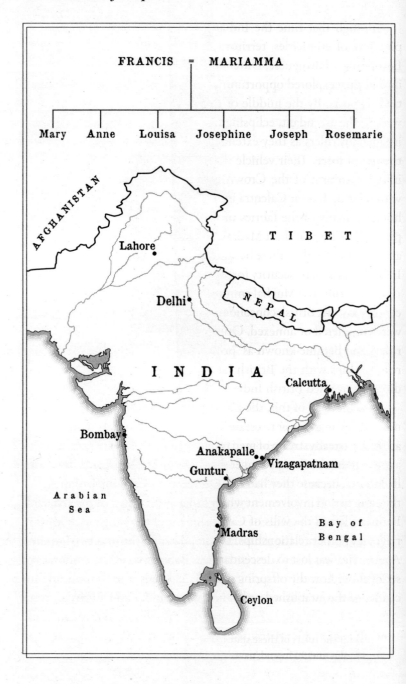

Through that time the Indian subcontinent remained a complex mix of ethnicities, territories and local rulers, a picture that Europeans – Portuguese, Dutch, French and British traders – fitted into as they explored opportunities in spices and textiles and set up trading posts. By the middle of the eighteenth century the British were in the ascendant, eclipsing not only other Europeans but also indigenous rulers as they extended their power through trade and the use of force. Their vehicle was the East India Company – not, initially, an arm of the Crown but a highly profitable enterprise with its main base at Calcutta in Bengal, the eastern region that was home to many of the fabrics most prized in Europe. It also had a presence further south, at Madras, and on the opposite western coast, at Bombay. Together, these became the three 'presidencies' of British India, backed up by security forces that were, in effect, a private army.

By this time the Mughal empire had declined, and the nineteenth century saw the British consolidate their presence, as more territories were conquered or annexed. Other areas remained under their own rulers and became known as 'princely states', developing their own relationships with the British Crown and existing in parallel with directly governed British India.*

To achieve all of this, the East India Company had skilfully harnessed local manpower to create its fighting forces, but its success also attracted a steady stream of men from Britain and Ireland, keen to play a role. Often, they were younger sons seeking a fortune or even a basic livelihood, because they had no hope of a family inheritance, and in the early period involvement with Indian women was commonplace. Bequests left in the wills of Company men reveal cross-racial marriages and other relationships, but later, British sentiment changed. As America was lost to descendants of the original settlers, concerns set in about how the offspring of mixed relationships in India might challenge the established order. New rules were introduced, barring

---

*Titles for the rulers of these states varied by religion, usually 'maharaja' for Hindus and Sikhs and 'nawab' for Muslims.

anyone without European parentage on both sides from almost all Company jobs.[1]

Still, children had been born and would continue to be born, growing into what became known – and recognised in the 1911 Indian census – as the Anglo-Indian community, people of mixed descent who might previously have been called Eurasian or 'country-born'. By 1935, they were defined in law as natives of India whose fathers or other male ancestors were, or had been, European, and often those origins were evident in French or Portuguese surnames as well as British or Irish ones. The other key marker was faith: Anglo-Indians were usually Catholic or Anglican, but the fact that this stemmed from heritage rather than conversion made them different to other Indian Christians.

They were not, however, regarded as equals by those in India who were fully white. Anglo-Indians' socio-economic status was lower, they experienced prejudice, and sometimes life chances were dictated by the shade of a skintone: those with paler complexions and greater ability to 'pass' as European gained opportunities denied to others.[2]

❈❈❈

It was the faith aspect of my grandmother Mary's heritage that was most apparent to me as a child, when she and Mumtaz were living in Saudi Arabia at the same time as we were in the UAE. Mumtaz was working for the World Health Organisation, and when they came to visit us Mary would always take the opportunity to go to Mass; unlike Saudi Arabia, which banned non-Islamic religious worship, the Emirates had churches. With her, we always spoke in English rather than Urdu, a language which remained difficult for her despite many years living in Pakistan, and I knew she came from a town in India which was also my father's birthplace. In his Pakistani passport it was noted as 'Anakapalle (India)', and I learned that it was pronounced *Anna-capa-lee*, the syllables sounding exotic and unusual compared to the place names I knew.

Mary had sisters who were by then living in England, and from the times I met my great-aunts, and from photographs, I could see, too, the differences between her and them. It was in their dress: she wore saris or long *kurta* tunics over trousers, while they wore skirts and seemed more Westernised. The obvious place to start tracing their story, I thought, was to establish how their father Francis had come to be in India by the time that Mary, the eldest child, was born in 1922. I knew that my father had been curious about this and had begun exploring his ancestry towards the end of his life, but I also had access to a precious, living, resource. Uniquely among my grandparents, Mary had a sibling who was still alive when I began my research: my great-aunt Anne, then aged ninety-six and living in Oldham, Lancashire.

'I'll tell you whatever you would like to know, my darling,' she said when I went to see her in the house she had occupied for the previous sixty years and where she and her husband Michael had brought up their sons. I was lucky that her knowledge of Mary was not restricted to childhood: she had also lived with my grandparents in Pakistan after independence and met Michael there. After Mary died in 1984 both Anne and Michael remained close to Mumtaz, and it was through her that I came to a startling realisation: the Quinn children's life chances would have been bleak but for something that happened in 1924, when Mary was two years old.

Sitting with Anne in her front room in Oldham, more aspects of Mary came back to me: they had the same accent, intonation and expressions, and even the shape of Anne's fingers was as I remembered my grandmother's. She was, by then, widowed and living alone, but maintaining a precise and admirable routine, taking care with her meals and managing her way up and down the stairs of the house.

She told me straight away that her father had not been the one to make the journey from Ireland: Francis had been born in India, and she thought it was *his* father who had migrated. From this I could immediately place the Quinn arrival in India in the nineteenth rather than the twentieth century, which made sense, given Irish emigration in the face of famine and poverty. India, I discovered, had been a significant destination once the East India Company set up soldier-recruiting depots in Ireland. By 1857, more than half of its white soldiers in India were Irish.[3]

That particular year, 1857, is a significant one in the modern history of South Asia, as a mutiny – often called a war of independence in India and Pakistan – took place among some of the Company's 'native' troops. Anne told me that her Quinn grandfather was a medical officer and came to India in that period, though she was not certain of dates and did not have old passports or other documents that might help me. But during our first conversation she suddenly asked if I wanted to see her 'Life Story', and took from her bookshelf a spiral-bound document compiled by an Age UK volunteer some years before. 'I was born on the 28th July 1925 in a little town called Guntur in south India,' it began, and, for me, it proved to be an invaluable resource. I kept it on my lap as we talked, flicking through the pages and using the content to nudge her from one point to another.

It was here that I saw for the first time a picture of my great-grandparents Francis and Mariamma, taken on their wedding day. I gazed at it for some time, noticing at once the difference in their ages: a man past midlife with a much younger woman, barely coming up to his shoulder in height, their clothing and faces telling a story of East and West. 'Mummy was about 5 foot tall and Daddy was 6 foot,' Anne had written underneath the image and I noticed what looked like a cigarette in Francis's left hand and Mariamma combining her sari with elements of European bridal style: a bouquet and a floral headpiece.

They had met, according to the text, because Francis's father Major Thomas Quinn was personal physician to the Maharaja of a princely state and Mariamma was a relative of that ruler. But when I asked Anne about her parents, a different version emerged. Francis

was a widower, she said, with two teenage children, Bobby and Kitty. 'They were living quite happily, close to the sea,' she told me. 'Daddy had a good job.' By then the rule of the East India Company had evolved into the British Empire and Francis was employed as a tax and licensing inspector in the Salt and Abkari Department, meaning he was responsible for alcohol, drugs and the hated taxation of salt, an essential food ingredient.* Their home was near

*In 1930 salt tax sparked one of Gandhi's major campaigns, and he led a protest march against it.

Madras and Anne told me Bobby and Kitty often went to the beach, which was where they met and became friends with Mariamma, a Hindu girl of about their age.

I thought Anne might have misremembered and I asked about the version of events in the 'Life Story': didn't Francis and Mariamma have a mutual connection to a maharaja? 'So they said,' Anne replied slowly, but it was not the truth. 'I think Daddy was a naughty man and she got pregnant by him. She was only a young woman, you see. And he kept her in the house with his children.' The marriage came later, she said, only after Mary was born, and that too only after the local Catholic priest remonstrated with Francis. 'Mr Quinn, you are a sinner,' he said. 'You've got a woman there and you've given her a baby. You've got to marry her.'

This was quite a revelation, and I asked Anne how she could be sure of it. 'Mummy told me,' she replied. 'I asked her years later, and

this is what she said.' We looked together at another photograph, this time of Mariamma with baby Mary, and she said that Francis seeing his own likeness in the child helped persuade him. 'Mary was very fair-skinned,' Anne said. 'She had blue eyes, nothing like my mother.' Francis was smitten and agreed with the priest that the baby should be baptised and that he should marry Mariamma. 'He went back to church and was blessed by the Bishop and became a good Catholic,' Anne said. 'Whereas before, he wasn't really.'

❦

I now had two versions of the Quinn story from Anne's written and oral accounts, and wondered if official records might help. I knew my grandmother's birthday from the headstone of her grave in London – 9 April 1922 – and I discovered that registers relating to the British in India are in the old India Office collections in the British Library. In the Asian & African Studies Reading Room I began to leaf through leather-bound volumes arranged according to the three presidencies of British India, able to focus on Madras, the Quinns' home region. In those times, it was baptisms rather than births which tended to be registered, but I found no record for a Mary Quinn in April 1922, or any time that year, only an Anne Quinn baptised in 1925, as well as an Ann Quinn the year before.

The librarians told me there was no guarantee records were complete, as some registers had not survived or had not been trans-ferred to London at independence, but one was kind enough to do some digging on my behalf. He emailed me back with details of what I became certain were Francis's two marriages. The first was in 1903, to Mary Woods Scawen, producing two children, Charles and Mary Catherine, baptised in 1904 and 1905. These could well be the full names of Bobby and Kitty, I thought, given that the dates would make them teenagers in the early 1920s. Then, a second marriage to Mariamma Myalapalla was registered in August 1924, and the librar-ian had spotted that this couple were also recorded as the parents of the 'Ann Quinn' baptised that same year. My great-aunt spelled her name 'Anne' and said she was born in 1925, so I had assumed this 'Ann' was a different person, but the full version of the entries was clear: our Anne was born in July 1924, not 1925, and her parents' marriage had taken place when she was two weeks old.

Of Mary there remained no official trace but I was sure her birth had been in 1922: it fitted with the age gap between her and Anne. It might be that she was never baptised, though I found that hard to imagine, and thought it more likely that that particular record had been lost. In broad terms, the registers backed up what Anne had told me: Francis did not marry Mariamma until after she had given birth to his child, or in fact, as I discovered, to two children.

When I saw Anne next I did not dwell on the fact that she was a year older than she thought, but we did talk about her childhood memories of other cross-racial relationships. Because of their faith Catholic men were more likely than others to marry the Indian women in their lives, she told me, but it was not a given. 'We had a neighbour, Mr Wright, who had a little house in the next compound to us and an Indian lady he kept there,' she said. 'He never married her.' Had Francis acted the same way, the family would have been destitute when he died a few years later, as Mariamma would have been unable to claim his property or his pension.

❧❦❧

On Anne's living-room wall in Oldham I saw a framed photograph recording another moment in her early life, when she and Mary attended a party to mark Francis's retirement from government service, in 1928. He would have been fifty-five and he and Mariamma had a third child, Louisa, that same year, followed by Josephine in 1930, Joseph in 1932 and finally Rosemarie at the beginning of 1935. He built a home for them all near the town of Anakapalle, and bought some land further inland, where he began farming as a way of supplementing his pension income. A second home, a small cottage, was built on the farm, and the family were all staying there together in the summer of 1935, when tragedy struck.

Anne was then eleven and Mary thirteen, and they were home from their convent boarding school for the holidays. It was the month of June and because of the heat the family slept outside on a *pindaal* or raised platform, set a little away from the cottage. It had a simple wooden frame, with open sides and coconut palm leaves draped over the top, which were kept damp so that any gust of air became cooler as it passed through. That evening seven beds were laid out for Francis, Mariamma and the five older children, as well as the cradle used for six-month-old Rosie. 'I don't know why it was on the ground,' Anne told me regretfully. 'Usually it was hung on long iron chains from the top of the verandah, and the baby could be rocked in it that way.' She remembered seeing her mother sitting down, feeding Rosie, while Francis tried to get three-year-old Joe into bed. 'Joe ran between the two beds where the cradle was,' she said. 'Daddy was chasing him and tripped and fell. And one of the big wooden knobs of the cradle hit him in his chest.'

Joe ran off in fright but the older children tried to help their father. 'Mary and I went to Daddy,' Anne said. 'I knew he had hurt himself badly because – I will never forget it – he didn't cry out. He couldn't breathe, and we didn't know what was wrong with him.' They tried to get him up off the floor, but his size and weight made it difficult. 'He was a very big man, over six foot,' she said. 'Mary and Mummy and I, it took all three of us to get him into a chair, like a deckchair. And that was where he stayed, in a kind of camp chair, all night, all the next day and until the morning of the day after that.'

There seems to have been little effort to call for a doctor. Perhaps there were none nearby, or Mariamma thought Francis would get his breath back as he rested, and it was not an injury that involved blood, at least not visibly. But there was to be no recovery; the fall had broken Francis's ribs and one had punctured his lung. I tried to imagine the thirty-six hours he spent in that chair, struggling amid the heat, with Mariamma and the children looking on, unaware that he was in mortal danger.

It was a Catholic priest called Father Dyas who intervened when he came by unannounced. 'He used to go around the area and into the villages, to try and get people to become Catholics,' Anne told me. 'He very rarely came to our house, because of course we were already Catholics. But suddenly we saw him coming up the garden path.' Seeing Francis slumped on the *pindaal*, he called out: 'Mr Quinn, what are you doing there in that chair?' It was everyone else who responded, Anne said, and as the details came flooding out Father Dyas took charge. 'He saw that Daddy was very, very ill,' she remembered, and a taxi was ordered to take Francis to a nearby convent of nursing sisters. 'Leave it to me, Mrs Quinn,' he said as Francis was carried off. 'The nuns will sort it out.'

Anne thought Francis was alive for another few days, for she remembered her mother going to visit him and taking the baby with her. But the nuns could not save him. 'If he had gone to the big hospital in Vizagapatnam, which was twenty miles away, he might have survived,' she said, sadly. 'They would have known how to look after him.' It seems that Mariamma was with him at the end, because Anne remembers her returning one day and breaking the news to the children. 'She came home and, honestly, it was just terrible, absolute hell,' she told me. 'I was crying. Mary was crying. Louisa and Josephine were too young. And Mummy was terribly upset. I'll never forget that night, it was just awful.'

Francis's body was brought back to Gandhavarum and he was buried there, on his land. Word spread, including to the girls' school, where he had been a benefactor as well as a parent, and not long after the burial the family saw two of the nuns appear on the garden path. One was Mother Marie-Joseph, the girls' boarding mistress, and the sight of her was astounding as well as unexpected: the nuns had no transport of their own and rarely left the convent, which was some distance away in Vizagapatnam. The children could see that Mother Marie-Joseph was in tears as she approached, and she called out to ask if it was true Francis had died. 'She didn't bother with my mother,' Anne said. 'She wanted to know where my father was buried and ran to the coconut grove. Afterwards the other nun told me she was crying over his grave.'

I wondered about the nature of the bond between these two people, my great-grandfather and one of the women who taught his daughters. The convent was a community of mostly French nuns, who had come to India as missionaries; with Francis's knowledge of the country and long government service, they probably relied on him for many forms of assistance and saw him as a friend to the Church and to them personally. All of that had gone, in an instant.

❧❦❧

For Mariamma, Francis's death brought about a financial as well as a personal crisis. If the birth date recorded on her 1924 marriage certificate is correct then she was thirty-three when she became a widow, with six children under the age of fourteen. Her native language was Telugu and, while she had learned English, it was not at a level which enabled her to complete official paperwork and deal with the family's affairs as her husband had. I think she may have struggled even to notify the authorities of his death, because while the register records it as taking place in June 1935, the copy I have seen has a date stamp of 1936. Several parts of the form are left blank, possibly because Mariamma did not have the information required: her husband's place of birth, the length of his service, and details of his son and daughter from his first marriage. 'The former is in Rangoon,' the entry reads, 'and the present whereabouts of the latter is unknown.'

Mariamma's links with her own family were also about to fade away, including a sister who had been part of the Quinns' lives until Francis died. Her name was Pentamma, Anne told me, and her husband Rajayar had been employed to help Francis on the farm. They lived there with their children, in a second cottage Francis had built, but it seems the Quinn siblings had little contact with their cousins. 'We were Anglo-Indians, because of Daddy being Irish, whereas they were Indian and lived in the Indian style,' Anne explained. 'We were quite different in our dress, and because we were Catholics and went to the convent for schooling.'

Francis's death changed the entire economic model of the farm. He had been hands-on and there was no way Mariamma could replicate his labour. Even after she managed to access his pension, she had bills to pay. Rajayar's salary could no longer be afforded, and he and Pentamma moved away. Anne could not tell me where they went and could not recall subsequent contact with any of Mariamma's relatives. The children's world now consisted of their mother – and the nuns.

❧❧

After that difficult summer the older girls went back to school in Vizagapatnam, further up the Bay of Bengal coast, a town known in earlier colonial times as Waltair. Anne had begun boarding there when she was only four, sent along with her older sister when Mary went at the age of six. It was possibly the only English-language school within striking distance of Anakapalle, and English was the language of the boarding house too, even though the nuns came from an order rooted in seventeenth-century France.[4] There were Hindu and Muslim girls from the local community among the day pupils, but the boarders were all Catholic – mostly Anglo-Indian – and the nuns were, effectively, bringing them up.

'We all had favourite nuns,' Anne remembered. 'We would copy them, try to walk like them and pray like them.' Whatever the hour, the nuns were only ever seen fully dressed in their white habits, with their hair completely concealed, and apart from a few specialist teachers they took care of the entire curriculum.

While Francis was alive he would come and collect the children by car for their two holidays: a month at Christmas and another month in the summer. Apart from that they were at school. Parcels of cakes and biscuits would be sent from Anakapalle to supplement

Mother Marie-Joseph with Mary and Anne

the school food, and Francis and Mariamma sometimes came to visit, though their social calls on the nuns seemed as important as seeing the children, if not more so. Anne described once being told that her parents were sitting with Mother Marie-Joseph, when she didn't even know they were on the premises: creeping close to the parlour door she peeped through to catch a glimpse of them.

She found the end of the holidays very hard and would cry bitterly at the thought of leaving Anakapalle and Gandhavarum, and again at the moment of departure. Once back at the convent her misery was compounded by separation from Mary, who was in the older girls' dormitory. 'I don't think we ever slept in the same bedroom, Mary and I,' Anne said sadly. 'She was always away from me.'

Her sister was also the nuns' favourite. 'I used to get spanked with a brush if I did anything wrong,' Anne told me. 'Once it was in front of the whole school, when I didn't even know what I had done. But Mary was a saint. She never got the brush.'

❦

By the time Francis died, there were four Quinn sisters at St Joseph's: Louisa and Josephine as well as Mary and Anne. That autumn the car had to be given up as Mariamma could not drive and, in any event, it was too expensive to maintain. The trips back and forth to school were now by train, and the food parcels stopped. 'After Daddy died we didn't have all those luxuries,' Anne said. 'It was just very difficult.' Mariamma would still visit from time to time and the girls would look out for her on the appointed day, knowing that she would walk from the station carrying baby Rosemarie. 'She'd come into the convent gate and Mary and I would run to greet her, and take Rosie from her arms,' Anne said. Often there was something Mariamma needed help with: she would bring letters and other documents and the girls helped her read them and compose replies.

At Christmas 1935 the girls were told by the nuns that they couldn't go home: it was too much for Mariamma to have them now that she was on her own. As time went on, Anne found she no longer missed

Anakapalle and Gandhavarum in the same way. 'When Daddy was alive, I wanted to be at home,' she said. 'Afterwards, it was different. I was older and I accepted that we had to be away.' She and Mary could see Mariamma's travails for themselves, including her struggle to secure ownership of the property. At one point the nuns helped by finding a lawyer, and I wondered if there had been court cases, perhaps involving Francis's children from his first marriage.

The worries about money continued as Mariamma tried to work out how to derive an income from the farm, and the girls were suspicious of any man who appeared on the scene, fearing their mother could be exploited. Eventually, she reached agreements with local people under which they cultivated parcels of the land and paid her based on their crop yields. 'They always cheat me,' she told Anne, suspecting under-reporting of harvests. 'But at least I have something.'

That something was not, however, enough to pay for the girls' schooling at St Joseph's and for their brother's at the Catholic boys' school in Vizagapatnam. It was the nuns themselves who found a solution, agreeing with Mariamma that all fees could be paid in arrears, at an unspecified future date when the Gandhavarum land was sold. Anne told me that only happened in 1960, which means the nuns waited twenty-five years for the debt to be settled.

Mary's school-leaving certificate, issued in 1938 when she was sixteen, is among the papers my uncle Ejaz has in Karachi, and it records her status as a 'Free Pupil' at St Joseph's. She must have continued to some form of higher study at a local college while trying to work out what to do next and, according to my grandfather Mumtaz's account, she was under pressure to join the convent and become a nun herself. Anne told me this was wrong: the nuns were pushing Mary towards nursing, already an established profession for Anglo-Indian women and within the Quinn family, as Francis's sister Alice and his daughter Kitty had both become nurses.

According to Anne the nuns also had firm views on where Mary should train. 'They said there was a special hospital in Lahore and one of the convent girls had already gone there,' she said. 'They thought it was a good place and sent Mary there.' It must have been a daunting prospect: Lahore was in the distant, alien region of Punjab, where Mary would not understand the local languages, and there would be no visits from home and few trips back. It was 1940 and she was only eighteen, but the training contract came with a monthly stipend and that meant she could step up and help her mother, lifting some of the financial burden Mariamma had been carrying alone.

2

Mumtaz

Mary and Mumtaz met within a few months of her arriving in Lahore, but their circumstances could not have been more different. It was not only that she was a Christian and he was a Muslim, but that unlike her mix of cultures, languages and background, he was rooted firmly in a single place and the product of a largely homogeneous environment. In fact, had he followed the path envisaged by his parents, he would have spent his entire life in the house in which he was born, in the city of Multan, in present-day Pakistan.

Multan, with its history as one of the oldest settlements in South Asia, was a source of great pride to my grandfather. It was in this area that Alexander the Great's advance into India was checked, when he was wounded as he tried to storm a citadel of the ancient Mallian people.[5] The city lies on the Chenab, one of five tributaries of the great River Indus, from which Punjab gets its name: *panj* means five and *aab* water. It is known for its monuments, including richly

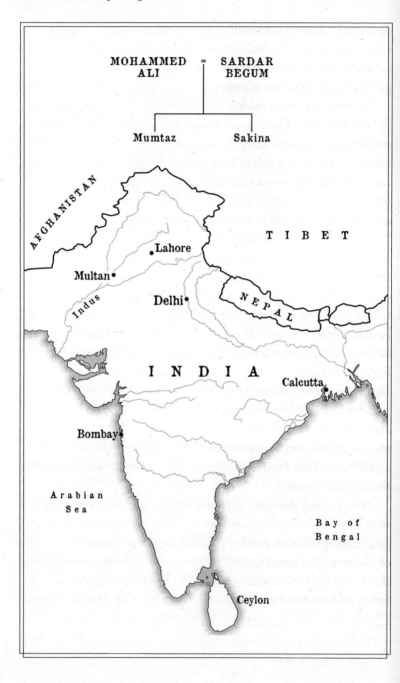

decorated tombs of thirteenth- and fourteenth-century Sufi Muslim saints, and also for a challenging climate: the summer is long and extremely hot, there is little rain even in winter, and beyond the irrigated areas lie expanses of desert.

Mumtaz was born during one of those punishing summers, in the last few days of July 1920. 'The month of July is not reputed for inspiring poetic outpouring in our part of the world,' he says in his memoir, a fact that seems to have bothered him. There was literature celebrating the blossoming of spring, the coming of the monsoon or the cool of autumn, but July was, he said, a month of 'in-between ordinariness, that fails to stimulate the imagination'.

Giving birth at that time of year would have been hard on his mother, he knew: the house had no electricity in those days and all she had to counter the heat was a block of ice placed nearby, so that cooler air might be fanned in her direction. There was nothing to relieve pain, and everyone was fearful because a previous baby had been lost at a late stage. 'The sufferings of my poor mother can only be imagined,' Mumtaz wrote. 'The stifling heat of Multan, the crowding in of relations, servants and hangers-on, the latter desiring to be "in on the event" and then rushing off to spread the news.'

That news, of his safe arrival, brought well-wishers to the house and one suggested names which his parents liked and adopted. He was called 'Mumtaz', meaning excellent, and 'Husain', in tribute to a grandson of the Prophet Muhammad, who had been martyred in the seventh century.*

When I read this early section of my grandfather's memoir I was struck by his ability to picture the scene around his birth so clearly, empathising with his mother's travails in a way unusual for a man of his time. This owed something to the nature of his upbringing, I think, and its physical setting. The house had been built by his grandfather and operated as a joint family system, with Mumtaz's father

---

*The murder at Karbala in what is now Iraq is a key moment in the development of Shia Islam.

and his uncle living under the same roof with their respective wives and children. Mumtaz grew up in close proximity to life events of all kinds and one of his earliest memories, aged four or five, was hearing an aunt in labour, with only a curtain between her and the rest of the household. 'Everyone was praying for her to come out of it safely,' he said, and one of the adults asked him to join in. He did so, but the labour then went on and on, in a way that baffled him. Pray again, he was told, but this time he refused, telling his elders that, really, one lot of prayers ought to be enough.

This environment set the tone for his life: it was a devout home and, even though he faced grave difficulties and almost a schism with his family later, he always retained a strong religious faith. Every day began with rising for the dawn prayer and reading from the Qur'an, he kept his fasts during Ramadan and he went on the Hajj pilgrimage several times. Alongside this was an equally strong conviction that faith was deeply personal: he had immense knowledge of Islamic history and doctrine, but I never heard him tell anyone how to practise their religion.

✺✺✺

By the time he was born, Punjab had been part of British India for just over seventy years, since the original Sikh-ruled princely state was annexed in 1849, after the Anglo–Sikh wars. Following the annexation Mumtaz's forefathers moved from rural areas in southern Punjab towards the city of Multan in search of work, and from around 1890 his grandfather was an inspector in the Canal Department and part of the local administration.

Mumtaz understood that further back his ancestors had been Hindu, part of the Rajput clan that spread across the north-west of India. In Multan, his grandfather chose to settle in an area known as Mohalla Kashigran, the neighbourhood of the potters, where those who produced the distinctive blue and white ceramics of the city lived and worked. It was an industry that had developed thanks to the easy availability of clay from the nearby riverbed, and its output was visible everywhere, from crockery and cups in people's homes to tiles and friezes on monuments. No artisan ever used a template or stencil, Mumtaz said with pride, as the point was not to copy but to paint freehand, taking inspiration from previous designs.

His own home was of traditional construction and layout, made of mud and brick, with rooms set around a central courtyard. His grandfather had not lived to see his sons bringing up their families there, but each nuclear unit had a room or two of their own, while cooking and eating communally. Mumtaz's own father Mohammed Ali worked in the Multan municipality and enjoyed a high social standing as a result, as people came to see him and sought his help in dealing with the British authorities.

Unusually, he and his wife Sardar Begum had only one son and one daughter, Mumtaz's younger sister Sakina, but because of the joint family system they grew up alongside five cousins, the children of their uncle. It was a secure, middle-class home and the two brothers expected to live out their days side by side, a plan shattered by the untimely death of Mumtaz's uncle. The cause had been a chill that turned into pneumonia, and it meant Mumtaz saw death at close quarters, as he had birth. 'The vivid memory is of sitting round the bed where he lay dying,' he wrote. 'My uncle breathed his last and the whole house was resonant with the most awful wailing. My father was crying like a baby and refusing to be consoled, his elder brother having looked after him in childhood and adolescence.'

⁓⁕⁓

Mumtaz was in his sixties by the time he was writing these words and his memoir paints a vivid picture of the Multan of his youth, in the 1920s and 1930s. 'Our homeland speaks to our most intimate memories, moves our deepest emotions,' he wrote. 'Everything that is a part of it belongs to us in some measure. And in a way we belong to it too, as a leaf belongs to a tree.' His own personal and professional choices were to take him away, from the age of seventeen, but when he looked back later he was able to appreciate the simplicity of his family's lifestyle, while always conscious of its privations. The lack of electricity made summers especially hard, when the only fans were date palm fronds suspended from the ceiling and agitated by hand from below. Nights were easier, as *charpoy* rope-strung beds were pulled out on to the roof and the open air was more comfortable than enduring the trapped heat of the rooms below.

All year round, the family would rise together and gather for the dawn prayer before each one set about their own work, play or study. For the women this meant domestic chores, most of which took place in the courtyard of the house, where water stored in an earthenware pitcher would be shared out for cooking and washing, and a buffalo brought in for milking. Mumtaz said his mother usually took charge of making the butter, perching on a low stool in front of a large clay pot of milk and churning it through a pulley action on the wooden rod set into it. Just as she completed a batch, he wrote, relatives who lived nearby and did not have their own source of milk would invariably appear, and have to be given a share. Then the family would sit down to breakfast and the butter would go with the *paratha* bread other women had made in the meantime.

His family were Sunni Muslims but had many links to Multanis from the Shia sect of Islam, and when Shia religious processions came past the house they would stand in the doorway and offer water. They enjoyed cordial relations with Multan's Hindu and Sikh communities too: Mumtaz said his father's Hindu friends would visit at Eid and send sweets and baskets of fruit to mark their own festivals of Diwali and Dussehra. There were customs in his own family which he thought were remnants of their Hindu ancestry, especially the way he had been taught to bend towards his elders' feet before each departure from the house and when greeting them on his return. 'The elder person would invariably reach out to embrace the younger almost halfway through the movement,' he recalled. 'Hindus practise this gesture to this day. I always found it very touching.'

There was not always a perfect atmosphere between Multan's communities, he acknowledged: incidents did arise at times between those of different faiths and sects. But the British authorities always responded swiftly, rounding up troublemakers and sending troops through the streets in a show of force.

❧❦❧

Mumtaz's education began at home, when he was four years old and his mother started teaching him the Qur'an. It was a mix of reading, reciting and understanding the underlying Islamic principles and expectations of behaviour, and it cemented Sardar Begum as the central figure of his early life. His father was much less present, partly due to his work but also because even when home, he would often be in the small annexe to the house which functioned as an office and a place to receive male visitors.

This was in line with the purdah requirements of the time, which kept women and girls away from the gaze of male strangers. The way it was observed depended on social class, geographical location, circumstances and preferences, and Mumtaz's memoir revealed to me how it worked in his family. For his mother it meant that any walk in the local park or excursion in a *tonga* horse-drawn cart usually took place after dark, when there was more privacy. A daytime outing required an elaborate ritual. First, people walking in the alley outside would be stopped and asked to wait at either end, while a *tonga* was brought in. Then, drapes – this is what the word 'purdah' literally means – were held up between the *tonga* and the front door. Only then could Sardar Begum emerge, clad in a burqa, a head-to-toe cloak, and once she was on board the drapes would be pulled over the cart's canopy.

Mumtaz was observant enough to spot that his mother relished any opportunity to cast off her burqa outdoors, but this was only possible when they were beyond the city limits, heading to their ancestral village east of Multan. Halfway through the journey she would fling the burqa off, ignoring the frowns and remarks of her husband, who preferred her to keep it on until they were closer to their destination. On the way back, she would wait until the last possible moment, when the city came into view, before covering herself again.

Conservative social mores could also affect boys, albeit to a much lesser extent, and Mumtaz saw this when he spent his last two years of schooling at Emerson College in Multan, which required Western dress as part of the uniform. There was a blazer, to be worn over the traditional shalwar kameez of Punjab, which was his first experience of European-style clothing. He found he liked it, and he purchased other novel items: shirts, ties and trousers. His family had no difficulty with this, but others struggled with what was perceived as the Westernisation of their children. One friend had to sneak his tennis kit out of the house to change into elsewhere, because his grandfather forbade any 'foreign' clothing beyond the school blazer. 'Poor Qasim,' remembered Mumtaz. 'He had to forgo quite a few sessions of tennis when it was not possible to have the appropriate wear smuggled out past ever watchful eyes.'

Emerson was an important place for Mumtaz, as it provided an entry into a significantly more diverse world, where he had British teachers as well as Indian ones from all religious backgrounds. His arrival there in 1935 also occurred at a time of wider change, as stirrings of political activity reached Multan for the first time. He was aware of this only from a distance, as his parents had given him strict instructions to avoid any of the meetings that took place in a park near their home. Attending carried a high chance of being caught up in a disturbance or a *laathi* charge, when police rushed forward with wooden staves to disperse the crowd, and intelligence men working for the Raj were also known to be present. They would be in plainclothes but quite obvious, Mumtaz heard, 'busy taking notes, sometimes not too surreptitiously, and reporting back to the district authorities, particularly anything bordering on the seditious or revolutionary'.

At this point in the 1930s all the political gatherings Mumtaz could recall taking place in Multan were organised by the Indian National Congress, a party then a few decades old whose most prominent face from 1915 was Mohandas Karamchand Gandhi. The younger Muslim League, founded to safeguard the interests of Mumtaz's own community – and which would later bring about the creation of Pakistan – seems to have had little presence in this Muslim-majority area. The leaders whose visits Mumtaz remembered were both Hindu: Gandhi and his younger associate Jawaharlal Nehru, whom he once saw mounted on a white horse in the Multan bazaar. 'People like Jinnah were either not around,' he wrote of the future founder of his country, 'or not well known as distinct personalities.'

❧❦❧

This was the period in Mumtaz's life when he had to start thinking about a future profession, and it was the example of his family doctor that nudged him towards medicine. The Multan of his childhood was one where infections were rampant and there had been many instances when the doctor had been called to attend to him: bouts of typhoid, dysentery and malaria as well as the odd injury from sport or play. He was an only son and perhaps for this reason his parents fretted in a way he found tiresome. The doctor, he realised, was the one person they listened to. 'Over the years,' he said, 'I came to look upon him not only as a role model but a father-confessor, who could shield you from wrath if you had come to grief through a forbidden pursuit.'

From an early age he had copied the doctor in play, with a pretend clinic in the courtyard where he would be the doctor and his cousins the patients, assigned injuries and ailments which he would purport to deal with. Then, at Emerson, he had the chance to study zoology, which gave him his first experience of dissection: earthworms, flies, mosquitoes and, later, frogs and rabbits. 'Study of the systems of these creatures could not fail to fascinate and enthral at nature's creations,' he said, and he became convinced that medicine was for him.

There was no possibility of pursuing this in Multan: it was 1937 and India still had few medical schools. The nearest option was the one founded as Lahore Medical College and renamed King Edward

Medical College after the death of Edward VII in 1910. Mumtaz knew that there was fierce competition for the 100 places available every year, that he needed a first-division result in his intermediate exams at Emerson to be in with a chance, and that there were faith-based admissions quotas: 40 per cent of places reserved for Hindus, the same for Muslims, and the remaining 20 per cent for Sikhs, Parsees and Christians.* There was an extra factor, though, which favoured him: his family's roots in Kabirwala, outside Multan, put them into the 'agriculturist class', whose children were being encouraged into higher education and given stipends. It was a colonial ploy to cultivate a particular group of people, Mumtaz thought, but if he was successful it would cover living expenses in Lahore, leaving only the annual fees for his family to pay.

He was called for interview in the summer, just after his seventeenth birthday and travelled to Lahore with his father. It was his first time in the capital of his home province, and he found the city 'a world apart, and totally alien'. His interview panel was made up of five professors – four of them British – which was intimidating, but he found their questions were quite general, more about his interests than about academic matters. It was probably, he thought, largely to gauge his proficiency in English.

Almost immediately he was told he had been accepted, an outcome that was a huge moment not only for him and his family but for their wider network of relatives, neighbours and friends. 'Multanis were known in those times to be timid,' he said, 'little inclined to go away from their city and their homes, regardless of any emergent, attractive opportunities elsewhere.' But everyone understood and respected the desire to become a doctor. As the news spread, extended family flooded in from Kabirwala, there were thanksgiving visits to local shrines, and a *diya*, a small earthenware oil-filled lamp, was lit in the next-door mosque. Vats of *pullao* – rice with meat – and

---

*Parsees are followers of Zoroastrianism, one of the world's oldest religions.

zarda – saffron-infused sweet rice – were cooked and distributed to the poor and there were purchases of bedding, linen, new clothes and new glasses, for which he chose the latest rimless style, giving him, he felt, 'a scholarly, sophisticated look'.

It was not until the day before his departure that the enormity of the undertaking hit him. He knew no one who had gone away from Multan to live elsewhere, apart from brides who had left to join their husbands, and those marriages were usually within the clan or extended family network. Apart from his foreign teachers at Emerson, everyone he knew fitted into the tapestry of a community linked by long-standing connections and relationships. At this eleventh hour, some of his family also wobbled. His maternal grandmother admonished her daughter for allowing this only son to go so far away, 'in pursuit of a richer career, as if God hadn't given enough for us to be content with'.

All this meant emotional scenes as he left the house to begin his journey to Lahore, and again at the station, where he leaned out of the carriage to wave goodbye to those who had come to see him off. Then, as Multan disappeared from view, he slumped into his seat. 'Unmindful of the other people in the compartment,' he wrote, 'I gave myself up to paroxysms of sobbing and crying out loud.' His father, too, was in tears, leading fellow passengers to enquire what was wrong and offer consolation and words of encouragement.

By then, Mumtaz felt drained, but his memoir records in some detail what he saw out of the train window during the rest of the journey and the emotions he experienced as afternoon turned into dusk. 'Menfolk carrying their ploughs and prodding their bullocks, having done the day's work in the fields; women with huge bundles of fodder on their heads, wending their way home, brought a peculiar sense of nostalgia for my own home,' he said. He found himself envying these people, who did not have to part from loved ones as he did. He recognised later that this was tone-deaf, that his teenage mind was oblivious to the trials of these rural people, who were at the mercy of feudal lords. 'They had to live with the

oppressive and selfish dealings of their *zamindars*, the pain of having to share the major part of produce from their sweat and toil with
an absentee landlord, never being able to call the soil they tilled
their own, and dealing with greedy and avaricious merchants and
money lenders,' he wrote. In contrast, he was on his way to a life of
new freedoms.

❦

That night, he and his father pulled into Lahore's main station, an
imposing building through which he would transit many times and
which in those days was a bastion of orderliness. The railway officials
wore starched white uniforms, gleaming shoes and sola topi sun-
hats, the porters red uniforms and turbans, each with an identifying
number on a brass plate tied to their upper arm. Passengers would
be collected by *tongas* appearing in steady sequence, and even the
outside precinct was spotless. 'No filth or litter,' Mumtaz said, 'the
road clean and well swept other than, perhaps, the droppings of a
wayward horse which the ever-present sweepers had not yet got to.'

The next morning they headed to the college, well located just
outside the walled city of Lahore with its captivating Mughal-era
monuments, and close to the grand buildings of the colonial period,
including the museum where Rudyard Kipling's father had once
been the curator. Mumtaz's heart leaped with excitement when the
clerk called him 'Doctor Sahib' as he registered, and he was sent
off towards his hall of residence, Broome Hostel. It was then that
apprehension set in again: he had thought rooms were assigned, but
discovered there was no such system. It was up to him to find people
to share with from among the young men gathered outside.

He watched as others bumped into friends, former schoolmates
or acquaintances and sorted themselves out. There was no one he
knew from Multan, and he felt suddenly aware of his social limita-
tions. 'My inherently hesitant nature did not encourage an approach
to any stranger,' he said, which left him with no option but to continue standing there, hoping someone might approach him. Eventually

someone did, a student who had to be from Delhi, he thought, given his perfect, formal Urdu and his attire – a straight white *pajama* and a long, buttoned-up *achkan* coat. If he did not have anyone to share with, perhaps they could team up, the young man suggested, and Mumtaz tried not to look too eager in response.

His roommate's name was Abid Hasnain and the two of them would be lifelong friends, a bond that began with settling into the last available and least attractive room in Broome, facing the busy main road. Only then did Mumtaz's father leave, heading for his train back to Multan with a parting plea to Abid to look after this 'much loved only son' who was away from home for the very first time.

Mumtaz squirmed, but Abid turned out to be a huge help: he had experience of student hostel life and knew how to organise laundry, barbers, provisions and – most importantly – budget, so that allowances lasted the month. Mostly they would eat in Broome's canteen, which was not a bad option, or indeed pair of options as it had two dining halls. The 'Muslim kitchen' served meat and there was a corresponding, vegetarian, 'Hindu kitchen', although meat-eating Hindus and Sikhs would often go to the Muslim side and Muslims would flock to the Hindu one on Sunday mornings for the sweet *halva puri* breakfasts.

Mumtaz's bigger problem was social adjustment. He continued to feel he was an outsider and his homesickness stayed with him for a long time, even as he made friends. Everyone else seemed to hail from bigger cities or more sophisticated backgrounds and he felt provincial, sometimes struggling even to follow what the others were talking about. His refuge was his bed, where he would pull the sheet over his face and hope no one heard his despair: 'Many pillows were left drenched with my silent tears in the night.'

❧❦❧

Eventually, his clinical studies would take him into Lahore's Mayo and Lady Willingdon hospitals, but the course began with two main subjects, Anatomy and Physiology. He was impressed by his professors, many of them Hindu and Sikh men who, within a decade, would be fleeing Lahore at independence. Mumtaz appreciated their knowledge and their skill, remembering one who had an extraordinary ability to help students understand the layers of the human body by drawing them in different-coloured chalks on the blackboard: first the bone structure, then the muscles and finally the nerves and vascular system.

Alongside this was dissection, where the first challenge was the smell: the bodies themselves and the preservative injected into them. However much students washed their hands, the odour stayed with them for hours, Mumtaz said, putting them off their food and causing some to drop out of the course. He discovered, too, that the dissection hall had its own customs. The courteous '*Salaam*, Doctor Sahib-ji' of the head sweeper as the students entered was a prompt: those smart enough to cotton on and pay him 5 rupees a month would have their assigned body part properly looked after, kept moist and covered. Those who ignored him would soon find theirs dried up and impossible to handle.

At Broome, Mumtaz found aspects of his new friends' lifestyles perplexing. Often they would come back late in the night and appear unwell, and when he heard someone being sick he would get out of bed and try to help, wondering what infection they had caught. 'Only after some time did I stumble on to the fact that all these upsets were merely due to over-imbibing,' he remembered ruefully. Later, he tried alcohol himself and found he liked it, but he knew his parents would be horrified. 'To see their one and only son fall from the pedestal if they were to know about the drinking would have been extremely painful,' he wrote. 'My overriding consideration was not to hurt their feelings.'

He was still only nineteen when his clinical studies began, in the autumn of 1939, and he was issued with a white coat and instruments for ward duties. 'It was a great joy to be cycling to the College with a stethoscope round one's neck, fancying that one was being viewed by passers-by with some awe,' he said, and it was the summer after that, in July 1940, that he met my grandmother Mary for the first time, at Mayo Hospital.

Mumtaz begins this part of his memoir with a heading – 'The anchor and focus of my life' – and I could see as I read how much it meant to him to be able to relive every moment of that first meeting. It had come during a night shift, when he and another student were supposed to be on a break but found themselves unable to sleep because of the stifling summer heat. They had gone in search of cold water and had approached Mary as she stood by a table in one of the wards, engrossed in patient charts.

They knew from the probationer's belt on her uniform that she was a newcomer, one who seemed to resent the request for water from the refrigerator, or at least regard it as a waste of her time. Mumtaz, however, appears to have been spellbound. She had, he wrote, 'the most elegantly shaped, beautiful, big, and most flirtish eyes I had ever seen'. He looked for her the next night, too, and waited for a moment when the senior nurse supervising her had walked away. Again, she rebuffed him – and he discovered later that she had been warned about medical students trying to chat up new nurses. Could she at least tell him her name, he pleaded? There was no reason he needed to know, she replied, but if he must, it was Mary Quinn.

That was how it began. Mary had come to Lahore knowing only one person in the city – the other convent girl – and it would have been much more of an adjustment for her than it was for Mumtaz, coming as she did from the other side of the country. Over time she looked beyond the dire warnings about amorous students and started to meet him, usually over coffee and a plate of chicken sandwiches at a café near the hospital. He told her about his family and she told him about her home, both aware of the contrast between their backgrounds. 'Here was a young girl from a faraway place, two nights' and three days' journey by rail,' Mumtaz wrote, 'meeting a boy from a laid-back, almost backward, orthodox city like Multan; with the radical differences of culture, language and – above all – religion.'

When she told him about her father he was able to understand the accident in medical terms, concluding that hospitalisation would not have saved Francis: in 1935 even sulpha drugs, the precursors to antibiotics, were only just starting to be used. She told him how close she had been to her father, regarding him as a companion, friend and teacher, and how her grief had led to terrible nightmares. He could also see she was lonely in Lahore, 'missing her family, the outdoor life, the farm and its fruits and even the nuns'.

Their meetings became more frequent, and soon, he said, the friendship matured into romance. Whether it could ever be more than that was still too difficult to contemplate. 'Whenever pros and cons raised their ugly heads,' Mumtaz wrote, 'pushing them out of our thoughts seemed the only thing to do.'

※※※

They had a two-year courtship, during which Mary went home once, in 1941, sending a basket of her favourite south Indian mangoes back by railway post for Mumtaz and his friends. His own trips home became less frequent, partly because of Mary but also because of the demands of academic work as his Finals approached. Then, early in 1942, he had a particularly insistent summons home and realised on arrival that something serious was afoot: alongside Mohammed Ali and Sardar Begum were an uncle and aunt who appeared to have been drafted in for a specific purpose.

It was the issue of his marriage, he was told, and he learned for the first time that one had been arranged for him, years before, with his cousin Rahima, the daughter of his late uncle. Their respective fathers had agreed it and now, Mohammed Ali said, it was time to complete the formalities, during this very visit to Multan. A celebration could follow later.

Mumtaz had not even suspected that there was a plan for him of this kind. 'Rahima had been a pleasant playmate since childhood, but I had never harboured any such thoughts about her, even after we grew up,' he wrote. He thought of her almost as he did his sister

Sakina and, at twenty-one, he also felt it was far too soon for marriage. For his parents it was the opposite: they wanted the matter settled and were probably fearful that once he graduated he would go further away from home than Lahore, and perhaps be lost to them.

'As forcefully as I could, I remonstrated that it was too early and the arrangement might distract me from my Finals,' Mumtaz recalled. After what felt like hours of argument his parents said they were willing to compromise: there could be an engagement rather than a marriage. Still Mumtaz refused, but when his frustrated father asked whether he had other plans or attachments, he said that he did not. This was, he felt, reasonably truthful: he and Mary had not, as yet, reached an understanding.

As I read this part of Mumtaz's memoir I remembered being told years ago that his parents had wanted him to marry his cousin. I knew I must have met Rahima myself on childhood visits to Multan, as she lived in the family home for the rest of her life. I had not known the details, and Mumtaz's description of the prolonged row made me wonder if Rahima had overheard it, given the way they all lived together. If she had, it could only have been upsetting and humiliating. From her point of view it was probably a good arrangement, for Mumtaz was on his way to joining a prestigious profession. In an age when women had little agency, and could be mistreated by their in-laws, marrying within the family also offered a degree of security.

Mumtaz would remember these days in Multan in 1942 as among the most consequential of his life: had he gone along with his parents' wishes he would have returned to Lahore either married or engaged. He would then almost certainly have come back to Multan once qualified, he thought, perhaps opening a clinic in the annexe to the house, building a reputation, even entering local politics. Rejecting his family's plans was a major step in charting a different course for his life – primarily driven not by Mary, I think, but by his discovery of a bigger, more compelling world.

❦

Back in Lahore, he was soon immersed in a separate problem, this time a financial one. For many months, perhaps even years, he and his friends had been living on credit, with the Broome canteen manager willing to roll over the negative balance on their accounts. In the early days in the hostel they had been able to economise towards the end of each month and make do until the next allowances came in, but expenses had grown steadily through their clinical years, not least because they now had girlfriends in their lives. With their Finals approaching, the canteen manager became nervous, worrying that they would suddenly disappear. It was time, he told them, for the debts to be settled.

Previously Mumtaz would have turned to his father, but the Rahima situation made that impossible: he could not risk conditions being attached to a request for money.

He was lucky: a lifeline emerged at exactly that point, when one of his friends spotted an Army recruiting poster. The dire position of the Allies at that point in the war had led to new incentives for final-year medical students to enlist: a stipend of 100 rupees a month, payable until they had passed their exams. It was a fabulous sum in those days, Mumtaz said, and he and Abid signed up, along with their friends Jimmy Manekshaw and Riffat Mahmood. They discovered an added bonus; as they were in the middle of their final year the allowance was backdated, allowing them to clear their debts and immediately live more comfortably.

Until then, the war had had little impact on Mumtaz's life, apart from when King Edward's teaching staff, both Indian and British, were called away to serve, as some belonged to the part-military part-civil Indian Medical Service.[6] But by the middle of 1942 no one could escape how grim things were looking. The December 1941 Japanese attacks on American, British and Dutch interests in Asia and the Pacific had been swiftly followed by the fall of Hong Kong and the invasion of Malaya. In February 1942 the Japanese captured

Singapore, taking tens of thousands of Allied personnel prisoner, and Burma would be next. The recruitment of more medics was just one part of what would be required to turn the tide.

❦

With his financial position suddenly eased, Mumtaz allowed himself to think more concretely about his personal life, and whether there could be a future with Mary. 'I was, by now, in love, but just did not know how she felt about me,' he writes in his memoir. He decided to drop what he thought was a subtle mention of Rahima, and his parents' hopes, into conversation. He regretted it immediately. Mary was already serious about him, he discovered, and had been refusing invitations from two young Catholics she knew from Mass. Now she reacted strongly to what she saw as his future already being decided and told Mumtaz they must stop seeing each other. 'No amount of explanations, cajoling and pleading could counter her despondency,' he said. 'She left immediately, asking me not to follow her or seek to meet her any more.'

He was shattered, wanting to explain to her that his future had *not* been decided, that he had refused his parents, but when she saw him waiting at the entrance to the nurses' quarters or in the wards, she ignored him. It was only through the efforts of his friends that she agreed, finally, to a meeting. Having heard him out, she asked for a promise: 'Take an oath that you will stick by me and not succumb to any further family pressures.'

In order for such a vow to be meaningful, Mary wanted it spoken in a holy place, and they went together to her church, close to the Muslim shrine from which their neighbourhood got its name: Neela Gumbad, the blue dome. It was Mumtaz's first time in a church and, as they sat holding hands and pledged to marry, he felt a sudden confidence. 'If difficulties were to beset our path, we would cross those bridges when we came to them.'

After that they met with more freedom, enjoying excursions out of Lahore to Shahdara, just across the River Raavi, where they walked in the gardens around the tomb of the Mughal Emperor Jahangir. This is one of Lahore's most important seventeenth-century sites, a low-lying single-storey building in sandstone and marble, with a minaret rising from each corner, and Mary noted the contrast between it and the nearby burial place of Jahangir's widow, Noor Jahan. Despite her status at the Mughal court, where she had first come as a child, with parents from Persia, Noor Jahan's mausoleum was simple, and more ravaged by time. Mumtaz and Mary stood at the tomb, and she asked him to translate the inscription, knowing that he had studied Persian at school. 'On the grave of this poor stranger let there be neither lamp nor rose,' he read. 'No moth wings will catch light here, nor birds sing.'

Mary reflected for a moment on the words and then, unusually for her, flew into a rage. 'There he lies, next door, in all his glory and majesty,' she said, 'while the poor woman who was ever so devoted and supportive to him all her life, lies abandoned in desolate circumstances, unsung and almost forgotten.' Mumtaz tried to explain that Jahangir had died many years before Noor Jahan, and her tomb was not of his choosing, but I think Mary's words came back to haunt him after her own death. She was buried in London, where she had come to see a cancer specialist in her final days, and he could visit her grave only on an annual visit from Pakistan. On those trips he would go to the cemetery every day and I remember him standing at the graveside, lost in prayer and thought, and – it always seemed to me – with regret as well as love.

❧

In 1942, as he and Mary became an established couple among their group of friends in Lahore, Mumtaz discovered new aspects of her, including, one night, her aversion to drunkenness. 'Each time my glass was refreshed,' he said, 'I noticed that Mary gave it a disapproving look.' At the third drink, she snatched the glass and, to his horror, threw it out of the window. He felt degraded, 'particularly with the smirking of the others, as if to say what a wimp I was'. She didn't seem to care, and he found out later she was scarred by memories of her father. 'Drinks were cheap and easy to come by in his job,' said Mumtaz, recalling that Francis had worked on alcohol licensing and taxation. 'It seems he did not come off well after some of his drinking bouts. She was, therefore, apprehensive that I might, someday, also have one too many.'

I think he generally knew his limits, but there's no doubt that he was by then a very different person to the shy teenager who had arrived in Lahore in 1937. He was part of a close-knit social circle, in a city with a thriving cultural scene, including centuries-old traditions of dancing girls and courtesans. He must have been studious when he first came to King Edward, but he acknowledges in his memoir that by this point in his clinical years he was not doing enough work, and in October 1942 he failed to get through his Finals at the first attempt.

The next opportunity was in January 1943, and in the meantime he and Mary tried to work out how to fulfil the vow they had made to each other in church. Mumtaz had told his parents nothing about her, but having a *nikah*, a Muslim marriage, would be of help when it came to breaking the news. For Mary, the sacrament of a church marriage was essential. They began to explore options, each according to their own faith, starting with their usual places of worship.

The obstacles became immediately apparent. Mumtaz's regular mosque, attached to the Neela Gumbad shrine, told him that his fiancée would have to convert to Islam. This he knew she did not want, nor was it something he would ask of her. 'To me, renunciation of one's faith for a matter of expediency alone has always been repugnant,' he wrote, but when other mosques gave him the same response he started to lose heart.

It was then that his friend Jimmy got involved. While not a Muslim himself, he went from mosque to mosque speaking to imams until he finally had a positive answer at the Australia Mosque near Lahore's railway station.[7] Here, the imam saw no difficulty: after all, he said, Muslims, Christians and Jews were all 'People of the Book', in the language of the Qur'an, and the Prophet himself had had a Christian wife.

Even this did not entirely solve the problem, as Mary was struggling with the church element; her priest had rejected outright the idea of marrying a Muslim. She had gone on to Lahore Cathedral, but there the response was even sterner: she should forget this boy and seek guidance from the Holy Spirit. Again, it was Jimmy who continued the search, convinced that more flexible priests might be found in the smaller churches.[8]

He was right. An Irish priest further out of the neighbourhood was more sympathetic, and willing to meet Mary and Mumtaz. 'He questioned us at length about the sincerity of our commitment, particularly mine,' Mumtaz said, and after that, he appeared persuaded. Pronouncing the Bishop and others they had consulted as 'rigid Englishmen', he said he was prepared to ask for a dispensation from the Pope and marry them – as long as Mumtaz allowed Mary to continue to practise her faith and any children to be brought up as Catholics. Mumtaz hesitated over the second condition but said that – if it was Mary's wish – he agreed.

Within a week, he heard that the dispensation had been granted and he rushed off on his bicycle to give the news to Mary, who was on shift at the Lady Willingdon maternity hospital. 'We threw caution to the winds and hugged each other in the middle of the ward,' he said, 'to the consternation and later applause of the patients and staff, once they came to know the reason.'

Dates were set for both weddings, within a day of each other in December 1942. The Muslim marriage came first: a simple affair witnessed by Abid, where Mumtaz and Mary were each asked three times, separately, for their consent, in the traditional way of ensuring free will. After a few prayers and the signing of the register, a *nikah-nama* marriage certificate was issued.

In church the next morning there was rather more ceremony, for even though it was a weekday the priest had asked nuns from the next-door convent to come and sing the Mass for the couple. Standing at the church door Mumtaz and Mary could hear the sound filling the church, and then he waited by the altar with Abid while Jimmy walked her up the aisle. Sadly, no photograph survives – perhaps none was ever taken – but Mumtaz describes Mary as wearing a white chiffon dress, despite the chill of the Lahore winter, and carrying a bouquet bought for her by Abid and Jimmy. Her expression was one he had never seen before: an enormous smile combined with an attempt to look demure and keep her gaze low. 'I cannot rightly recapture in words our tremendous relief,' he wrote. 'Mary and I belonged to each other in the eyes of man and God, the union having been cemented in the manner our respective beliefs ordained, in the mosque and now in church.'

She was still only twenty and he was twenty-two, and the Quinns, as well as the family in Multan, had been kept completely in the dark. As I reached this point in Mumtaz's memoir, I could combine it with what I knew from Anne of Mary's childhood, and I felt I understood a key aspect of the bond my grandparents had formed. Mumtaz was trying to spread his wings beyond the confines of his background, and a wife from a different culture was part of that journey, while Mary's family life had largely fallen apart when she was thirteen. This was a chance to build a new one.

A few days in a Lahore hotel had to suffice as a honeymoon, and then it was nearly Christmas and Mary set off for Anakapalle, where she had to break the news to Mariamma not only of the marriage – to a Muslim – but of the end of her nursing career. 'In those days you couldn't be married, or have babies or anything like that in your training days,' Anne told me, and it was her account of the weeks that followed which revealed elements of the story completely absent from Mumtaz's version.

Mariamma was deeply upset when Mary came home and said that she was dropping out of her course, Anne recalled. 'Mummy hadn't sold the land and money was short. Daddy's pension wasn't enough to cover costs and I was still in school. And Mumtaz was still a student, he wasn't qualified as yet. So it was very difficult. There was no money on either side.' Like me, Anne felt that Mary's disrupted childhood had played a role in the way she fell in love with Mumtaz and chose to make a life with him, despite their differences of culture, language and religion. 'She was a convent girl, and she had gone straight from the convent to this hospital. And this young man showed her affection, which nobody [else] had. Who was there to do

that? There was only Mummy, and she always had a baby. And in the convent nobody shows you affection.'

Anne's own feelings about the situation were more positive than Mariamma's. To her, the story felt wonderfully romantic and she already knew of Mumtaz from Mary's letters, where she had mentioned a young medical student who was kind to her. This must have been a support to Mary, but there was also the convent to consider: for the previous seven years, since Francis's death, Mother Marie-Joseph and the other nuns had almost been surrogate parents to the Quinn children. In many ways, they were more influential and more determining of their futures than Mariamma could ever have been, given the circumstances of her background and marriage. I think Mary put off going to the convent for as long as she possibly could, to avoid facing the women who, with so much pride and belief, had chosen not just any old place for her to train as a nurse, but the best possible one.

When she could delay no longer, she went up to Vizagapatnam on the train, accompanied by Anne. By then, she knew she was pregnant – with the baby who was my father Tazi – but given how much else the nuns had to absorb she did not want them to know at this stage, and she tried to hide it with bandages. 'Mary was not very big, she had just started to show,' Anne told me. 'But these nuns have very sharp eyes. We went up to Mother Marie-Joseph and she looked at Mary and burst out crying. She blamed herself in the end for sending Mary so far from home. A young, innocent girl who had never had a boyfriend.'

Back in Lahore, Mumtaz had a little time in hand between Mary's departure and his retakes, and he decided to go to Multan and study there. Feelings were still raw after the upset over Rahima, but everyone understood how important these exams were, and he was left in peace. He used the annexe to the house as his study space and found an unprecedented sense of purpose: it was not only his own success he was working towards but security for Mary and their future family.

He wrote to her in Anakapalle, and found a way for her to write back, using the address of the one Multan friend he took into his confidence. Then, as the exams approached, he headed back to Lahore and joined forces with his friends for the last stage of revision, pooling any information they could gather from the hospital about preparations for the practicals. Nurses could often be helpful, revealing examiners' pet topics or which specimens had been removed from departmental displays and were being prepared for use. Even patients used as live examination cases were known to nudge the students in the right direction: 'Doctor Sahib, look at my kidneys,' or 'There was a long discussion on my urinary problems the other day.'

Mumtaz must have been under intense pressure through this time, as a student stipend would not go far towards supporting a wife – he desperately needed to pass and start earning a professional salary. And yet with his personal life settled, he felt a new contentment. 'Consider, if you will, the two of us,' he wrote. 'Myself from the provincial town of Multan, with ultra-conservatism woven into the society, staunchly believing and practising Muslims, hardly a contact with the outside world, an only son to whom hopes and aspirations were attached. And then there was Mary, a total stranger from miles away, with a completely different socio-cultural background, ethnicity and religion, venturing out to distant and unfamiliar lands.' With his deep faith, he believed in guiding forces and therefore that this unlikely union was somehow ordained.

3

Shahid

Like Mumtaz, my mother's parents Shahid and Tahirah were Muslims, but they grew up as part of a minority community in the north Indian region which covers a large swathe of the Gangetic plain and was known in their time as the United Provinces. A significant part of the push for Muslim rights that developed into the demand for a separate homeland came from this area, gathering force at the end of the 1930s and developing further in the 1940s.

My grandfather Shahid was born in 1911 and regarded two places within that region as central to his life: his home city of Lucknow and the town of Aligarh, close to Delhi, where he went to university. Both were lost to him in 1947, after which he managed to visit India only once, thanks to a kind diplomat in Islamabad who allowed him a visa to visit his father's grave.

His parents Hamid and Feroze were both natives of Lucknow whose families could trace their origins back to the Prophet

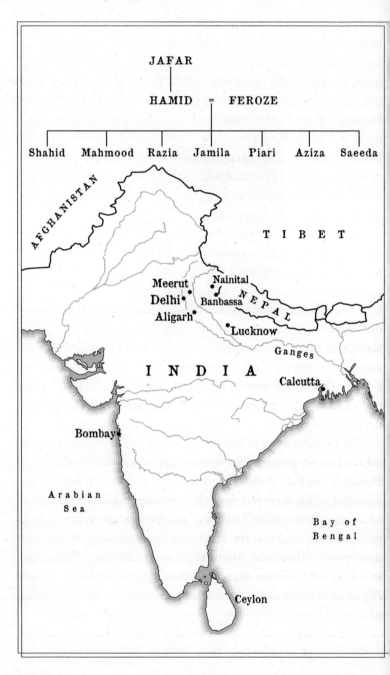

Muhammad, which is why he used the honorific 'Syed' before his first name. He had a family tree detailing the ancestry on his father's side and, once in a while, this very long piece of paper, folded multiple times because of the many generations recorded upon it, would be taken out for us grandchildren to inspect. It started with the Prophet himself, followed by his daughter Fatima, her son Husain and so on until, in the final three generations, there were names we recognised, including our own. In between there had been three great migrations: from Arabia to central Asia in the thirteenth century, then on to Badakshan, in present-day Afghanistan, and finally into India, at the beginning of the nineteenth century.

The last move came about because Shahid's forefathers had a reputation as men of learning and they were invited to the Mughal court in Delhi. By that time the dynasty's power was fading and soon the ancestors had to travel on, searching for new patronage. They found it in Lucknow, a city within the same region of India but governed differently as it was part of the large princely state of Avadh.* But there, too, times were changing and it was not easy to earn a living as writers, religious scholars and poets. The family had a precarious time until new professions were found in the 1870s, and for Shahid's paternal grandfather Jafar this meant funding himself through engineering college.

The circumstances of Shahid's mother's family in the same period were more comfortable. Feroze's ancestors had fought for the British in the First Anglo–Afghan War and then in the 1857 uprising, after which they were rewarded with a gift of land.[9] This *taluqa* or small estate outside Lucknow was later inherited by Shahid's grandmother, who was the dominant figure of his early years. His description of the way she travelled between the *taluqa* and her home in the city of Lucknow seemed to come straight out of the *Arabian Nights* rather than the early twentieth century: she was carried on a palanquin borne by eight men, he said, with others accompanying

---

*This is the phonetic spelling. The British in India spelled it 'Oudh'.

on horseback. She was a Shia Muslim, while most of the rest of the family were Sunnis, and she had many superstitions, particularly about travel: no one in the family was allowed to begin a journey on a Thursday, and if a cat crossed their path they had to turn back and start again.

Beyond his own childhood memories Shahid must have asked many questions of his elders, for he was able to set out the antecedents of his family in detail in a book he published in Pakistan in the 1980s. He saw it as 'a procession of memories', a way to chart not so much his own life as the fortunes of his community in the tumultuous period after 1857. 'From an era where the Muslims were still groaning under the after-effects of the war of independence to their awakening as a nation,' he wrote. 'From a time when scientific and purposeful education was considered a taboo to the realisation that without it we would be lost. It was a period when the Muslims struggled to find their identity and their rightful place among the nations.'

He also knew what he wanted to avoid. 'Most autobiographical accounts degenerate into ego trips,' he said. 'At times the writer drifts into fantasy and self-glorification in which the readers are least interested.' He felt it was important to describe not only key influences but *how* people lived: 'In our own humble way we are all part of history,' he wrote. 'Our writings should be indicative of the socio-economic ethos of our times, so that the story can be adequately interpreted by latter-day historians.'[10]

❧❧❧

By then he had explored several historical subjects himself, in other books: cavalry regiments in South Asia, the period around independence, and the early years of Pakistan. He wrote in English, a language he had acquired in school and used throughout his professional and adult life, but his native tongue of Urdu was very close to his heart. It was also central to the milieu of the Lucknow he knew, when the influence of nawabs who had ruled the princely state of old was still keenly felt.

Under these rulers, a dynasty of Shia Muslims, Avadh managed to flourish for a time, even as the Mughal Empire fragmented and the descendants of its emperors were reduced by the East India Company to nominal 'Kings of Delhi'. Lucknow became a pre-eminent place for art, culture and knowledge of all kinds, right up to the time of the last Nawab, Wajid Ali Shah, credited by Shahid with patronising essential aspects of a civilised society: 'Education, encouragement to men of letters, libraries, publishing houses, newspapers, religious institutions, calligraphy, poetry. Most of all he encouraged respect, courtesy, good manners and tolerance of views and beliefs. He gave a code of human behaviour.'[11]

The Company saw him differently, or certainly portrayed him differently as they targeted Avadh for annexation to British India. This was a tactic frequently employed in the first half of the nineteenth century, often under the pretext that a ruler had no obvious heir or was incompetent. But few thought it would be used against Avadh, a large, high-profile state with a seemingly stable and mutually beneficial relationship with the British. A garrison of Company troops was stationed in Lucknow and its officials enforced the nawabs' revenue demands; in return the British had access to the Avadh state treasury, which helped finance their military campaigns.[12]

In the end it was Wajid's personal fondness for the arts – his love for staging plays inside his palace and for writing poetry – that was used against him. He was accused of self-indulgence and a lack of interest in his subjects' welfare, and given an ultimatum to sign over his state in 1856. He was unwilling to comply, but faced with a forced annexation he left Lucknow for Calcutta, planning to appeal to the British Governor-General based there, and perhaps go on to England and put his case to Queen Victoria.

He never made that journey, but remarkably his mother Kishwar did, sailing out of Calcutta without the Company's knowledge and arriving at Southampton that August. It was always unlikely that she would get much of a hearing from Victoria and she was kept waiting for months. By the time an audience took place it was July 1857 and

Avadh's fate was mixed up in much bigger troubles for the British in India, as the Mutiny was under way. Kishwar was not permitted to talk to Victoria about politics and the meeting involved little more than the presentation of gifts. She died on her way home and is buried in Paris, while her son spent the rest of his life in exile in Calcutta, forbidden to return to Lucknow.[13]

❈❈❈

I did not intend to go as far back as this when I started tracing the lives of my grandparents, who were not born until the early part of the following century. But it soon became clear to me that the thirty years from 1850 had a crucial influence on the environment in which they grew up. Many of their families' choices arose out of events that took place in that period, from annexation to rebellion, and to the ultimate illustration of British power as Victoria became Empress of India in 1877.

The most familiar Mutiny narrative is that the uprising was sparked by new gun cartridges introduced for Company troops. Lubrication with pig and cow fat made these abhorrent both to Muslims, for whom the pig was forbidden, and to Hindus, for whom the cow was sacred. In truth, the events of 1857 developed in a wider context. There was the steady expansion of Company reach – including through annexation – as well as more interventionist British attitudes to Indian society, including a desire to 'civilise' through law, Western learning and Christianity.[14] India's economy was also changing; industries such as weaving had declined, as had opportunities in the old royal courts, and some of the new ways of raising revenue were contentious. It was also a time when many omens and prophecies were circulating, including one which declared that British rule would last for 100 years after the victory at the landmark Battle of Plassey, in 1757.[15]

In the early months of 1857 unrest among sepoys – the term comes from the Urdu *sipahi*, meaning soldier – had been noted in several parts of the Company's Bengal Army, which operated across a wide expanse of northern India. In May, serious trouble erupted in the garrison at Meerut, after a group of sepoys were court-martialled and paraded in public. Their outraged colleagues rose up, liberated them from jail, and then, significantly, chose to ride to Delhi and seek out the man who still resided in the Red Fort as the descendant of Mughal emperors. That 'King' was Zafar,* an eighty-two year old who had little stomach for trouble with the British and was less than pleased to hear that cavalrymen in Company uniforms had been spotted approaching.[16]

At first he told the sepoys who rode into the fort that they had behaved wrongly, but later he relented and placed his hands on their heads in a form of blessing. For the next four months the mutineers held Delhi and a Mughal restoration took place: old robes and a throne were taken out of storage, the royal mint was reactivated and titles and honours were awarded.[17]

In September 1857 the Company recaptured the city, after a siege and fierce battles that scarred and destroyed historic neighbourhoods and killed many civilians. Any man found in Delhi by Company troops was treated as a suspect; some were bayoneted or shot as rebels or collaborators. Zafar, who had sought sanctuary at the tomb of his ancestor, the Emperor Humayun, was arrested, imprisoned, tried and later sent into exile in Rangoon. The fate of his male descendants was worse. Three, who had surrendered to British officers, were ordered to strip and were then shot dead, their naked bodies displayed as conclusive proof of the rebels' defeat.[18]

In Avadh, it took longer to put down the uprising, as news of the sepoys' revolt tapped into anger about the way the state had been taken over. Lucknow was among the places which remained in rebel hands into 1858 and saw its own intense battles, especially around the besieged British Residency, where a large number of European

---

*Known in South Asia as Bahadur Shah Zafar, or 'Brave King Zafar'.

women and children were killed. As areas came back under Company control, retribution was fierce: tens of thousands of suspected mutineers were hanged, shot or tied to cannon so that their bodies were blasted to pieces. And, with two prominent symbols of the old order being Muslim – Zafar in Delhi and Wajid in Awadh – it was that community which faced being perceived as a continuing threat.[19]

Shahid's grandfather Jafar was born around this time, when it was clear that the British were strong enough to see off a challenge to their rule, and were not going anywhere; personal and professional choices needed to be made accordingly. After qualifying as an engineer he worked on land surveys, railway electrification, the development of the hill station of Nainital and canal irrigation, one of the big enterprises of the time. His son Hamid, Shahid's father, followed him into these projects and both would later be given the title of 'Khan Bahadur' by the Raj, in recognition of their work.[20]

The profession they shared had a considerable impact on their personal lives, as building canals required long periods moving from one remote location to another, as construction expanded across large areas. These were not places where families could be accommodated and when Jafar's wife died during this period of his working life, the impact on Hamid and his siblings was severe. Effectively homeless, they were passed between different family members: something I discovered not from Shahid's memoir but from the writings of his uncle Rafiq, Hamid's younger brother. 'My childhood was very disturbed,' he said. 'Sometimes I lived with my sister, sometimes with an aunt and at other times with sundry relatives. When my father remarried, life became settled again. By then, my education had been completely disrupted and this was never remedied.'[21]

This probably explains why no one in the family has any record of where Hamid went to school: he might not have attended one, or at least not for long, and his engineering skills were developed on the job, as an apprentice to his father. His later projects brought separation from his own wife and children, when he lived among farming

Feroze and Hamid

communities far from Lucknow, seeing how canals or small dams could help them with their crops. The work meant he was deeply rooted in the outdoors, and Shahid was influenced by this, seeing the landscapes and the way of life on visits to Hamid, when the family travelled deep into rural areas on *tongas*.

In 1922 Hamid began work on a major new project, to construct headworks for the Sarda Canal at Banbassa, on the Nepalese border. Unusually for Muslim parents of the time, he and Feroze chose a boarding school, in Nainital, for their daughters, but Shahid and his younger brother Mahmood had much of their education in Lucknow. They were enrolled in an elite school, founded in 1889 by a British civil servant with a mission to educate the sons of *taluqdars*, the landowners of Avadh.[22] Even though the princely state was long gone, these families continued to live in the old style as far as they possibly could, forming themselves into an association which was headquartered in Qaiserbagh, Wajid Ali Shah's old palace. When the Viceroy visited they would dress as if for court and pay homage in the way that their forefathers had to the nawabs.

Shahid and his brother must have been admitted to the school on the basis of their grandmother's small landholding, but their circumstances were entirely different to those of their peers. The ones who came from the richest landowning families had stables not only for horses but for elephants, and garages for cars, which were becoming the ultimate status symbol. This was despite a lack of roads to drive them on, or mechanics to maintain them. Shahid said a fleet of cars was often described as containing a certain number of 'runners' – functional vehicles – and 'non-runners', although the latter were never sold, as this would imply the owners were in need of money.

The more substantial estates even had what he described as 'little private armies, equipped with matchlock guns, swords and spears, dressed in the livery of their masters'.

At school the sons of such families were usually accompanied by servants who carried their books from one class to the next and held sun umbrellas over their heads outdoors. Unlike Shahid and Mahmood, who knew they needed to do well at school in order to earn a living one day, the landowners' sons tended to have little aptitude for lessons, or even interest in them. At exam time many simply disappeared to their estates, knowing they had little chance of passing.

Shahid, though, soaked up everything the school had to offer, which was considerable, quite apart from academics: a swimming pool, a riding track and even a farm. His school reports describe him as bright, intelligent and keen on games, and I know that Shahid was fond enough of some old friends and teachers to keep writing to them after independence – I found their replies, right up to the 1970s, in his papers.

In his 'procession of memories' are some that made me pause and wonder if they could be correct. He describes being friends with three Sikh brothers at school, adding that the middle one 'became a communist, left India for Russia and married Svetlana Stalin'. I discovered that Stalin's daughter did indeed fall in love with an Indian, Brajesh Singh, in Moscow in the 1960s, and – while forbidden to marry him – regarded him as her husband. It was on a visit to India in 1967 to scatter his ashes that she went to the American Embassy in Delhi and defected to the United States.

❧

Beyond his school environment, the main influence on Shahid in these years was the atmosphere of his grandmother's home and of the city of Lucknow, which was still redolent with the legacy of the old Avadh court. 'Lucknow was recognised as the metropolis of good manners and civilized behaviour,' he wrote. 'Courtesy to the old and young, humility towards all.' Children were taught to stand for an elder entering the room and told that they, as the younger person, must be first with a greeting of *salaam* (peace) or *adaab* (respect). Each salutation had a specific response, and the older person usually acknowledged the younger with *jeetay raho*, wishing them a long life.

Shahid's description of these expectations made perfect sense to me because it was what he and Tahirah inculcated not only in their children but in us grandchildren, too, later in Pakistan. While no one in the family seemed able to visit Lucknow, for reasons I did not understand as a child, I knew that our links to it were the reason for particular forms of address being drilled into us. There were specific ways to address aunts, uncles, the extended family and even older cousins and siblings, who were always 'Bhai' – signifying an elder brother – or 'Apa' – a sister. Raising your voice was also considered bad form, and although Urdu has two forms of 'you', similar to *tu* and *vous* in French, any use of the less polite one was frowned upon, even when talking to children.

Shahid writes, too, of his immersion in cultural events and the traditional arts in 1920s Lucknow. He was taken to poetry evenings, where people would recite Urdu and Persian couplets, whether their own compositions or from well-known works, and he saw masters of *dastangoi*, or oral storytelling. For this, skilled women and men would go from house to house to tell stories in instalments: if they were especially good and their tale particularly gripping, they might be asked to stay overnight and continue the next morning, in a version of today's TV binge-watching.

Elsewhere, he describes domestic routines and of how people in Lucknow coped with the intensity of the seasons, with summers not far off what Mumtaz experienced in Multan. His grandmother's home had a basement where everyone retreated during the hottest part of the day, and where there was a well, with brick alcoves for the storage of food. Water was cooled by wrapping the earthenware pitchers in wet cloth and leaving them in the open to catch the wind: Shahid said the hotter and fiercer the wind was, the colder the water became.

In winter, hot water was poured into terracotta bowls and left out overnight: in the morning the resulting ice would be buried in deep pits, where it would remain until required the following summer.

❧❧

He finished school in 1928 and moved on to the Muslim University in Aligarh, an institution founded in the wake of 1857 and driven by a belief that modern education was required for a new phase of the British presence in India. He found Aligarh to be a close-knit place, 'where a common heritage converted a student into a useful member of the community'. Here he saw a teaching faculty which was highly respected but not hierarchical, and a place that prized sport as well as academic knowledge. 'The captains of games were the uncrowned kings of Aligarh,' he said, and he played his own role in that, captaining the university tennis team.

Distracted by the tennis and, probably, like Mumtaz, by the new liberties of living away from home, Shahid did not do enough academic work. The results of tests ahead of his first-year exams were a shock: 3 per cent in his chemistry paper, 3 per cent in physics and zero in mathematics. There was no chance of hiding any of this from his parents, as they had received the results separately, direct from Aligarh. Shahid's father forwarded a copy to him, with a note in the margin: 'This hardly requires comment.'

To have any chance of progressing to higher study or a career Shahid needed to turn things around, which he achieved by bolting himself into his room in the evenings to study, his friends assuming from the locked door that he was out. At this point his father Hamid was keen that he take an entrance exam for the prestigious engineering college at Roorkee, but Shahid was certain that the profession of his father and grandfather was not for him. The problem was that alternatives were limited: the business world was largely dominated by Hindus and Parsees, while middle-class Muslims – of whom there were few – generally went into teaching or government service. Shahid would have known something about the police, for he had

an uncle who was a police officer in Aligarh, but he became interested in the Indian Army, possibly through his soldier brother-in-law
Anis. Opportunities in the Army had expanded after the First World
War, with Indians able to become King's Commissioned Officers for
the first time, and Anis had gone to Sandhurst in the early years of
that programme.*

Shahid set out to see if he could do the same. The chances were
slim: the highly competitive process was based on exam and interview, but it favoured candidates who were either the sons of soldiers
or had graduated from the Indian military college established in
1922. Shahid was neither, but went to Delhi to try his luck alongside
300 others in November 1931.

Two months later he was woken up early one morning in Aligarh
by a friend brandishing a copy of the newspaper: the results were
out and his name was on the list of successful candidates. 'Within
an hour the news had spread across the university,' he said, and it
sparked incredulity as people wondered who this Shahid Hamid was:
the one they knew was more into sport than academic work. His
room filled with well-wishers, who picked up his bed and carried him
outside in celebration. He was deeply touched, feeling as if the whole
university was taking pride in his success, and he kept the telegram
sent by his father: 'Heartiest congratulations. Parents and sisters very
proud of you. God bless you.'

In the full breakdown of results – which my uncle Ali still has
– you can see the complexity of a process that had to assess appli-
cants from across India, whose ethnic and religious backgrounds had
affected the languages they spoke and the subjects they studied at
school and university. All were tested on their English and general
knowledge, but beyond that there was leeway. Hindu and Sikh candidates were examined on oral and written Hindi, Muslim candidates
on their Urdu. All had to take a history paper, but they could choose

---

*Sahibzada Anis Ahmad Khan was from Aligarh and married Shahid's
sister Razia in 1931.

between general, modern or Indian history and they could avoid the requirement for Latin, as this had not been part of their schooling. They did need to be able to present their work properly; marks were deducted for poor handwriting and everyone was tested on their drawing skills.

The competition had selected for three military colleges in England: Woolwich, Cranwell and Sandhurst, where the biggest contingent, of ten, was going. Shahid was twenty-one and his journey to England would be his first time overseas, as well as the start of a long love affair with the country he came to regard as his second home. As he prepared to travel he applied for his first passport, in the summer of 1932, and by a stroke of luck my family in Islamabad found it, in the back of a drawer in an old piece of furniture, just as I was writing about Shahid's life. The faded navy-blue cover is a little battered by time, but the words 'British Indian Passport' and 'Indian Empire' remain visible, alongside a golden coat of arms. Inside, each of the pale pink pages bears a circular 'Empire of India' watermark, but the part that interested me most was how Shahid's national status was recorded: 'British subject by birth.'

Beneath his photograph in that first passport of his life is a note that appears to be an extra confirmation of identity, added in urgent circumstances nearly a decade later. 'Captain S. S. Hamid, the holder of this passport, is an officer of the Indian Army and is known to us', an official has written on 16 December 1941, probably a hurried attestation as Shahid prepared to head to Burma in the wake of Japan's wartime attacks. It was not until the post-war period that his admiration for Britain and the British was dented, when he could not understand how a country with such a great sense of justice and order could be so deficient in its leaving of India.

4

Tahirah

My grandmother Tahirah was born in Aligarh in 1920 and would have been at school when Shahid arrived to attend university in the same place. Her parents were not from Aligarh but had moved there in 1914, when her father was employed as the Medical Officer for what was still then a college rather than a university.

Its origins lay in the period after the 1857 uprising, when Muslims had to decide how to adjust to an era in which the Crown was taking over from the East India Company and placing India firmly within the British Empire. There were Muslim responses that looked inward, to theology and the founding of religious schools, and those which were more interested in community advancement.[23] The founding of Aligarh was part of the latter approach, and the environment that had sprung up in and around it by the 1930s was a central influence on Tahirah's life.

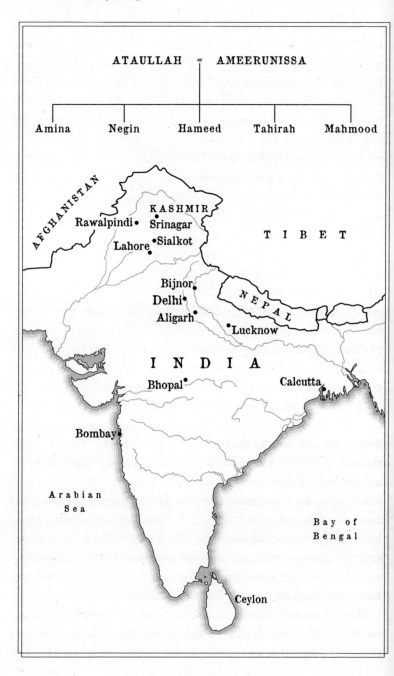

The man who had made it happen was Syed Ahmad Khan, later knighted by the British, who had witnessed the violence of 1857 while employed in the Company's judicial system. Based at Bijnor, near Delhi, when the rebellion took hold, he saved a group of Europeans besieged by mutineers, negotiating their release and leading them to safety. His own background was more closely connected to the old order than to the colonial one, as his family had held senior positions in the Mughal court. But as a young man he had sensed the changing times and chosen to work for the British. His heritage remained important to him and he reflected this in his writing, producing books on monuments, historical figures and interpretations of faith.

When he acted in defence of European lives in 1857 it was without knowing the fate of his own family, who were in besieged Delhi. After the British victory that September, he managed to obtain a special permit to enter the city, discovering that an uncle and a cousin had been killed by Company troops and that his mother was close to death, having hidden in the house during the battle for Delhi and survived by eating animal feed. By the time he found her, she had gone without water for three days.[24]

Afterwards, the British offered him the confiscated estate of a sepoy-supporting landowner, as a reward for what he had done in Bijnor. He refused, but the memory of that summer drove him for the rest of his life. He embarked on two parallel tracks: trying to influence the British and counter negative perceptions of Muslims, while telling his own people that they needed to pick themselves up and make progress in education, as Hindus were already doing to a much greater extent. 'Muslims had fallen behind,' Tahirah says in her tapes. 'No one was studying, no one was learning English, or going to school. They were pining for the old society and old times – Persian, Urdu, the Mughals. Sir Syed realised all of this.'

Among his early attempts to influence the British were two essays, one about Muslims who, like him, had not joined the uprising and the other about what had sparked it. The primary cause was, he said, the lack of voice or representation in decision-making for the people of India, and he accused the authorities of being out of touch. 'Government has not succeeded in acquainting itself with the daily habits, the modes of thought and of life, the likes, and dislikes, and the prejudices of the people.'[25]

In this early post-Mutiny period, it was dangerous for an Indian, especially a Muslim, to comment publicly on 1857, and Syed Ahmad's friends feared for him. He reassured them that he was not distributing these views in India but having copies printed and sent to England, where he hoped they might come to the attention of members of Parliament.[26]

In 1869, he had the chance to travel to England himself, when his son Mahmood became one of the first Indians to win a scholarship to Cambridge. He used the opportunity to look at books and papers in the India Office Library, to visit English universities and public schools, and to observe the English, paying particular attention to the level of literacy.[27] 'Look at this young girl Elizabeth Matthews,' he wrote home about one of his landlady's maids, 'who, in spite of her poverty, invariably buys a halfpenny paper called the "Echo" and reads it when at leisure. If she comes across a "Punch", in which there are pictures of women's manners and customs, she looks at them and enjoys the editor's remarks thereon.'

These letters were intended for publication and he used them to tell his fellow Muslims that they needed to move with the times. But he was also shaken to discover on the trip the extent of the educational gap between Britain and India. Colonial rule had, he said, 'despoiled us of our mother tongue and our hereditary sciences' while failing to set up schools in line with what was available in England.[28] He started thinking about a school or college of his own, a place that could develop along the lines of what he had seen in Oxford and Cambridge: residential settings where there was a sense of shared endeavour and worship, each college with its own chapel. This could be a model for Muslims, he concluded, distinct both from madrassah Islamic schooling, which he felt did not equip young people for the modern age, and from the missionary approach, which did not reflect indigenous culture.[29]

Where such an institution might be located was also important, and he decided on Aligarh, a town he knew, which was small compared to Delhi and Lucknow, but also therefore free from the distractions to be found there. He persuaded British officials to release land and he battled religious leaders who opposed teaching in English, which they called the devil's language. In 1877 his college was formally established and, within a decade, admiring British friends were calling him 'the foremost Mohammedan in India'.[30]

❧❦❧

Syed Ahmad, or 'Sir Syed' as he is known in India and Pakistan, had died by the time Tahirah's parents came to live in Aligarh, moving there from Lahore. Their own ethnicity was Kashmiri, but their families had moved south in the mid-nineteenth century, as Sikh rule came to an end and the British sold the Kashmir valley to the ruler of a neighbouring state.[31] 'We came down from the hills' was the way I remember Tahirah describing this migration and, like my grandfather Mumtaz, her ancestors had once been Hindu. They were Pandits, she told us, a term often used for the Kashmiri Hindu community.

Tahirah's father Ataullah and mother Ameerunissa were from two different Kashmiri clans and they settled in different parts of Punjab: Ameerunissa's in the city of Lahore and Ataullah's in Sialkot, a town already becoming known for metalwork and manufacturing.[32] His forefathers had difficulty finding their feet in a new, urban environment, away from networks of relatives or land that could provide a source of food or income. As I tried to work out how they had made a living I discovered that Ataullah's father was known as 'Master' Abdul Aziz, suggesting that he was a tailor. A contract to supply uniforms to the Raj seems to have been a game-changer, financing his children's progression from school into higher education, and the family lived alongside others from the same background, in the Kashmiri *mohalla* or neighbourhood of Sialkot.*

Tahirah's mother Ameerunissa had a more chequered childhood, one that my grandmother either didn't know about or didn't share with her children, and which I only discovered through talking to the wider family. In what would soon become a familiar pattern to me as I researched, her troubles were again due to the untimely death of a parent – her father – in 1906. Ameerunissa was fourteen at the time and saw her mother cut off by her in-laws from her husband's share of the family income. Despite the restrictions of purdah she ventured out into Lahore's markets and bought baskets of whole wheat and unhusked rice, which she and her daughters hand-processed and sold back into the bazaar. It must have been back-breaking but it tided them over a period of financial insecurity and enabled the younger children to stay in school.[33]

❧❦❧

Ameerunissa is the only great-grandparent of whom I have any real memory, as she spent the last decade of her life living with Shahid and Tahirah in the Rawalpindi house. We called her 'Ama-ji', meaning the respected mother, and I recall her quiet presence in the house, as well as the differences between her and my grandmother. I realise now that these went to the heart of how the lives of middle-class Muslim women changed within a generation at the turn of the twentieth century, particularly in education and dress: Ameerunissa had been educated at home while Tahirah had gone to school; Ameerunissa kept her white *dupatta* scarf drawn over her hair, while Tahirah covered her head only for prayer.

By the time she was born in 1920, the fourth of five children, her family were well settled in Aligarh. When she described to me

---

*Mohammed Iqbal, later a celebrated poet and philosopher, grew up in the same neighbourhood, a little before Ataullah and his siblings, and went on to study at Cambridge, Munich and Heidelberg.

the home in which she grew up there was one surprising detail: her father had hung large portraits on the walls, of a family he had lodged with when he was a student in Germany. My mother, her siblings and cousins all remember these, and how odd it felt to have these unknown Europeans gazing down on them.

I thought I should perhaps try and learn more about this period in Ataullah's life, as I was especially curious about how he had managed to fund it. He had been to Humboldt University in Berlin, Tahirah had told me, but I did not know when, or for how long. I contacted Humboldt to ask if they had any record of an Ataullah Butt, and the answer came back almost immediately: yes, he had studied in the Faculty of Medicine of what was then the Friedrich Wilhelm University from April 1923 to July 1924, gaining a doctorate on tuberculosis of the lacrimal gland of the eye. There were very few non-European foreign students at that time, they said, and there was an address in the file, in Weissenburgerstrasse, south of Spandau – presumably the home of the beloved German host family.

The dates were surprising, much later than I had imagined. By 1923 all five of Ataullah's children had been born and I couldn't see how he had financed even a year away, given his responsibilities. Humboldt must also have been challenging academically, for the university told me Ataullah would have had to defend his thesis with a spoken viva, in German. For more details I should try the Berlin State Library, they said, where his thesis would still be held, prefaced with a *Lebenslauf*, a short biography of the author.

When the library sent me a scan of that page, I could see in the few lines of text how my great-grandfather had presented himself to his examiners in 1924. 'I Ataullah Butt, born in Sialkot in India', it began, in German, explaining that after ten years of schooling he had obtained a medical degree and licence from the University of Punjab and spent a year as a house surgeon in Lahore. Then came the job in Aligarh, and it was after nine years there – presumably saving some money – that he had come to Berlin, aged thirty. Even then, I was sure that his study abroad was possible only because of its timing: hyperinflation and the state of the German economy in the 1920s transformed the relative value of the Indian rupee, making the opportunity suddenly affordable.

❦

Even though I spent a considerable amount of time with Tahirah throughout my teenage years and twenties, and we often talked about the past, I could not have pieced together the story of her life without the audio tapes found by my mother. They gave me Tahirah in her own words once again, and I could hear a sense of wonder in her voice as she spoke of the Aligarh of her youth and had an excuse to travel back in time. 'I think the great contribution of Aligarh was the simplicity and elegance of life and the feeling of brotherhood,' she said. 'There was total respect for one who deserved it – not for rank, wealth, or anything else. No one thought in terms of money and no one missed it.'

Most of her parents' friends were members of the Aligarh faculty, who prided themselves on their accessibility to the young people they taught. 'Every student was welcome to go and question the professors, to spend time with them,' she remembered. Many had studied in Germany, like her father, a choice that often led to work in universities when they returned home, as German degrees were not recognised in government service in British India. Some had fallen in love in Europe, and the Aligarh community therefore included a number of German wives.

Like Shahid, who experienced Aligarh as a student, Tahirah also saw it as a place which prized community spirit, considering it to be as important as individual excellence. There was a 'Duty Society', which gathered contributions towards bursaries, and the governing body was always looking out for alumni or other supporters with specialist skills: in an earlier time Shahid's engineer grandfather Jafar used his annual leave to oversee the construction of new buildings on campus.

I found more of this ethos in the memoir of Shahid's cousin Hameeda, who grew up in Aligarh and wrote about the way her parents took on responsibility for an underprivileged boy who went to school with her brother Shaukat. The child had been employed by another family as a playmate for their son, and followed him into school. But when the family had to move away he faced being sent back to his home village and his education coming to an abrupt end. Shaukat wrote to his parents, asking them to step in. 'If you don't,' he said, 'a great mind will be buried forever under the rubble of physical labour.' They agreed, supporting his friend not only through school but into higher education.[34]

Tahirah's own school was the first to educate girls in Aligarh, a mission that was still developing in her early years. She was proud of having witnessed it, remembering the educationalists who went on bullock carts into the poorest parts of the city and then on foot from alley to alley, persuading families to allow their daughters to learn. 'Education is important for daughters too,' they would say. 'Place your trust in us, we will come every morning, take them to school and bring them back to you at the end of the day.' Parents gained confidence that their girls would be safe, and slowly the carts filled up. 'I never saw Sir Syed or knew that generation,' Tahirah says on tape. 'But these were people I knew in my childhood and when I witnessed their commitment I felt I had a glimpse of those who had gone before. By my time there was a school bus and a boarding house too.'

Every day when she walked to school, she would see her headmistress sitting under the tree outside the gate, whatever the weather, checking how the girls looked. If there were absences she would follow up with the families concerned, and she had opened her own home to girls who were orphaned or destitute. 'The narrow-minded Muslims would regularly badmouth her,' Tahirah remembered, 'but in the face of all the untoward things people would say, she and her husband were steadfast.'[35]

❦

In 1927, when Tahirah was seven, her father was offered a new job: setting up a college in Aligarh that would be devoted to traditional medicine, the *yunani* system brought to India by the Arabs and dating back further to Galen and Hippocrates in Ancient Greece.[36] Ataullah led this college for more than twenty years, while continuing with a small private medical practice. 'At the end of the month my mother would ask him who bills should be sent to,' Tahirah said. 'He would say he hadn't seen any patients, when of course he had been out from morning till night. But he did not feel these were the kind of people bills could be sent to.'

Most of his patients were friends, and some time in the late 1920s one of them came to see Ameerunissa, driven by a desire to do something for the doctor's family. My great-grandmother was not in purdah, but she was also not entirely comfortable sitting down with a man one to one, and thus the visitor was given a chair on the verandah while she remained on the other side of an open doorway: apart but able to see each other. He addressed her as a sister and said that, as he was of advanced years and had no surviving children, he would like to put some land he owned into the names of her sons, Tahirah's two brothers, whom he thought of almost as his own. This was too big a gesture to accept, Ameerunissa said, but he insisted, saying dramatically that otherwise he would shoot himself. 'He was a Pathan, you see,' Tahirah says ominously on tape, referring to the tribesmen of the North-West Frontier, known for carrying guns as well as for their code of honour.

This was how the family home came about, the house that my mother and her siblings continued to visit for years after independence, and in which Ataullah and Ameerunissa continued to live until the India–Pakistan War of 1965 led to their final departure from Aligarh.

In Tahirah's childhood it was a house full of books, in both Urdu and English. 'My three elder siblings were all prolific readers,' she said. 'I remember trying to get to grips with the books belonging to my sisters and my elder brother and thoroughly enjoying novels.' A love of reading stayed with her throughout her life, although when her eyes started troubling her she turned to audio books, sent by my mother from England. 'I have always loved good fiction, I can't resist it,' she says on tape. 'I think it's the closest thing to human life.' She remembered grappling with Tolstoy when she was fourteen, 'skipping over where it was about war', and then discovering writers who could bring faraway places to life. 'I think my most undiluted joy is reading books on travel,' she said, 'from Ibn Batuta to Fitzroy Maclean to Thubron and so many others.'

As a teenager, much of what she devoured in Urdu came via Ameerunissa, who had been taught to read and write at home in Lahore by her own mother. 'Urdu literature reduced me to tears,' Tahirah said, 'because at that time most of it was based around the plight of Muslim women. My mother was a great one for the rights of women and she used to receive all the magazines and the books that were coming out. Some of it was emotionally upsetting, the lives of the nicest girls, forced to marry or treated badly at the hands of their in-laws.' All three of Ameerunissa's daughters devoured this material, much to the displeasure of their father. 'He used to say to my mother, "Please keep your books to yourself. I don't like these young girls reading them, it's not good for them." He didn't understand why this sort of book should be going around.' For Tahirah however there *was* a societal good: these books, she felt, were raising awareness of women's rights and capabilities. 'Muslim families didn't really wake up until, sadly, the partition of India took place,' she said, remembering the instability of 1947 and the vulnerability of those still living under variations of purdah. 'It was so difficult for women to get out and be able to fend for themselves.'

Much of the siblings' reading took place on the verandah of the Aligarh house, where they sat together after school or in the holidays, supposedly with their textbooks. Once in a while Ameerunissa would emerge to check on them. 'She would come and have a peek and see who was working and who wasn't,' Tahirah said. 'She would point at one or other of us and say "*You* are reading a novel!" And invariably she was right. We were convinced that she was very well versed in English and could spot the book from a distance.' Years later she realised Ameerunissa's grasp of English was very limited and she was relying on her powers of observation. 'She said when she saw us reading with great attention and really lost in our books, she knew it was a story, not a school book.'

⋇⟨⟩⋇

In 1929, a member of Sir Syed's family took on a key role at the institution he founded, as his grandson Ross Masood became the new vice-chancellor. Masood had gone from his own studies at Aligarh to Oxford and returned to India to become both a lawyer and an educator. He was also central to the publication in 1924 of E. M. Forster's *A Passage to India*, which opens with the dedication: 'To Syed Ross Masood, and to the seventeen years of our friendship'.

That friendship tells its own story, of a generation who were at the forefront of links being created between Britons and Indians on a more equal basis. Masood had grown up immersed in the Aligarh created by his grandfather and had been given a Christian as well as a Muslim name in tribute to an English friend of the family.[37] Forster met him in England, when he had needed some Latin tutoring before Oxford, and it was thanks to Masood that he gained the impressions and insights he channelled into his novel: 'He woke me up out of my suburban and academic life, showed me new horizons and a new civilization, and helped me towards the understanding of a continent.'[38] Visiting Masood in India in 1912, Forster listened to conversations of all kinds between him and his friends, absorbing their woes about forging careers in a system with the British at the top, and about how careful they had to be around European women.[39] He also witnessed the early throes of what would become a significant political movement during and after the First World War, as Indian Muslims agonised over the fate of the Ottoman Sultan, custodian of Islam's important holy places, of Mecca, Medina and Jerusalem.[40]

When Masood became Vice-Chancellor of Aligarh he boosted fundraising, placed the university on a more solid financial footing and expanded provision for the sciences. Like his grandfather, he was unafraid to speak frankly to his own community: in a 1930 speech to a Muslim educational conference he called for an end to 'the unnecessarily early marriage of our girls' and warned the almost certainly all-male audience that women's expectations and aspirations were changing. 'It is safe to predict that in India purdah as an institution is now doomed,' he said. 'I refuse to believe that Muslim women in India will be content to lead secluded lives behind purdah walls when all their sisters in other Mohammedan countries of the world do the very opposite.'[41]

He died only seven years later, at the age of forty-eight, and Forster, who was almost certainly in love with him, mourned him deeply and publicly. 'When his services to Islam, to India and to the Urdu language are commemorated,' he wrote, 'it must not be forgotten that he was loved and indeed adored by men and women who differed from him in creed, race and speech, but were able nevertheless to recognise his genius and the greatness of his heart.'[42]

❦

The constraints of purdah would never affect Tahirah or her two sisters, apart from a brief period when the eldest, Amina, went to stay with her in-laws shortly after her marriage in 1932. Her father-in-law was employed as the Prime Minister of a small princely state in Rajasthan and Amina found herself in a tiny, conservative circle around the court, expected to stay at home or, if out, to wear a head-to-toe burqa. Her sister Negin visited and reported back to Aligarh, where the household reacted with shock. Amina never lived like that again, but Tahirah, the youngest sister, was the one who gained the most freedom, living away from home as a student and single woman.[43]

Her decision to go to medical school in 1937, when she was seventeen, was primarily driven by a sense of duty. Ataullah had hoped that one of his children might become a doctor and, after Amina had married very young, Negin had gone into teaching and Hameed into the film industry in Bombay, Tahirah felt it was up to her to fulfil that wish. 'I hadn't really studied science,' she said, 'but I told him yes, I would do it.' She may also have been influenced by the family's devastating experience of serious illness in 1935, when Amina's firstborn child, a little girl they all doted upon, died of pneumonia at the age of two.

Her closest option for medicine was Delhi, which gave her a new experience of a place to which she was already attached. 'From childhood you were aware of the glory of Delhi and we were all made to visit the Mughal Fort, the Mosque and the Qutub Minar,' she says in her tapes. 'We heard stories of the ruins of seven Delhis and how, when the city's boundaries expanded, it heralded the end of an empire. And so as children, when we heard of New Delhi being built, we believed it would end the mighty British empire as well.'[44]

That purpose-built capital of British India was inaugurated in 1931, and Tahirah would live in the heart of it, as a student at the women-only Lady Hardinge Medical College.[45] In Tahirah's time it did not award degrees of its own, which meant that students had to travel to Lahore and take their exams at King Edward. There, Mumtaz remembered the excitement generated by the annual arrival of the Lady Hardinge girls. 'Students used to get attracted to them like bees to a flower,' he said, 'much to the disdain of our own female classmates.'

In Delhi, Tahirah revelled in new freedoms. Being away at college allowed her to be out in the evenings, mix as she pleased and also soak up the political atmosphere that was building at that point in the late 1930s. Significant elections were taking place and Tahirah was influenced by Gandhi's campaigning on cloth, as he told Indians to shun British imports and wear local fabrics, ideally hand-spun; in the shops on Connaught Place she would seek out saris of this rough *khaadi* cotton.

For a while, all of this masked the difficulty she was having with the content of her course. She had a core group of three close

medical-school friends, and she noticed how enthusiastic they were compared to her. 'It took me about three months to start work in my Anatomy class,' she recalled. 'I just wasn't born to it. The other three would do my dissections for me until finally I steeled myself. Then came the hospital years and they would say "Come, let's go to the maternity ward." But I had no curiosity, no desire.'

When war broke out it refocused her for a while, adding a frisson of excitement as she and her friends wondered where they might be sent as doctors qualifying in the hour of the Empire's need. But by the end of 1939 she was deeply unsure about whether she could stomach the rest of the course. Her parents must have known, for her professor uncle Khalifa Abdul Hakim, Ameerunissa's brother, stepped in. 'Medicine is not for everyone,' he said. 'And, it would appear, certainly not for you.' He suggested she try studying languages and philosophy with him in Hyderabad, and she did visit that winter before concluding that this, too, was not her thing.

❧

It was at that point in her life, in early 1940, that she became engaged to Shahid. The story I heard growing up was that they had met at a dinner in Delhi and decided there and then to get married. I thought it wonderfully romantic, particularly in an age when marriages were arranged by elders. But the full tale as I discovered it through her tapes, and the letters he kept filed away, had more of a backstory.

In his autobiography Shahid writes of the autumn of 1939 and resisting his sisters' efforts to nudge him towards marriage: 'I had been telling them that a war was on and I could be sent abroad at any time.' He was then twenty-eight and their letters before and after the outbreak of war show how much they pressed him to give the matter proper attention. 'We do so want you to marry a sweet girl like your own self,' his second sister Jamila wrote in the summer of 1939. She was married to their cousin Shaukat – the Aligarh boy who had persuaded his parents to fund his friend's education – and she had two young women in mind. One was Tahirah, 'who apart from being a pretty girl has a lot of depth in her', she wrote. 'You should try to see her. She will be in Lady Hardinge, Delhi, in September.' Only he could decide, Jamila acknowledged, and if he had met another girl somewhere, he only needed to let the family know.

Nothing happened in September, and another sister, Razia, wrote to him later in the autumn, relaying conversations with their mother. 'Bee and I sit for long hours talking about you and what we ought to do,' she said, clearly frustrated.* 'Nothing yet has been arranged about the great event, when we thought this winter would be the happiest winter.' She, too, had her eye on Tahirah. 'I think she would suit you very well ... She is in her habits very much like us and I know you would like her. If you have no objection we can write and fix up soon, for if she gets engaged somewhere then we really do not know of any nice girl, in U.P. [United Provinces] anyway.'

The war was adding to the family's worries. 'Every time there is news of Indian troops, we think of you,' Shahid's brother-in-law Shaukat wrote to him in November 1939. 'If you should see action I feel certain that you will give a good account of yourself and carry the name of your family with honour. Unlike other members of the family I do not feel anxious, as I believe that nothing can happen before one's time.' He was under pressure from his wife, I think, to do his bit to nudge Shahid towards Tahirah, and he complied. 'Some people after a few years of marriage get fed up with it all and begin to regard it as a necessary evil,' he wrote. 'Perhaps it is due to my good luck in having a girl like Jamila as my partner in life that I take the opposite view. As the years roll along, life with her is getting fuller and deeper.'[46] Wishing the same for Shahid, he recommended Tahirah from a position of knowledge, as both had grown up in Aligarh. 'I need not enlarge on her outward beauty and charm,' he said. 'I will only say this: she will stand her ground with any girl in the country. It is her keen fresh mind, modern outlook,

---

*Feroze's children called her 'Bee Ama' – another way of saying respected mother – and 'Bee' for short.

and deep and sincere character that distinguishes her most. She is the type of girl who will be equally at ease in a sophisticated drawing room or a simple little cottage – the type that sticks to one's side through thick and thin.'

⁂

This might have been the decisive communication because the next few letters in Shahid's files are no longer concerned with trying to persuade him, but are dominated by the practicalities of engineering a meeting with Tahirah. It finally happened in February 1940, when he came to Delhi en route to a training course in Rawalpindi and Jamila and another sister, Piari, organised a dinner. 'Tahirah left a deep impression on me,' Shahid wrote of that evening. 'To this day I cannot account for it but I really felt I could share my life with her.'

On tape, Tahirah mused aloud on the same theme: what had given her the confidence to say yes to Shahid's proposal the night they met. She was certainly at a crossroads in her life, and knowing his sisters gave her an idea of what the family was like. But she was ignorant of his professional world, which would dictate so much of their future. 'Do you know, I had never known anybody in the Army?' she says. 'I didn't know what an army was, because the place I was brought up was an undiluted little university town, with little semblance even of police. I had no idea of life as an Army officer's wife.'

After that dinner Shahid continued to Rawalpindi, while Tahirah dropped out of Lady Hardinge and went home to Aligarh. They began to write to each other and she scrutinised his handwriting for clues to his character, feeling alarmed to see the meticulous way he formed his letters and wondering if he might be overly exacting in his habits. Other letters flew back and forth: Shahid's parents wrote to Tahirah's to confirm the proposal, and Ataullah wrote to his future son-in-law. 'We feel happy to know that both of you love each other, love is the essence of life,' he says in one letter Shahid kept. 'From what Tahirah has told us I have no hesitation in feeling that she will be happy with you, and I am sure she will make you happy as well.'

There was one difficult matter. Shahid wanted to get married as soon as possible, but Ataullah's family had been recently bereaved, by the death of one of his brothers. 'My old mother is so full of sorrow that to tell her of a marriage so soon would be a desecration of her feelings,' he wrote to Shahid. 'If you have waited so many years for a girl of your choice then you could wait for another six months. Dear heart, you should not be impatient.' It was April 1940, coming into the hottest part of the year, and this was another reason to delay: 'Let us all wait until October and make the occasion a source of happiness and joy for us all.'

❦

Shahid might have left it there, except that the wartime orders he had long been expecting arrived. 'He was asked to proceed overseas,' Tahirah said, 'and he had the nerve to write to my parents and say he would very much like to marry me before he left.' They were not happy: 'You can imagine during the war the reaction any parent would have to that sort of a proposal.' The household erupted in debate, and Tahirah's younger brother Mahmood was sympathetic to Shahid. 'If I was in his place and you didn't marry me now,' he told her, 'I'd never marry you.'

I think this made a significant impression, although Tahirah says on tape that she had already decided to tell their parents she was going ahead. 'It was a hurriedly arranged affair,' she remembered. 'But India was far from the war so there was the normal excitement of such a moment. My sister and I were given some money to go and buy clothes for my trousseau and we had a happy few days doing that in Delhi and Lahore.'

Shahid came in from Rawalpindi and his family from Bhopal, the princely state where they were then living, as his father was work-ing for its ruler. There was a simple wedding meal, prepared by the Aligarh dining-hall cooks, and with his love of the university Shahid

felt at home: his old teachers were among the guests and his new father-in-law was the doctor who had once stitched up his lip after a hockey injury.

Only one photograph survives of the wedding, and a framed copy of it used to sit on the hallway table in the Rawalpindi house. Compared to the brides I saw in Pakistan, Tahirah wears remarkably little jewellery and her outfit is simple: a tasselled chiffon *dupatta* which she wore with a brocade *gharara*, the floor-length divided skirt which was courtly dress for the women of Avadh. In many ways it is Shahid who is stealing the show, in what looks like a silk *achkan* coat and a *saafa*, a turban tied in the expansive Lucknowi style from a particularly lengthy piece of material.

They left Aligarh on a night train to Bhopal with all of Shahid's family, for the reception Hamid and Feroze would host there. It was May and the intense pre-monsoon heat had set in, but the *motia* jasmine was blooming and Shahid's sisters filled the newlyweds' compartment with baskets of the scented flowers. From that day on, all five of the sisters no longer called Tahirah by her name, but addressed her as 'Bhaabi Begum' – lady wife of my brother – in line with Lucknow etiquette. To their children, Tahirah was 'Dulhan Mumani' – bride of my uncle – and thus it continued right to the end of her days, when there was hardly anyone still alive who could remember her as a bride.

They were supposed to have only a week together before Shahid reported for duty in line with his orders. But during those first days of their married life something remarkable happened: the orders were rescinded. Such a turn of events was unknown, Tahirah said, no one had ever heard of it happening in wartime or could explain it. But Shahid's delighted and relieved parents linked it immediately and firmly to Tahirah's arrival in their lives, as if she were a talisman. 'I was accepted in the family', she said, 'as a bride who was going to bring good luck, all her life.'

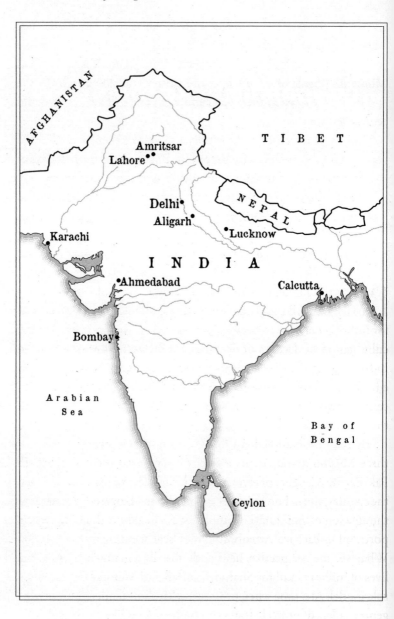

5

Jinnah and Gandhi

By the time independence came Tahirah, Shahid, Mumtaz and Mary were all the parents of young children, making decisions for future generations as well as for themselves. That moment was the culmination of decades of demands for greater self-government in India, to which successive British administrations felt they responded. And of all those who led the call in the first half of the twentieth century, two stand out: Jinnah and Gandhi, a Muslim and a Hindu, the founding fathers of independent India and Pakistan.

By 1947 Mohammed Ali Jinnah, born in 1876, was the man my three Muslim grandparents trusted to safeguard their interests. In Pakistan he is a figure of reverence, in India he is the man who divided the country, and in Europe and the United States he is largely unknown, though some would have formed a view based on the unflattering portrayal in Richard Attenborough's Oscar-winning movie *Gandhi*. Whatever the perspective, he is undoubtedly a man who shaped the lives of millions, and for Shahid, Tahirah and Mumtaz he was also a role model. At a time when prominent Muslims tended to be landed gentry, rulers of princely states or unique figures like the Aga Khan,*

---

*Spiritual leader of the Ismaili Muslim sect.

he represented a rising Muslim middle class: a professional, a man whose wife and female relatives were not in purdah, and a symbol of what the community could be in the modern age.

◈◈◈

Jinnah was born in the Arabian Sea port of Karachi, now Pakistan's biggest city, to parents who had come there from Gujarat in western India. His father had worked as a small-scale trader, buying goods and selling them on, and he had moved to Karachi because he wanted a bigger market for his business. It was a good decision, and, as the family became more prosperous the children's educational options widened. Mohammed Ali was the eldest child and was sent away to school in Bombay for a time, but he failed to show academic promise either there or on his return to Karachi. This was a grave disappointment to his father, who hoped his son would have the acumen required to one day take over the family firm. Then an opportunity emerged via an English business associate in Karachi, whose firm's head office in London was willing to offer an apprenticeship to the young Jinnah.

This would be valuable commercial experience, and the family could just about afford to fund it. Jinnah took the cheapest possible sea passage, arriving in Southampton in 1892 and lodging with a landlady in west London.[47] He found himself in England at a landmark moment in British parliamentary history: Dadabhai Naoroji, a businessman from Bombay, had become the first Asian elected to the House of Commons, representing the constituency of Finsbury Central.* Naoroji and his Liberal Party circle were a focal point for Indian students in London and Jinnah found himself among interesting people and absorbing new political rather than business ideas. 'I grasped that Liberalism,' he said later, 'which became part

---

*The House of Commons Library notes that MPs of ethnic minority heritage before Naoroji included David Ochterlony Dyce Sombre, elected in 1841, who was Anglo-Indian.

of my life and thrilled me very much.'[48] He attended proceedings in Parliament, including Naoroji's maiden speech, had a reader's ticket to the British Library and soon began to consider a new professional direction, in the law. This was tricky: entrance requirements for the Bar included Latin, which he had never studied, but he got in after writing to Lincoln's Inn to request a dispensation.[49]

He was called to the Bar in 1896, aged nineteen, and returned home the same year to find his family in crisis. His mother had died and the business was struggling with unpaid debts and a number of lawsuits. To support his father and younger siblings he needed to start earning immediately, and he decided to practise in Bombay rather than Karachi: not only was it a bigger city but the spectre of his family's business failure would not haunt him there.[50]

For three years he earned almost nothing, but once clients came he did well, and was in a position to send money home and fund the education of his younger brothers and sisters. Soon, he began taking an interest in politics in India, as he had in England, and went along to gatherings of the Indian National Congress. He was, one biographer says, part of a 'swiftly expanding pool of educated young men, fired with the liberty-loving ideals of British literature while faced with the depressing realities of Indian unemployment, political dependence and abysmal poverty'.[51] In 1906, members of his own community formed the Muslim League amid concerns about how they would fare in the nascent age of representative institutions, given that around 70 per cent of India's population was Hindu. Not long afterwards a set of political reforms expanded the number of Indians on the Viceroy's legislative council and Jinnah won a seat reserved for a Muslim from Bombay.

He was still only thirty-three as he took this first step into politics, and he proved combative from his first council meeting, challenging the Viceroy over reports coming in about conditions for Indian labourers overseas. His words on 'the harsh and cruel treatment that is meted out to Indians in South Africa' were widely reported in the newspapers and Jinnah gained a reputation for being unafraid to speak out.[52] He would do so on many issues in the years that followed, including one directly relevant to both my grandfathers – equality for Indians in the armed forces.

The First World War was the next development which focused minds, as Indians began fighting and dying for the Empire in large numbers. In 1916, knowing that the conflict was likely to redraw Europe's borders, Jinnah began thinking about what it should lead to in India. He worked on a blueprint for much greater political reform, envisaging India with a status 'similar to that of the self-governing Dominions', countries such as Canada and Australia. He thought it imperative that the plan should win the support of India's 'two great sister communities' – Hindus and Muslims – and as a member of both Congress and the Muslim League, he spearheaded its adoption by the two parties in Lucknow. This 'Lucknow Pact' was a milestone in relations between the parties and the communities, but it failed to gain traction with the Raj in Delhi or with the government in London. The war was still raging, which meant little administrative capacity for other matters, and a moment of opportunity faded away.[53]

❧❦❧

In the same period M. K. Gandhi, soon to be a key leader of Congress, returned to India from South Africa, where he had honed his campaigning and political instincts over many years.

He was a few years older than Jinnah and, on the face of it, the two men had significant things in common. Both were lawyers, with roots in Gujarat: indeed Gandhi was born not far from the Jinnah family's ancestral village. Both men had trained as lawyers in England, and it was Gandhi's campaigning on behalf of fellow Indians in South Africa that had led to the reports Jinnah raised with the Viceroy in 1910. Beyond these commonalities, of background and purpose, the two men had contrasting styles. Jinnah used his skills as a lawyer, debater and creative drafter of documents to gain concessions from the Raj, while Gandhi favoured simple, homely communications and was interested in spiritual matters and religious reform as well as rights and politics.

Back in India from 1915, Gandhi chose to base himself in the city of Ahmedabad, and to live with a group of followers as well as family in an 'ashram', the term for a Hindu religious retreat. His return had attracted considerable attention, although what he could achieve in India was uncertain.[54] 'All of us admired him for his heroic fight in South Africa,' Jawaharlal Nehru remembered – he was then a 26-year-old who had begun to make speeches and appear at Congress gatherings. 'But he seemed very distant and different and unpolitical to many of us young men.' Then in 1917 Gandhi launched his first significant Indian campaign, on behalf of a rural community who were being forced to grow indigo, despite the crop's low market price. He forced the Raj to change its approach, impressing Nehru and his peers. 'We saw that he was prepared to apply his methods in India also and they promised success.'[55]

Gandhi's campaign on cloth – which struck a chord with Tahirah in her student days – was one of his most enduring. It stemmed from his beliefs that countries should be self-sufficient and manual labour valued, but it was also a reminder to India that it had previously been a world leader in textiles. From gossamer-like Dhaka muslin to elaborately dyed, woven or block-printed material, cloth had been at the heart of the East India Company's eighteenth-century sales, until industrialisation changed the picture. Once raw materials started going from India to British mills the finished products often stayed there, reducing demand for Indian textiles, and British-made cloth was also exported *to* India, reaching a vast pool of consumers under colonial rule.[56]

In the face of this, Gandhi called for people to wear fabrics made in India and, even better, to learn to use a spinning wheel themselves. The campaign caught on: in 1919, Shahid's first sight of political activity as an eight-year-old in Lucknow was activists going from house to house, urging people to throw out imported cloth.

By then, the conflict that had seen more than a million Indians serve on the Western Front, in the Middle East and in Africa was over. Troops had come from the princely states, offered up by rulers keen to please the Crown, and from the Indian Army. All were technically volunteers, but with recruitment focused on communities regarded by the British as 'martial races', and with financial incentives on offer for village headmen, there were many instances of coercion or force. Even if men were signing up of their own free will, they often had little knowledge of what war would involve.[57]

In the latter stages the government in London had tried to send positive signals to India about political change, not least because more troops were required. In 1917 Edwin Montagu became the first Secretary of State for India to actually visit the country, recording his impressions in a diary. He met Jinnah, describing him as 'young, perfectly mannered, impressive-looking, armed to the teeth with dialectics ... it is of course an outrage that such a man should have no chance of running the affairs of his own country'.[58] Then, in the spring of 1918, when Jinnah and Gandhi were asked to back a fresh recruitment drive, both pushed for further reforms. Otherwise, Jinnah said, India's young men were being expected to fight for principles denied to them at home.[59]

For India's Muslim soldiers there was an added dimension. Turkey was on the same side as Germany and that meant fighting for the British pitted them against fellow Muslims. Even before the outbreak of war, the Ottomans' loss of territory in North Africa and eastern Europe* had alarmed Indian Muslims who felt strongly about the Sultan: he was not a faraway foreign ruler but a figure to whom they felt connected. His lands included the Islamic holy sites and he was seen as a leader of Muslims across the globe – the Khalifa or Caliph, a position of historic moral and religious authority. This sentiment turned into the Khilafat political movement, led by Shaukat Ali and

---

*Libya's capture by the Italians in 1911 had been followed by the Balkan Wars of 1912–13.

Mohammed Ali Jauhar, brothers who were both alumni of Aligarh. When Gandhi returned to India in 1915 they found him sympathetic to their concerns, but not long afterwards they were arrested and interned, as the British considered their activities dangerous to wartime morale.

In their absence their mother, a woman who had been born in the 1850s and spent most of her life in purdah, helped to keep the cause alive. The shouts Shahid heard in Lucknow in 1919 were in her name: 'Mohammed Ali's mother urges all to sacrifice their lives for the restoration of the Khilafat!' Even though Turkey had by then been defeated, the movement was trying to influence the terms of the peace, and tying it into the effort to get self-rule for India. 'The First World War had ended and the people were expecting great political changes,' Shahid wrote, remembering the imported fabric he saw being thrown on to bonfires. 'None were in sight.'

In truth, reforms were being introduced, including some powers devolved to the provinces, which would have legislators elected by a limited franchise of male voters. But after India's contribution to the war, this was widely considered to be insufficient. Worse, it came alongside an effective continuation of wartime restrictions on civil liberties, amid concern about agitation in India and possible spillover from the revolution that had taken place in Russia.[60]

These measures would become known as the Rowlatt Act, after the judge who recommended them. When they were put before the Viceroy's legislative council its Indian members all objected, with Jinnah setting out no fewer than seven reasons for doing so. He resigned in protest, accusing the Government of India of violating fundamental principles of justice at a time when there was no longer an external threat.[61]

Gandhi also lodged his objections with the Viceroy and publicly rejected the Act. He started to travel and speak out about the repressive measures, and he could see how people responded: not only with anger but with donations, which he used to fund posters, travel and organising a network.[62] This became his first nationwide *satyagraha*, a campaign that began in earnest in early April 1919 with a widely observed day of action that saw shops close and people gather for meetings.

In the days that followed, unrest continued to grow, particularly in Punjab, home of many First World War veterans who had returned to shortages and high prices, some feeling that their service had been insufficiently recognised. In Amritsar in eastern Punjab, and on Gandhi's home turf of Ahmedabad, anger led to attacks on Europeans and on buildings; when he learned of these, he said those responsible had disgraced him.[63]

Then, in Amritsar, the situation developed into one of the Raj's most notorious episodes, which unfolded in an open area that I saw when I filmed a series on Gandhi's life for the BBC. In 1919 Jallianwala Bagh, or the Jallianwala Garden, served as a place of recreation and fresh air within a busy urban centre, and on Sunday 13 April a large group of men, women and children were gathered there, some attending a political meeting, others socialising and picnicking. It was not only a weekend but the Sikh festival of Vaisakhi, which had brought people into Amritsar from the surrounding villages.

Prompted by the prevailing climate of agitation and protest, the Punjab authorities had banned public gatherings, but not everyone present in the Bagh would have known that. A column of troops moved in, under the command of an officer named Reginald Dyer, who said later that he perceived those before him as 'the same mobs who had looted and burnt three days previously'. As far as he was concerned they were violating rules that he had had proclaimed throughout the city in Urdu and Punjabi, that public meetings would be dispersed 'under military law'. Within thirty seconds of entering the Bagh he ordered his men to open fire, sending bullets tearing through a confined space. At least 500 people were killed and three times that number wounded.[64]

❧❦❧

As Punjab was under martial law it took some time for the news from Amritsar to filter out, but when it did the revulsion was widespread; it was the most significant use of force since the uprising of 1857. Gandhi's call for civil disobedience gained new adherents and came together with Muslims agitating over post-war Turkey and the future of the Caliphate. 'It was the time when Hindus shouted *Allahu-Akbar* and Muslims shouted *Gandhiji ki jai* [Glory to Gandhi],' wrote my grandparents' contemporary Shaista Suhrawardy Ikramullah, as she remembered an 'emotional hysteria' taking hold and being taught poems about Turkish valour at school in Calcutta.[65]

Jinnah's focus was on process and governance rather than the streets. He went to London to try and make the Prime Minister, David Lloyd George, understand how Muslims were perceiving events. 'First came the Rowlatt Bill – accompanied by the Punjab atrocities – and then came the spoliation of the Ottoman Empire and the Khilafat,' he said. 'The one attacks our liberty, the other our faith.'[66]

As the Jauhar brothers were released from internment they made similar appeals, and Britain was accused of going back on its word because, in 1918, Lloyd George had emphasised that the war was not about depriving Turkey of its lands.[67]

Mohammed Ali Jauhar also travelled to London to appeal to the Prime Minister, and made public speeches in England and France. He reminded audiences that the peace they enjoyed came after a war fought with the assistance of Indian soldiers, many of whom were Muslim. They looked to the Turkish Sultan as the successor of their Prophet, he argued, and thus he should be allowed to retain 'adequate territories, adequate military and naval resources, adequate financial resources ... not for aggression, nor even for the defence of Turkey, but for the defence of our Faith'.[68]

None of these appeals was successful. At the San Remo conference in 1920 the principal Allied powers made their decision, confirming that Turkey was to lose the territories of Palestine, Syria and Mesopotamia. Meanwhile to the south, the Arab Revolt against the

Ottomans – supported by Britain through the liaison officer known as 'Lawrence of Arabia' – was turning into an intra-Arab battle that would affect control of Mecca and Medina and ultimately lead to the birth of Saudi Arabia.*

❦

The Viceroy had told Indian Muslims to brace themselves with patience and resignation over the misfortunes of their 'Turkish brethren,'[69] but a climate of dissent persisted across India's communities. Gandhi worked closely with the Jauhar brothers as a non-cooperation campaign developed: honours and titles bestowed by the Raj were returned and there were plans to boycott law courts, foreign goods and the legislative councils.

Educational institutions which received grants from the Raj were also targeted, and when the campaign came to Aligarh in the year of my grandmother Tahirah's birth, it caused a deep fissure. At that moment the college was on the brink of fulfilling a key part of Sir Syed's dream, as legislation that would turn it into a university was in the process of being passed. Gandhi and Mohammed Ali Jauhar's joint visit to Aligarh threatened to derail that, as they asked students, faculty members and the institution itself to join them and sever links with the British.[70] Immediately, the community was divided: the student union and some teaching staff agreed, leading to a boycott of classes and the non-cooperators setting themselves up as an alternative mini-university on campus.

As word of this turmoil at Aligarh spread, the students' families were, for the most part, horrified and ordered them home. For the college authorities it was disastrous: ahead of an inauguration ceremony for the new university, they were also battling a vocal splinter group, and trying to do so in a way that maintained the founder's standards of courtesy. 'My dear Maulana Sahib,' began one

---

*Turks themselves cast the Ottomans into history when the Sultan was deposed and then a republic founded in 1923.

letter to Mohammed Ali Jauhar, addressing him as a learned Islamic scholar. 'Some of your students have been visiting the boarding houses attached to this institution. Kindly warn all your students and prohibit them from entering the premises of this institution to avoid a friction.'[71]

What was happening went from friction to breach, and one that could not be repaired. Sir Syed's college formally became Aligarh Muslim University in December 1920, with a woman, the ruler of Bhopal, serving as its first Chancellor. But the non-cooperators never returned, evolving over time into a separate university, now based in Delhi.[72]

That same month the differences in style and approach between Jinnah and Gandhi became a gulf. Jinnah was aghast at the idea of mass civil disobedience, regarding it as a route to 'complete disorganisation and chaos', but his was an isolated view at a time when people were flocking to Gandhi. At a Congress meeting at the end of 1920 Jinnah was publicly shouted down, and he spent the next ten years largely absent from the Indian political scene.[73]

❧❧❧

Civil disobedience continued throughout 1921, a period 'full of excitement and optimism and a buoyant enthusiasm', Nehru wrote, although there were times he felt troubled by the way Hindus and Muslims were bringing faith into Indian politics. Gandhi was among those using religious terminology, including references to Rama Raj, the period in Hindu mythology when Lord Ram ruled, as a golden age that would return. Nehru consoled himself that Gandhi wanted to communicate in terms widely understood by the people, but Jinnah, too, was uneasy.[74] A 'false religious frenzy', he said, 'would ultimately lead the country to confusion'.[75]

That winter non-cooperation would mar a visit by the Prince of Wales, the future Edward VIII, who was accompanied to India by his cousin Louis Mountbatten. The tour was aimed at thanking India, on behalf of the King, for its wartime efforts, but the Prince was greeted by strikes, boycotts and what Shaista Ikramullah described as 'sullen resentment' as his procession arrived in Calcutta. 'Full of colour and pageantry though it was, even my child's mind could sense the tension in the air,' she wrote. 'I can still clearly remember the awful feeling of unspoken fear and not understanding why it should be so, why something that was outwardly so gay should make people look and feel so mournful.'[76]

In Bombay there had already been clashes between non-cooperators and those who wanted to welcome the Prince, and Gandhi was deeply upset by the violence. As 1922 began he was planning a new phase of action, but that February there was a terrible incident: twenty-three police officers burned to death when their police station was set on fire by a crowd chanting pro-Gandhi and pro-Khilafat slogans. Gandhi began a five-day fast in atonement and suspended the campaign.[77]

❧❦❧

Mohammed Ali Jauhar later became disillusioned with Gandhi and the Congress Party, and drifted away from them. He was not someone I had imagined writing about when I began digging into my grandparents' story, as he is a relatively marginal historical figure – although India and Pakistan both put him on stamps in 1978, the centenary of his birth. But reading his speeches and seeing the power of his oratory in English drew me towards wanting to know more, and I wondered what role he might have played in the last phase of the Raj had he not died in 1931.

His final political appearance was in London in the autumn of 1930, at a Round Table conference on the future of India convened by Prime Minister Ramsay MacDonald. By then Jauhar was chronically ill, with diabetes complications that had worsened during his imprisonment, and he asked permission to remain seated as he spoke. Dominion status was no longer sufficient, he said: it was time for complete independence for India. He favoured the country becoming a federation, because of its diversity of faith and the many princely states existing alongside British-ruled provinces, and he spoke of his own faith and identity. 'I belong to two circles of equal size,' he said. 'One is India and the other is the Muslim world.' With memories of the First World War still fresh, he tried to put perceptions of his faith in that context. 'Nationalism divides, our religion binds,' he said. 'No religious wars, no crusades have seen such holocausts and have been so cruel as your last war, and that was a war of your nationalism and not my *jihad*.'[78]

Jauhar knew at this point that he was dying, which made him speak in stark terms, declaring that he wanted to return home only with 'the substance of freedom' in his hand. 'If you do not give us freedom in India,' he said, 'you will have to give me a grave here.'

When he died in London a few weeks later his family and friends felt that those words barred them from taking his body home, but they struggled, too, with the prospect of a burial in England. They took him instead to Jerusalem, where he is interred close to the Al Aqsa Mosque, one of the sites at the heart of the Khilafat movement. The Arabic inscription on the gravestone reads 'Mohammed Ali Al-Hindi' – Mohammed Ali of India.[79]

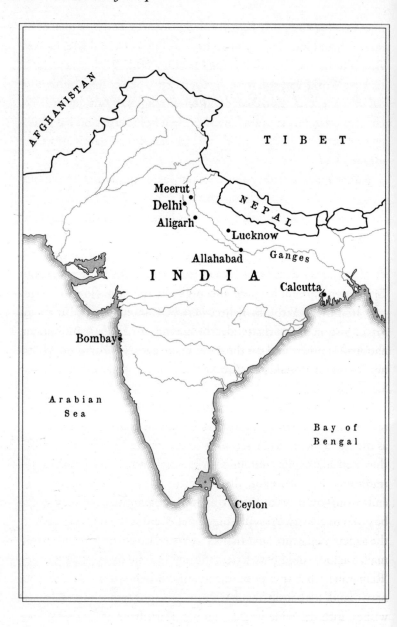

6

A Passage to England

That Round Table conference was the first of three such events organised by the British government at the beginning of the 1930s. The second was attended by Gandhi, who was by then internationally known, and the third was in the autumn of 1932, soon after my grandfather Shahid had arrived in England as a cadet bound for Sandhurst.

The opportunity to go overseas was a first for his family, and he records in his memoir some of the apprehension they felt as well as the excitement. As he set off by train to join his ship at Bombay, they tied silk bands containing gold coins to his upper arm, in the traditional way of seeking divine protection for someone on a new endeavour: on news of his safe arrival, the equivalent money would be given to charity. Press photographers were at the docks to capture the cadets' departure, and thanks to the relatively new service of airmail, Shahid would have letters throughout the three-week journey. 'Remember that this poor, disorganised, half-fed country is your native land,' his cousin Shaukat wrote. 'You go forth with our deepest wishes, into the wide world, and yes, learn from it all that can be learned. Bring back to its shores the accumulated experience of other people.' There must have been worry at the time that those who went abroad would forget their roots, but Shaukat had confidence in him. 'I feel sure there is no fear that you will come back with contempt in your heart for the ways of your people at home,' he said. 'Our Shahid is not so superficial.'

The voyage took him past Aden and through the Suez Canal into the Mediterranean, stopping at Malta, Gibraltar and Casablanca before turning north. He found it hard going, as he grappled with seasickness and faced the monotony of English-style food at every meal. This part, at least, was assuaged by the cadets discovering that the engine crew were all Indian Muslims, cooking their own food below decks and happy to share. Finally, at Tilbury, the group of ten were met by a Sandhurst officer and as they drove through London Shahid marvelled at the brightness of the street lights.

His experience as a cadet began with the obligatory military haircut, the issue of a canvas jacket and trousers, and a swimming test in the lake, before the routine that would dominate the first term: hours of drill on the parade ground, followed by more indoors after dinner. 'We cursed in our hearts and felt like running away,' he said, discovering that instructors were exacting on every front. Any speck of dirt spotted on a uniform was described as 'a ton of fluff', resulting in a punishment of extra drill, while rifle, belt and shoes really did have to be polished until you could see your face reflected back.

His group of fellow Indians were a mixed bunch, he thought; a few were clever and clearly had aptitude for their chosen career, but one from a princely state family was nervous and seemed unsuited to the Army. Shahid also formed impressions of the British cadets, and this was his first experience of mixing with Europeans on an entirely equal basis: he had come from a world where 'whites only' signs were commonplace and where part of a main shopping street in his home city was accessible to Indians only at certain times of the day.[80] In England, he found that there were other dividing lines. 'There was a certain snobbishness among the cadets,' he said. 'Those who came from public schools looked down on others.' He made some lifelong friends, including John Masters, later a bestselling novelist, who took little interest in his studies, he said, but kept everyone amused.

Apart from the Indians there were other international cadets: a Siamese prince who could barely hold his rifle, and a Chinese cadet who placed orders with military tailors in London for the dress uniforms of several British regiments. Shahid was curious, and asked why he would need so many. 'He replied that in his country any uniform could be worn, and the more gorgeous it was, the quicker the promotion.' In 1942 Shahid encountered him again, in command of an entire Chinese division in Burma, and concluded that his assessment of how to advance must have been correct.

By Shahid's time the 'Indianisation' programme that had begun after the First World War was well established: he was among scores of Indians who attended Sandhurst between the wars. In 2020, nearly ninety years after he was there, I found myself looking through his record in the Sandhurst archive, while filming a BBC report on the Indian Army in the Second World War. I stood in the spot where he had posed for a group photograph, discovered pictures of him in the tennis team, and looked at his academic file, thinking how bemused he would be at a granddaughter poring over his marks. The classroom work was more wide-ranging than I had imagined, from geography, military history and map-reading to economics and book-keeping, because future officers would need to monitor the expenditure of their units or regiments.

Towards the end of the first term the cadets were given more freedom and Shahid was able to head to London, making straight for a restaurant called Shafi's, near Piccadilly Circus, which he had heard was the place for all Indians in London to meet. With the latest Round Table conference under way it was also where word went out about opportunities to meet the delegates, and Shahid found himself invited to a number of events. By chance, he also met Jinnah, while having tea with a friend in a hotel one afternoon. 'A rather well-dressed man came in,' he remembered. 'We looked up, and wondered who he was, and said amongst ourselves that he did not appear to be an Englishman. He must have noticed that we were scrutinising him, and when he came up to our table, he greeted us. Out of respect for his age we stood up, and he introduced himself as Mohammed Ali Jinnah.' They knew his name, of course, but had never seen a photograph or had any means of recognising him. 'Little did we realise then', Shahid wrote, 'that we were talking to the maker of Pakistan.'

⊰⧉⧉⊱

His course would keep him at Sandhurst all through 1933, which meant he missed his sister Jamila's wedding, though frequent letters from home kept him in touch with events. One, from his father Hamid, reflected how changed the family home was, now that two daughters were married, Shahid was in England and his brother Mahmood at Aligarh. 'With four of you away the house is not much of a house for one who has lived for his children,' Hamid said, comparing parenthood to being a *maali*, a gardener tending to plants. 'The only difference is that when the children grow up they leave the *maali*. He would like to keep them and admire his produce. But if he did so he would be a selfish *maali*, while an honest one would send the produce into the world to be admired and cherished.'

By the beginning of the following year, 1934, Hamid would at least have Shahid back in the country, after he passed out from Sandhurst with his King's Commission in the name of George V. 'It was with a heavy heart that we left the college where we had come as raw recruits,' Shahid said, reflecting on how much Sandhurst had grown on him since the early days of endless drill. He came home on a troopship and Army life began not with his chosen Indian Army regiment but with a year-long attachment to a British Army unit in India. This meant he would be commanding white rather than Indian troops, and he was apprehensive about it – taking orders from a 'native' was still a novel idea. His men were mostly Liverpudlians of Irish descent, whose previous officers had all been British, and they scrutinised him carefully. Shahid made a point of being attentive to their welfare and playing hockey with them: both went down well and he had no difficulty.

The regiment that should have been his permanent professional home proved to be much harder. He had been able to fulfil his dream of joining the cavalry only after his father offered to supplement his pay, for such regiments always involved significant extra costs. In the old days men would have joined with their own horses, and while that was no longer the case, the many uniforms required in the cavalry, the style of living and the cost of pursuits such as polo all added up.

Wanting to stay relatively close to home, in the United Provinces, Shahid had chosen 3rd Cavalry, which was based at Meerut, the historic garrison from which the mutineers rode to Delhi in 1857. He discovered too late that the regiment was dysfunctional. It had been formed by the merger of two others in 1922, but more than a decade later the original sets of officers still did not mix. Evenings in the mess were awkward, as they chose opposite sides of the table and rarely spoke across it, and the presence of people like him was another sore point. 'The British officers were unhappy over Indianisation and resented the presence of the natives but could do little about it,' Shahid said. Orders were however given that no Urdu was to be spoken by Indian officers in the mess and there was to be no interaction with civilians, which may have been a way of limiting contact between these officers and their families and friends.

Shahid found that, despite long service in India, British officers were often unable to communicate with their troops and made mistakes that were embarrassing or even insulting. A common one was mispronouncing *sowaar*, the word for a cavalryman or mounted soldier, as *sewer*, which meant pig; one British general's Urdu address to his men was therefore heard as 'You are all pigs and I am one too.' Another officer's retirement speech, after twenty-seven years in India, began with '*Jawano*' – men – before he switched to English, saying he had not been in the country long enough to learn the language. He might as well not have bothered speaking to the troops, Shahid thought, for they understood nothing after that first word.

It had not always been so. In a previous age those joining the East India Company as officers were told language skills were essential 'to secure the faithful energy of the native army. You must acquire their language first of all. You must learn their customs. You must respect their religious ceremonies. You must not only be their officer, but their friend.'[81] Some of this approach was still evident in Shahid's time, among officers such as Claude Auchinleck, the Army Chief he worked for in 1947. Auchinleck had learned Urdu and when his duties took him near his men's home villages he would visit their families and eat with them. 'There are no bad soldiers, only bad officers,' he would say. As Chief he had to inspect troops across India and, when he did so, he looked out for men answering his questions with confidence and ease. Afterwards, his highest possible tribute was to say it was 'a happy unit'. This meant, Shahid said, that it was battle fit.[82]

❦

When he joined 3rd Cavalry in 1935, horses were still an integral part of training for warfare, but Shahid would soon see significant change as the age of mechanisation began. In the 1980s he wrote about the history of South Asia's cavalry regiments and traditions that went back to the Mughals and beyond – a book that led to an interview on the BBC Urdu Service. I would have known nothing of this, had it not been for an email from a colleague who had been tasked with digitising the BBC Urdu archive. One clip was labelled 'Shahid Hamid', and when he discovered that this was my grandfather, he sent over the audio.

It was indeed Shahid, speaking in his distinctive Lucknowi Urdu, his voice coming back to me with a flood of recognition thirty years after his death. 'It was only when the Second World War began that armoured cars and tanks came in and the horses were removed,' he said. 'I remember to this day the scenes when they were led away from men who had ridden them and cared for them for seven, perhaps ten years. They flung their arms around the horses' necks and kissed them, with tears in their eyes, because together they had been a team. I have never been able to forget the sight of that farewell.'[83]

As he started his time at 3rd Cavalry he had been required to immerse himself for several weeks in the routine at the heart of such a bond. It began before dawn at the stables, where he would clean the yard and groom, water and feed his assigned horse before returning, shaved and in uniform, for mounted parade. After breakfast there would be musketry, dismount parade and office work, and, in the

evening, a march to the stables and a final feed for the horses. He found it exhausting but could later appreciate that it helped him understand exactly what was expected of the men under his command. Alongside this, new cavalrymen had to learn manoeuvres such as how to operate along the flanks of a formation, and absorb a new language, as orders needed to be transmitted by trumpet, whistle and hand signal.

❦

Serving in his home region of the United Provinces meant that Shahid could use his local knowledge when it came to interaction with the civilian population, which was at its most sensitive when troops were called out amid political unrest or cross-community tension. His main experience of this was at Allahabad, a city on the confluence of the great Ganges and Yamuna rivers, where he and his colleagues were stationed in the old Mughal Fort. From his description it sounds like an extraordinary place to live: he refers to one part as an 'air palace' six storeys high and the officers occupying large rooms with fountains, Mughal paintings on the walls and views of the two rivers.

The importance of the rivers as sites of Hindu pilgrimage meant that they woke to the sound of *bhajans*, religious songs, coming from passing boats, while the Fort itself contained the access route to an underground temple. Shahid saw it for the first time when he was invited in by the resident priest, and he was captivated as he approached through a passageway lined with magnificent statues. This led to the inner sanctum, where there was a tree said to remain the same size for ever. Some time later, the priest made an unusual request, asking for permission to bring a truck up to the temple late one night. This was how Shahid discovered how the legend was maintained: every two years the tree was secretly replaced with one very slightly smaller.

He did have to deal with Hindu-Muslim tension on at least one occasion, and seems to have deployed his personal skills and his family's long-standing links in the area to maximum effect. When a dispute arose over a Shia Muslim procession that local Hindus wanted to keep away from their homes, he went from one community leader to the other, addressing each as 'Uncle', and begging them to agree a route, for his sake. 'Good-humouredly they cursed me, and said they would tell my father what an impossible person I had become.' The march passed off peacefully, but in the winter of 1936–7 he had to deal with a much more serious incident, this time sparked by political rather than religious tension.[84] Important elections were about to take place for eleven provincial legislatures and Allahabad, the home of the Nehru family, was a centre of Congress activity. 'Troops were called out in aid of civil power and we were ordered to patrol the narrow streets of the city,' Shahid wrote. He suggested a foot patrol, fearing that the horses would panic if projectiles were thrown from rooftops, but he was overruled and set out with a mounted squadron. 'We wore our steel helmets,' he recalled. 'But no sooner had we started patrolling than we became the target of every conceivable object – bottles, stones, bricks and even pots and pans. Both the horses and men were soon bloody.'

Exactly as he had feared, the horses became difficult to handle. Just then, the alley they were in opened out into a park, where Shahid could see a large crowd assembled and recognised what he called 'Congress leaders and the local elite' at the front. He mentions a magistrate being with him – perhaps in line with post-Jallianwala Bagh protocols – and he was told to disperse the crowd. He tried to do so, first using the trumpeter to achieve quiet and then giving the instruction to those before him, with a loudspeaker. 'They took no notice of my words but showered me with the worst abuse imaginable,' he said. He followed procedure and repeated the instruction three times: 'The only visible result was the increased hostility of the crowd.'

Shahid knew what was supposed to happen next: he was to use 'minimum force' to achieve his objective, which included, he says, authorisation 'to fire one or two rounds at the leaders, not in the air.

Casualties were therefore inevitable.' He looked again at the crowd. 'I had to think very hard,' he writes. 'I ordered the trumpeter to sound "Draw Sabres", which the troops did. There was a deathly silence and I once more requested the crowd to disperse. The leaders shouted back that they were ready to die rather than disperse.'

It was then that he thought of a brief cavalry charge: completely against procedure but, he felt, a means of dispersal that would avoid anyone getting hurt: the crowd would surely scatter as soon as the horses came towards them. He told the trumpeter to sound the note for trot, and the troops lowered their sabres and advanced, before racing forward on his second command. Everyone leaped out of the way and immediately he called halt: 'Not a single shot was fired and no one was injured.'

Back at barracks he was upbraided for his unorthodox method and told he had endangered those under his command. Then, privately, the senior-most officer congratulated him: 'Officially I had to give you a rocket. But it was a damn good show nobody was hurt, otherwise we might have found ourselves in a most awkward situation.' That alternative reality haunts me: had Shahid not acted according to his conscience it might even have been another Amritsar-style horror.

⋙❖⋘

The 1937 elections were a significant moment for pre-independence India, both constitutionally and politically. The franchise had been extended to 35 million voters – still only about a sixth of the adult population – and more powers were devolved to the provinces. When the results were announced, Congress was the big winner, with a strong enough showing to form governments in seven provinces. From being unsure whether to even contest the elections, the party had found the process an invaluable way of spreading its message across the country.[85]

The Muslim League found itself in a very different position. It had hoped to form a coalition with Congress in the United Provinces but found its support was not required, nor had it gained enough of a hold in Muslim-majority areas elsewhere.[86] Jinnah had lived in London for a time, practising law, but had been persuaded to return to India. Now, he needed to regroup, and his thinking and ideas were also developing. Rather than the legalistic, technical way in which he was known to speak and operate, Jinnah began to use Islamic symbolism such as the crescent moon in his speeches, and adopted a visibly Muslim identity in his clothing.[87] By then sixty years old, he began a major reorganisation of the Muslim League and tried to grow its base, tapping into Muslim student groups, particularly at Aligarh.

In the summer of 1937 Congress provincial administrations began governing and a fresh source of tension emerged: complaints from Muslims in those areas, particularly the United Provinces, of maltreatment by officials or the undermining of their identity. Schools became flashpoints; it was said that Muslim children were being made to salute the Congress Party flag and sing 'Vande Mataram', a song closely associated with the freedom struggle, which included Hindu imagery. These issues and other grievances, such as moves against Muslim butchers and marginalisation of the Urdu language were taken up by the Muslim League and became a running sore in its relationship with Congress.[88]

Resentment also crept into social relations between the two communities. Muslim girls who might previously have adorned their foreheads with a *bindi* mark now found it was frowned upon by their families, while Hindus eschewed words like the Persian-origin *khuda hafiz* for goodbye, or the respectful greeting *adaab*, which was associated with the old court of Lucknow.[89] Opinion and sentiment were becoming entrenched along enduring lines, with many Muslims seeing Congress as being for Hindus, and Congress regarding the Muslim League under Jinnah as 'aggressively anti-nationalist and narrow-minded'.[90]

Some Muslims' attitudes were also being affected in this period by what they were hearing from Europe, as they followed Nazi

Germany's treatment of Jews and commentary on it within India. In 1939, just before he became the leader of the Hindu nationalist RSS group, the lawyer M. S. Golwalkar wrote of Germany's 'purging' of Jews being a manifestation of 'race pride at its highest'. The 'Hindu Race' had evolved a noble culture despite contact with 'debased' Muslims and Europeans, he said, and he put forward views on India's 'foreign races' – by which he meant non-Hindus. They must either 'lose their separate existence and merge in the Hindu race', he wrote, or otherwise be subordinate, 'deserving no privileges, far less any preferential treatment – not even citizen's rights.'[91] It was a time of negative perceptions, fears and tensions setting in and in a different international climate perhaps the Raj authorities, or the British government in London, might have tried to address it. But attention was focused elsewhere: on Europe, and the prospect of another world war.

PART TWO

Before Midnight

7

Burma's Descent

Britain's declaration of war on Germany in 1939 was followed by an announcement from Lord Linlithgow, the Viceroy, placing India in the same position. Despite being a serving soldier, Shahid, surprisingly, did not hear the news through official channels. Instead, driving out in the early morning to go shooting with friends near Poona, in western India, he was flagged down on the road. 'Our car was stopped by a party of police and the inspector asked if we had any Germans in the car,' he remembered. Seeing their bewildered faces, the inspector explained: 'Have you not heard? Great Britain has declared war on Germany.'

Initially, Shahid said, the prospect of going into battle was something of a thrill for him and other young officers who had never seen combat, but they were set right in the mess that night. 'A senior major of my regiment, who had been in the First World War, walked in with a long face and told us that this was not an occasion for rejoicing but rather for anxiety,' Shahid said. 'War brought many hardships and miseries.'

Politically, it brought immediate upset in India, as the Viceroy had said the country was at war without consulting its political parties. For Congress this was proof that Britain saw India as a creature

of its will, but Linlithgow felt he had no choice; he had acted in line with India's constitutional position at the time and called the leaders in for talks immediately afterwards.[92] Elsewhere, the Raj felt the response was heartening: several prominent princely states made immediate pledges of troops, and Indian businessmen knew the war was likely to bring lucrative contracts for supplies.[93]

From Poona, where he had been on a course at the Army Signals School, Shahid returned to 3rd Cavalry, and found that the outbreak of war had brought little immediate change, other than wireless sets being issued and motorcyclists being trained as despatch riders. Regimental life continued, initially, with centuries-old traditions of man and horse. 'We did not know when we would be mechanised and still hoped that in some part of the world horse cavalry might be required,' he wrote. 'The theatre of war seemed remote and far away.'

I don't think his family felt that way. In his files there is a letter from his uncle Rafiq, his father's younger brother, written in October 1939 and revealing his agitation over the possibility of Shahid being sent overseas. 'In the smoke and dust covered trenches, in the muddy dugouts, I will search out my gem, my Shahid, and will pray and pray for him,' he writes. 'And even if he will pass, I will see him among the angels.' But the first orders that came for a family member were not for Shahid but for his brother-in-law Anis, who sailed for Marseille in December 1939, only to be taken prisoner by the Germans the following June.[94]

Shahid thought his own most likely destination was the Middle East or North Africa, but the war came as his relationship with his regiment reached a new low. Apart from the generally icy atmosphere between officers, he felt his immediate superior was itching to find a way to throw him out, and he put in for a transfer, no longer minding where he went. The option that came up was the Royal Indian Army Service Corps, which meant leaving the world of cavalry behind. It turned out to be one of the best decisions of Shahid's life, as 3rd Cavalry were sent to Malaya in 1941 and became prisoners of the Japanese, many dying during their long captivity.

His brother-in-law Anis survived the war, but his capture was not known to his family until eight months after the fall of France. The families of Indian prisoners were particularly vulnerable to long periods in limbo, as the process of notifying them was especially prolonged: names given to the Red Cross were sent to London, where they went from the War Office to the India Office and only then on to Delhi. It was not until February 1941 that Shahid's sister Razia received a brief cable at her parents' home in Bhopal: 'Please inform family Captain Anis Ahmad Khan, Prisoner number 996 Stalag 111D 700 Germany. He is well. No need worrying. Letter follows.'

When I saw the date I knew that my grandmother would have been in the same house when this longed-for news arrived, as Shahid and Tahirah's first child Hassan was born there that month. 'No one went to the hospital in those days,' Tahirah says in her tapes, describing her mother Ameerunissa travelling from Aligarh to be with her. 'It was about a week before I was twenty-one years old. He was my twenty-first-birthday present.' Shahid was away, serving at a remote base close to the Afghan border, but I imagined the joy of his parents and their entire household at the twin pieces of good news: the safe arrival of a grandson and the relief that Anis was alive.

By then, the war had seriously affected Indian politics. Beyond being angry at the way the 1939 announcement had been made, Congress linked any potential support for the conflict to constitutional change for India. When that was not forthcoming, it pulled out of provincial governments, in a move celebrated by the Muslim League as a 'Day of Deliverance'. Jinnah, meanwhile, was sensing an opportunity. Some of the Raj's most important soldier-recruiting grounds were Muslim-majority areas in Punjab and the North-West Frontier, and this would make him relevant to the British in a way that had been impossible after the weak election performance of 1937.

The early period of the war also saw the League formulate and pass a resolution that came to be seen as a milestone in the road towards a separate homeland. Adopted at a gathering in Lahore in March 1940, it declared that any constitutional plan for India should be based on the principle that majority-Muslim areas in the north-west and east should be independent states, autonomous and sovereign. The text came to be known as the 'Pakistan Resolution', even though the word 'Pakistan' – coined by a Cambridge-based law student in 1933 – does not feature in it.*

❧

After Hassan's birth in 1941 Shahid and Tahirah had a series of short postings with the Supply Corps, moving three times in six months. In her tapes she explains how there was a system to ease the disruption of this: furniture and household items were rented afresh at each base, which meant only personal luggage needed to be transported. Families travelled by rail, often across huge expanses of the network, but Railway Traffic Officers at all the main interchanges were there to greet, direct and see them on to the next destination.

Shahid's work was mostly in support of armoured divisions, where he was gratified to see that there was still a need for horses: officers who were training tank crews found them a swift way to keep across a formation, allowing them to gallop up and quickly correct any wrong moves. He thought his own next move would be to North Africa, and the campaign against German and Italian forces in the Western Desert, but then came the Japanese attacks of December 1941. Within days, he received orders for Burma, and travelled with Tahirah to Delhi, where Hamid and Feroze came to say goodbye. 'It was a tense period,' Tahirah told my mother Shama. 'Your grandmother was beside herself, in a state. I look back now and think how strangely confident youth is. I must have been nervous, I certainly should have been. But somehow I was never frightened. I just felt Shahid would come back, that nothing could happen to him.'

In his memoir, the only emotion Shahid records is disappointment, verging on annoyance, because he did not see how he could be

---

*Chaudhry Rehmat Ali came up with it as a loose acronym for areas that he hoped would form a Muslim homeland: Punjab, Afghania – meaning the North-West Frontier – Kashmir and Sindh, with the final 'stan' for Balochistan. As *paak* means 'pure' in Urdu, there was also a literal meaning: 'Land of the Pure.'

useful in Burma. 'I had no knowledge of the country or the Burmese,' he wrote, yet his orders said he was to command a unit of the Burma Army, a force created in 1937 when Burma was formally separated from British India.

On 20 December 1941 he reported to the docks at Calcutta, joining a troopship that steamed towards Rangoon in darkness, to avoid being spotted by Japanese planes. As they approached port they were caught in what I think was the first Japanese air raid on Rangoon. From the deck, Shahid saw the bombers and their fighter aircraft escorts come in and calculated that, if the ship was hit, he was close enough to swim to shore.

He soon realised that ships were not the target. Instead, the raid concentrated on the docks and warehouses, which were full of US supplies destined for the Chinese troops who had already been fighting the Japanese for several years. He saw the stores explode and catch fire as they were hit and then watched a dogfight, as American aircraft stationed nearby came into view.[95] He was fascinated: after nearly a decade in the military, this was his first sight of battle.

Later, once docked in Rangoon, he discovered the extent of the panic the air raid had caused and the exodus of civilians that had begun. From being a prime colonial posting and an Englishman's paradise, as well as a place where many Indians had come to trade or work, Burma was now a war zone. Rangoon's Burmese population vanished into the outlying villages, while British and Indian civilians headed west towards India, using any available transport.

❦

More strikes continued in Shahid's first few days in Rangoon, but he did not expect to experience them for long, thinking that he would soon be travelling on to his new unit. When no details came through, he discovered policy had changed: Indian officers were not to command Burmese troops after all. 'I requested a posting to an Indian unit and that, too, was not forthcoming,' he wrote.

Instead, he was made a liaison officer, linking Army Headquarters to troops in the field. Based in a university hostel that had been requisitioned as Army accommodation, he took stock of his surroundings and the wider environment. He saw what had made Burma so attractive to the British: resources including the finest teak, silver mines, precious and semi-precious stones, superior-quality rice and fine handicrafts. At the same time he saw a lack of the infrastructure required to repel an invasion: 'Communications were based on river transport. The railway network was poor and little used, the roads few and mostly neglected.'

By the middle of January 1942, within three weeks of his arrival, Japanese forces were known to be advancing across the eastern border with Thailand, a region of mountains, rivers and dense jungle previously assumed to be impassable. 'Burma seems in grave danger of being overrun,' Prime Minister Winston Churchill cabled the Indian Army Chief Archibald Wavell – also responsible for Burma – urging him to make the most of assistance from Chinese allies.[96] But Shahid could see how different the two sets of forces were, and how difficult it was to make their relationship fruitful. 'Nobody could understand the control and command structure of the Chinese Army,' he wrote. While their soldiers were courageous and hardy, they came with few weapons and little equipment: 'no logistics support, no transport, no supply system and no administration'.

His work regularly took him out into field, where he saw the extent to which British and Indian units were being outclassed by an enemy trained for jungle warfare, using bicycles and pack animals to move with ease and stealth. 'They often lay concealed in the villages where our troops were stationed, and during the night created confusion,' Shahid said, remembering how the Japanese used Burmese and Urdu phrase books to call out to Allied soldiers and mislead them. 'Our forces were frightened, depressed and bewildered when entering a jungle,' Shahid said. 'They hated the silence and isolation.' When the enemy was known to be close, he told Tahirah later, even the animals seemed to hold their breath until morning came.

❧❦❧

She had remained in Bhopal in this period, living with Shahid's parents, looking after Hassan and pregnant with their second child. Remarkably, post between India and Burma continued to be delivered – she wrote to Shahid every day and his letters home described both the beguiling nature of Rangoon and its anguish. 'He said it was the most beautiful city he'd ever seen,' she remembered. 'But the retreat was starting. You'd walk into houses and the fridges were going, the clocks were going, they were full of the most beautiful china and carpets. And the owners had just gone.'

By February 1942 it was clear that Singapore, the base regarded as Britain's impregnable fortress in Asia, was in danger, as the Japanese moved south through the Malay peninsula. It was an astounding advance, and although the remaining British, Indian and Australian units were greater in number, they were confined to Singapore Island and looking vulnerable. 'There must at this stage be no thought of saving the troops or sparing the population,' Churchill cabled Wavell on 10 February. 'The battle must be fought to the bitter end at all costs.'[97] A day later, the Japanese were in control of half of Singapore Island, and Wavell was sending final messages to his commanders. 'So long as you are in position to inflict losses and damage to enemy and your troops are physically capable of doing so, you must fight on,' he wrote on the 15th. 'When you are fully satisfied that this is no longer possible I give you discretion to cease resistance ... Whatever happens I thank you and all your troops for your gallant efforts of last few days.'[98]

That same evening the surrender document was signed and 85,000 Allied soldiers became prisoners of war. The news was a great blow to morale in Rangoon, Shahid said, and it also had immediate adverse consequences for units in Burma, as Japanese planes that had been in action over Malaya were now diverted against them.

He continued to travel out to troops in close proximity to Japanese land forces in eastern Burma, finding them depleted in both manpower and supplies, and lacking stable lines of communication. As a retreat towards Rangoon began, there was one terrible incident when a bridge over the Sittaung river was blown up before all the Allied troops had managed to get across. The stranded soldiers tried to make rafts from bits of timber or bamboo, all the while under fire, and some plunged into the water without being able to swim. Many died, and the survivors could do little but drag the bodies into hollows and cover them with whatever they could find.[99]

By then, Shahid was witnessing a further deterioration in conditions in Rangoon. 'Local services had broken down and there was no law and order. The civil authorities had left, looting and burning were rampant, jails and asylums had been opened, corpses were lying in the street. It was sad to see this beautiful city in that mess.' Most of those now trying to escape to the Indian border were travelling on foot, and the long journey left British and Indian civilians at grave risk from hunger and disease, while being preyed upon by criminals. One teenager walked for three weeks but arrived in India only to find that his mother and five siblings had died elsewhere on the route.[100]

Events were now moving fast, so much so that any orders issued quickly became obsolete. Shahid saw a new commander arrive in Rangoon on 3 March and tell the gathered officers that, on Churchill's orders, the city was to be held at all costs. Within three days that position was unsustainable: the Japanese were so close that Rangoon had to be evacuated and he found himself in a long, slow-moving column as Army Headquarters moved out in its entirety. Assets such as the oil refinery were destroyed and they took the road north, towards Mandalay.

Their new base was Maymyo, Burma's summer capital, which at first glance seemed astonishingly untouched by the war, with a still-functioning club, golf course, polo ground and racecourse. But here, too, conditions soon worsened and an exodus began. Shahid saw people prepared to barter fistfuls of rubies for the same of rice, and one wealthy Indian offered him the keys to his house as he abandoned it, leaving with a single suitcase and his two dogs.

By then the pitiful state of those who had already made it back from Burma – and the tales of military families evacuated from Malaya – was being noticed in India. The Army became concerned about public opinion, as well as internal morale, and began radio broadcasts from Maymyo in order to allow troops to send messages home. Shahid was also asked to go on air and describe the situation in Burma in Urdu – presumably a sanitised version of the true picture. From Bhopal, Tahirah continued to write, and tried to be as strong as she could, for the sake of her mother-in-law Feroze. 'I stayed with her,' she says on tape, 'writing my daily letter to Shahid and waiting for my letters back from the war-struck zone. But she was beside herself with worry, anxiety and sorrow.'

In the middle of March 1942, Headquarters at Maymyo gained a new commander, General Bill Slim, who had been sent in from the Middle East. Slim thought the place surreal: it was picturesque, with houses 'in the best Surrey stockbroker style', but full of unnerved and demoralised colleagues.[101] Shahid watched him get to grips with the new command and found him impressive, as he swiftly visited a number of units before announcing his plan to hold the Japanese along an east–west line. From there, Chinese forces would withdraw north along the Sittaung river and his own troops would do the same along a second, the Irrawaddy.

This was the theory, but everyone knew the perils involved in what would be a long retreat across difficult terrain. Units away from the main formations were especially vulnerable to being attacked, either by the Japanese or by their allies in the Burma Independence Army, led by Aung San.* 'The troops were exhausted,' Shahid wrote. 'Malaria was becoming our worst enemy and casualties as a result of disease were heavy.' Even air support was disappearing: one RAF and American strike on a Japanese-held airfield triggered large-scale retaliation, which destroyed many Allied aircraft. Afterwards the

---

*This later became the Burma National Army. Aung San, father of Aung San Suu Kyi, switched his allegiance away from Japan in 1945.

Americans withdrew their remaining planes and the RAF moved to a new base further west, before pulling out of Burma completely.

From Shahid's account it seems that the Army still had access to some aircraft for supply purposes, because he writes of going on drops on these planes, flying with open doors towards isolated pockets of troops. One such trip took him to Mandalay on the morning of 3 April 1942 and he describes arriving shortly before an intense three-hour Japanese bombing raid began. When I looked this up I discovered that it was a terrible day in the history of Burma's second city, where most of the buildings were made of wood. When a correspondent for Life magazine arrived two days later she wrote of an apocalyptic scene: blackened human remains in the streets and a place almost obliterated by fire.[102]

Shahid describes seeing the flames take hold and spread quickly along rows of houses, and then feeling the force of a large explosion himself, as an ammunition dump caught fire. He was blown into a trench, where he lay for some time, struggling to open his eyes, until he was able to get himself up and back to Maymyo. There, Headquarters was in a state of flux and about to evacuate again but he found himself unable to be of use: the eye problem that had affected him in the trench was acute, seriously impairing his vision. One doctor prescribed rest, which was impossible, and as his eyes worsened he was admitted to hospital.

In his memoir he deals swiftly with what happened next, saying only that a medical board decided to evacuate him to Calcutta – I think that even years later, he was uncomfortable at having had a way out of Burma before the final, grim retreat.

It is Tahirah who tells the full story in her tapes, of a doctor who almost certainly saved Shahid's sight, and possibly his life. The evacuation order he signed is dated 7 April 1942, four days after the bombing of Mandalay, and Shahid told Tahirah he questioned it: 'Sir, there are many here wounded much worse than me.' At that point the doctor lifted his spectacles away from his face, revealing his own serious eye injury. 'This happened to me in the last war,' he said.

'To my mind you are the worst off here. You'll leave for Calcutta by plane at five o'clock this evening.'

Within hours Shahid was at an airstrip at Shwebo, north-west of Mandalay, carrying a slip of paper stamped 'Immediate' in red at the top. 'Capt. S. S. Hamid, 3rd Cav.Attd.R.I.A.S.C., B.I.Lines Mymo' it reads, detailing his original regiment as well as the Supply Corps, and that he had been with the infantry lines at Maymyo. 'You will be evacuated by Amb. train. Kindly be in readiness to move at a moment's notice.' It is signed by a B. B. Holden from the Royal Army Medical Corps, who may or may not have been the doctor who made the decision. 'I had just one bag with me, my entire luggage,' Shahid remembered, and as he flew towards India he must have looked down and seen many others less fortunate, heading in the same direction on foot.[103]

In Bhopal, Tahirah was six months pregnant with the baby who would be their first daughter, Shahnaz. With the news from Burma worse by the day, her desperately worried mother-in-law Feroze had decided to go to Ajmer in Rajasthan, to the tomb of a thirteenth-century Sufi saint, and pray for Shahid's safe return. 'She was there for a day or two,' said Tahirah, 'and when she returned to Delhi she found Shahid.' Tahirah's own reunion was to come the next day, after Feroze travelled to Bhopal with the person they had all been waiting for and praying for. 'You can imagine the joy with which she arrived back by train the following morning,' Tahirah remembered. 'She looked at me and said, "I've brought him back."' Shahid was home.

8

Mary and Mumtaz

That first half of 1942 was a terrible shock for the Raj and for the people of India, as Japan proved its military capability in one location after another. Parts of the British Empire, which had appeared as securely under colonial rule as India itself, were now occupied by another power.

Mumtaz and Mary were in Lahore in this period, still trying to work out how to get married, but on the Bay of Bengal coast her family were directly affected by the new threat from Japan. In April 1942 Vizagapatnam, where Mary's younger siblings were at school and college, was bombed. This was the moment that made the war real, Anne told me, when she looked up while walking on the beach to see small planes following a ship coming into the harbour and then opening fire. As explosions were heard, people around her started running inland, and at the convent her eleven-year old sister Josephine also saw the planes from the terrace where she was playing. 'I was filled with amazement and wanted to carry on watching, but the nuns rushed us all downstairs to take shelter,' she said in an account given to her local BBC radio station in 2005. 'As I was running, I saw the bombs being dropped from the planes and lots of light.'[104] Nine people were killed in Vizagapatnam that day, and

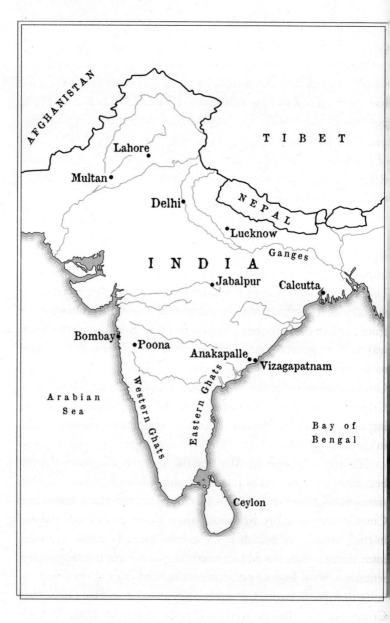

air strikes that destroyed twenty-three merchant ships off the coast caused further loss of life, with corpses washing up on the beach.[105]

Prior to that, the war had provided a net benefit to Vizagapatnam, which was well connected by rail to both Calcutta and Madras and had a natural harbour big enough to accommodate larger vessels. Its port was used to export minerals and coal mined further inland, and a new shipyard had opened in 1941. But after the air strikes the sense of risk led some people to leave, and for a time Josephine, Louisa, Rosemarie and the other boarders were evacuated with the nuns into the Eastern Ghat mountains.

❦

Japan's advance in Asia sparked another stage of the war's political impact on India. Britain came under pressure from two allies – the United States and China – to produce a vision of the future that would incentivise maximum war effort by Indians; it was clearly far from ideal that the biggest political force in the country, Congress, was not onside. From London, Churchill's government decided to initiate a new offer of constitutional change, and sent Stafford Cripps, a member of the War Cabinet, to Delhi with a draft plan. Cripps was fresh from negotiating the Allies' pact with Stalin and, importantly for this mission in India, he already knew key figures in Congress.[106]

His plan, set out in March and April 1942, involved India becoming a Dominion of the Empire after the war, finally equal in status to countries such as Canada and Australia. There would be a Constituent Assembly, whose members would be elected by voters in the provinces of British India and the princely states, and more immediately, there would be a national government involving representatives of the leading political parties.[107]

It didn't work out. Congress objected to two elements of the Cripps plan: for Britain to retain responsibility for India's defence while hostilities continued, and for provinces or states to be able to opt out of joining the post-war union. With the idea of a Muslim homeland increasingly being talked about, this particular option was regarded by Gandhi as 'an invitation to the Muslims to create a Pakistan'.[108]

Even decades on, it is impossible to say whether there was ever scope in this 1942 moment for a different outcome. Some thought Gandhi's philosophy of non-violence made the whole exercise academic, that it was impossible for Congress to really contemplate supporting a war; others felt Britain was the one going through the motions, in order to keep President Roosevelt and the Chinese leader Chiang Kai-shek happy. And, once again, there was little capacity to spend time on India, with Europe in darkness, intense fighting in North Africa and the Germans heading into southern Russia.

Afterwards, Gandhi focused on a new idea, a demand for Britain's immediate withdrawal from India. This was highly contentious even within his party, as it was certain to be regarded as seditious – some worried that it might encourage the Japanese to launch an invasion.[109] But in August 1942 the 'Quit India' resolution was adopted by Congress, calling for an immediate end to British rule, after which an independent India would be part of the Allies' 'joint struggle for freedom'.[110] The British response was swift. Under wartime rules arrest warrants were served the next day on Gandhi, Nehru and other Congress leaders, most of whom would not emerge from detention for another three years, when the war was nearly won.

⊰⊱

At the beginning of 1943 Mumtaz resat his medical school finals, and had a little time in hand before the results came. Mary was in Anakapalle and as her family knew by then about the marriage, he set off from Lahore to visit her home for the first time.

The long journey across India was an education in itself, showing him a vast swathe of the country beyond his native region of Punjab. Thirty-six hours after boarding an eastbound night train, he was looking out over Bengal. 'The crossing of the Hoogly River, a tributary of the mighty Ganges, was an awe-inspiring sight,' he wrote, but even then he still had a way to go. From Calcutta he travelled on for a further night and day on a southbound train, watching the landscape change from plains into hills and knowing from the salt in the air and the appearance of seagulls that they were close to the ocean.

His instructions were to 'alight at Waltair Junction' – the name of the station at Vizagapatnam – and as the train slowed on approach he saw Mary waiting. 'My heart nearly stopped with excitement to see the sight of my dreams and desires on the platform, waving frantically as she caught sight of me,' he remembered. They went yet further south, together, changing at Anakapalle for the even smaller line to Kasimkota, the station nearest to the Quinn home. She had time to brief him: while her siblings were looking forward to his arrival, her mother was in a less accommodating mood.

As they walked from the station he took in the sight of sugarcane fields and coconut palms, before the whitewashed house came into view. The times of the trains were well known and his new in-laws were assembled on the verandah to greet him: four girls, one boy, and his mother-in-law Mariamma, wearing a white sari, her jet-black hair swept back into a bun. She was younger than he had expected and he thought her face remarkably unlined, especially given what she had lived through. The two of them conversed in English, but apart from Anne, none of the other children said much. 'I did feel a bit odd and ill-at-ease under the scrutiny,' he wrote. Louisa told him later that they were unaccustomed to having a man in the house: he was the first since the death of their father, eight years earlier. That night the table was beautifully laid for dinner: a damask tablecloth, linen napkins, silver cutlery and wine glasses – though no wine was served – and Mumtaz thought the atmosphere eased a little when he poured Mariamma a whisky from the bottle he had brought with him.

When I asked Anne about this first meeting, she was characteristically blunt. She and Mumtaz would later become close, especially after Mary died, but in 1943 she told me she had been less than impressed by his appearance. She had imagined a 'great, handsome man' from the faraway lands in the north, a strapping Punjabi, whereas Mumtaz was not much taller than Mary and of a slight build. 'My God, Mary,' she told her sister. 'Is this the man?'

Mumtaz records his main sentiment on that first visit to Anaka-palle as one of relief, that he faced no hostility. 'I was made to feel almost at home,' he said. 'Only a few questions about my background and the place I came from, and my prospects of becoming a doctor.' Mariamma seemed to be reconciling herself to the marriage, although there were times when she switched into Telugu and exchanged sharp words with Mary. He could see that the others were chipping in on their sister's side, and he found himself grateful for the language barrier, which protected him from knowing what his mother-in-law was saying.

❦

Mary took him to explore Anakapalle and the area beyond, and he continued to be struck by the many points of difference between this region and his home. The town was smaller and much less developed than Lahore or Multan, and people seemed poorer: he noticed that the women balancing baskets of produce on their heads had economised with the amount of material they used for their saris, expertly winding shorter lengths of fabric around their bodies. In the market he saw coffee beans for the first time, and a thriving trade in coconuts, coconut water and toddy, an alcoholic drink made from fermented palm sap. He was amazed to see that this one town had several cinemas – film was clearly the main source of entertainment – and he noticed a great number of Hindu temples, as well as statues of deities at street corners, to which people would bow and fold hands as they passed. He had never been inside a temple and when he entered one now with Mary he found it fascinating: 'the spectacle, the colours, the devotion of the visitors and the continuous sound of the ringing bell'.

She wanted him to see the farm at Gandhavarum, too, and they went there together on a *jhatka*, the southern Indian equivalent of the horse-drawn *tongas* he knew. The acreage was substantial and he could see immediately why it had been a trial for Mariamma, while also being certain that Francis would have done well out of it. 'The Irishman in my deceased father-in-law gave him a passion and love for the outdoors and an inherent know-how about care of the land,' he wrote. Francis's long service to the Raj would also have left him well placed to navigate the inevitable bureaucracy over what he wanted to do.

Neither the Anakapalle house nor the farm are in the Quinn family's hands anymore and I am sure Francis's grave must be long gone, as a road was eventually built through the Gandhavarum land. After independence Mary went home only twice more in her life, but by the mid-1950s it does seem that her mother had a good grip on the farm. In a series of letters that Louisa wrote to her fiancé Jack between 1956 and 1957, when he was in England and she was on a trip home, the scene she describes is idyllic. 'I wish you were here, my darling, to see the fields all green with paddy, which will ripen in two weeks,' she wrote of the rice crop. 'The flowers are beautiful and all morning I have been watching the huge butterflies hovering around. One settled on my dress, as it thought the blue flowers were real. The air is full of different sorts of birds, there must be over 50 different species. We have cows, two buffaloes, calves, lambs and all our own poultry and vegetables, so we rarely buy anything from outside for our daily fare. I never realised the beauty around us until my return from England.'

❦

On Mumtaz's 1943 visit, it was not only Mariamma he needed to win over but the nuns. He was anxious about visiting the convent, knowing how much the nuns had supported the Quinns, and conscious that he was the man responsible not only for Mary marrying outside the faith but failing to fulfil the nursing dream they had for her.

On the agreed day he and Mary went back up to Vizagapatnam together, accompanied by Anne. As they approached the convent he was impressed by the scale of the building and by its well-established garden, and then the three of them were shown into the parlour. 'One by one the nuns started trickling in,' he said, and he was able to attach faces to names and stories, identifying an elderly nun as the one who would take a ruler to Mary's knuckles if she hit a wrong note on the piano. Then the most senior came in: not Mother Marie-Joseph on this occasion, as she was away in Europe, but Mother Thérèse-Marie, who had also known the Quinn girls for years. 'She looked amiable, with a lovely smile on a handsome face,' he said, but it didn't take long for the pleasantries to turn into more of an interview. Was he going to be steadfast in caring for Mary, allowing her to practise her faith, and would he stand by the undertaking he had given on the religion of their children? Here he felt confident: he had already made his promises and they were sincere.

The nuns appeared reassured but then one, Sister Bridget, went further: might he consider becoming a Catholic himself? He struggled for a moment, trying to think of a way to be truthful as well as polite. 'If the light comes,' he said finally, and they seemed pleased with this. Sister Bridget offered to provide him with literature to help the process along, and for several years she was true to her word, with books and Catholic pamphlets regularly coming to him in the post. When they met she would ask him if the light had now come, and he would say 'Not yet.' He never minded the questions, nor the packages, and when he heard she had died in a road accident he felt he had lost a true friend in the convent.

After this meeting I think he began to relax into life in Anakapalle, and almost lost track of time, because he appears to have been unprepared for the telegram that arrived from Lahore, bearing both good and bad news. It was from Abid and Jimmy, informing him he had passed his exams and was now officially a doctor, but also that he was overdue for commissioning. Questions were being asked as to his whereabouts and there was even a risk of being labelled a deserter.

Suddenly the conditions attached to Mumtaz's stipend the year before were real and pressing. He still had access to his old Lahore lodgings, and he and Mary travelled back there together, leaving the temperate climate of her home region behind and feeling the chill of winter in the northern plains as they went west from Calcutta. Mumtaz soon discovered that married accommodation in the services was out of the question – officers were not supposed to marry until the age of twenty-eight, and he was still only twenty-two. Mary would have to return to Anakapalle, but in the intervening few days in Lahore she did something entirely unexpected and, for him, highly problematic: she wrote to his parents and announced herself as their new daughter-in-law.

Now that they had been married in the mosque and in church, Mary no longer saw a reason to hide their union from anyone, and she had used the address Mumtaz had previously given her, for the friend who conveyed their own, secret, letters. When Mumtaz was told, he was horrified. 'Mary had initiated a storm, the intensity of which she had no clue,' he said, knowing that the efficiency of the postal system meant his parents could already be on their way to Lahore, in a rage.

Mary maintained that she was ready for their arrival. 'What is wrong with trying to gain the confidence of what is going to be my family as much as yours in the years to come?' But Mumtaz could not cope with the prospect of a family showdown in her presence. Yet again their friend Jimmy stepped in to help, this time finding Mary a hotel room so that Mumtaz could deal with his parents alone.

As he expected, they had left Multan immediately upon receiving the letter, bringing his sister Sakina to Lahore with them. Brushing past him at the door of the apartment, they demanded to know where Mary was, referring to her only as 'she'. Mumtaz did his best to keep calm: his marriage had been an Islamic *nikah*, he told them, and had to be accepted. He offered to take them to see the register at the Australia Mosque, where the imam, tipped off by Jimmy, delivered a mini sermon on marriages between Muslims, Christians and Jews.

Even this brought about only a short lull, after which his parents continued to press him: he must divorce Mary, or abandon her, or take another wife, if he had any regard for the family's honour, indeed for their very existence in Multan. Finally, Mumtaz said, a mood of 'disdain and disappointment bordering on contempt' set in, and his parents said they would leave by the next available train.

From now on, he told Mary, she was to leave such matters well alone: the situation would have to work itself out in its own time.

Despite the rift, when his first paycheck arrived that month he sent a portion of it to Multan. This was with Mary's knowledge and blessing, and the gesture continued for years, even when the needs of their growing family made it difficult. Mumtaz's parents did not necessarily need the money but receiving it was a source of pride, enabling them to tell people that the boy who had gone away to become a doctor still felt a bond with his home.

❧❦❧

After completing the formalities of signing on – and seeing Mary off to Anakapalle – Mumtaz travelled to a training centre in Lucknow, where he and Abid would begin their service. Uniforms had been purchased, and wearing them, they discovered, immediately opened doors: suddenly they could walk past 'Indians and Dogs Not Permitted' signs and into establishments from which their skin colour had previously barred them.

My grandfather was now, in the words of his emergency commission, King George VI's 'trusty and well beloved Mumtaz Husain', a lieutenant in the Indian Land Forces. He found the course designed to turn him into a soldier tough, but all those with him were in the same boat, young doctors who 'had never thought they would have to carry anything heavier than a stethoscope or do much more than stand around an operating table'. Preparing for their new lives alongside fighting men meant drill on the parade ground at dawn, clad only in vest and shorts, having baffling instructions barked at them. There were comical scenes, Mumtaz said, as people marched off in different directions, sparking the fury of their sergeant. 'You bloody fool, sir!' he would shout, the 'sir' included to stay just on the right side of military etiquette. In many ways Mumtaz could understand the frustration: the medics were 'a bedraggled bunch of people, drawn from all parts of the subcontinent, without even a passing acquaintance with army discipline and quite difficult to mould into an orderly final product'.

Even worse than drill were the route marches, which took them out into the countryside for up to twenty miles at a time, carrying medical kits as well as a weapon, food and water. Mumtaz found himself too exhausted to write much to Mary, but her letters came every day, each one a comfort. He turned to Urdu to describe their effect in his memoir: *koozay may darya bharna*, like having the contents of an entire river poured into your cup. As the weeks of her pregnancy rolled by she kept him updated on check-ups and baby movements, until one day there was a telegram: their son had been born. He was a beautiful boy, Mary told him, who had inherited his curly hair. She asked about names and Mumtaz chose 'Imtiaz', meaning distinction, and she chose 'Joseph' as a Christian name for the baptism.

Judging by the photograph I found in my father's files, he was about three months old when Mumtaz managed to get some leave and travel to Anakapalle to see him for the first time. Again, Mary came to meet him at Waltair and this time, when he walked up to the Quinn house, his mother-in-law Mariamma was standing on the verandah with his son in her arms. 'He was in his swaddling clothes and I turned the cloth from his face,' Mumtaz wrote. 'My expectations were more than borne out. He was a beautiful baby, with the cutest face I had ever seen.'

Tazi was wearing blue and white, and Mumtaz knew why. Mary had been deeply worried by a bout of infant jaundice and had prayed to the Virgin Mary, promising that if the baby was saved he would be dressed in her colours for seven years. When Tazi recovered, she was certain it was divine intervention. 'There seemed no point in

attempting to convince her otherwise,' Mumtaz said, knowing that newborns often got jaundice and usually recovered as feeding was established. 'In any case I myself was happy that our baby was safe and well.'

❦

As his training course came to an end, he had feared being sent to a front line, but instead he and Abid opened their orders to find that they were staying in India, at least for now – not that they had ever heard of the places they were going to. They had to look them up in an atlas and both turned out to be in central India, where they were to support troops training in jungle warfare.

Chindwara, Abid's destination, was especially remote. Getting there would involve travel on a narrow-gauge railway, through a forest where tigers were known to wander into the train's slow-moving carriages and out the other side. In comparison, Mumtaz felt fortunate: he was going to Jabalpur, a bigger town with a military hospital. Still, the wards there came as a shock. Apart from a few patients evacuated from front lines, most had come from the training battalions and the state they were in filled him with horror. They had obviously been in areas of thick bush, undergrowth and ponds, and there was little evidence the Army's Field Hygiene manual was being observed. He was treating scabies, boils and foot rot, and soldiers were often suspected of deliberately trying to get themselves infected as a way out of the field. Worse was the high incidence of malaria, cerebro-spinal fever and dysentery, which all contributed to the hospital's high fatality rate.

The doctors had few tools that might enable them to try to save lives, for penicillin was yet to be introduced. Early on, Mumtaz had an experience that left him badly shaken, when a young soldier was brought in and he was the doctor in sole charge. He began carrying out a lumbar puncture, his first time doing so unsupervised, and while he was withdrawing the needle his patient shivered and suddenly died. 'I had the most awful feeling that I was, somehow, responsible for this,' he wrote, despite being sure that he had gone into the right space in the spine. 'Even after I returned to my lodgings the image of that poor man kept cropping up wherever I looked and whatever I did,' he said. 'Sleep would not come either. I sought some relief in writing a miserable, guilt-filled letter to Mary.'

A fatal case report the next day declared that, given the condition of the patient on arrival, the outcome was inevitable. But Mumtaz never forgot what had happened and when he ran hospitals later in his career he would make a point of drilling young doctors on lumbar punctures.

By the time he was writing his memoir he was also able to compare his early experiences to the subsequent transformation of his profession, although there were aspects of the old ways that he missed. When he started out there were few tests, let alone scans; doctors needed to encourage patients to talk to them, to elicit every possible bit of information and combine it with clinical knowledge and examination in order to reach a diagnosis. There were also fewer specialisms, which meant the whole person was looked at, and Mumtaz disliked seeing how, later, doctors might order a battery of tests and scans and spend less time with the patient. 'I am not trying to deride the present,' he wrote. 'Modern research and treatments have, no doubt, opened up new vistas, but I do have a problem with a patient becoming a mere case or a number.'

✥

Later in 1943 he was moving on again, this time to field training, a prospect he dreaded. Wartime security meant he was told only that he needed to get to Bombay, where he was met at the station and directed to an Army truck that took him out of the city on a dirt road. 'The sense of despondency escalated with each passing mile,' he said, as inhabited areas were left behind and they headed towards the Western Ghat mountains.

The camp that would be his base was almost entirely tented, apart from a few prefab buildings, one of which would serve as his Medical Inspection room. At least he had a tent to himself, he thought, and it came with an orderly, who unpacked the camp kit he had brought and set it up: a bed, chair, trestle table and even a bathtub and wash-basin made of reinforced canvas, to be suspended on foldable metal frames.

The tent had a single electric lightbulb, which he was told would come on for exactly three hours after dusk, while the camp generator was running. That evening, he walked to the mess tent for dinner, nervously navigating the overgrown path and discovering that he was the unit's only Indian officer. No one was especially friendly and he found he had little to contribute to conversation: his new colleagues were all engineers and spoke mostly of bridge-building, explosives and minefields. He learned later of their personal circumstances, which no doubt affected the atmosphere. One had suffered a personal tragedy when his wife and two children were killed in an attack on their ship in the Mediterranean, as they travelled to India to join him; another was smarting from his wife abandoning him for a fellow officer. Meanwhile their Colonel had a wife back in England and a mistress in Bombay, and Mumtaz said one of the unit's youngest officers 'would waylay any available local woman and had earned himself a vile reputation'.

This was not a place where he felt he would make friends but there was, at least, a well-stocked bar, and he took solace from the fact that he would be able to save some money, as meals in the field were all free. He adjusted to new uniform requirements: shorts rather than trousers but the exposed leg covered entirely in *putties*, cloth bandages, to protect the skin. Simulating being in a combat area also meant replacing all metal pips and badges with less visible cloth-covered ones, which meant no belt buckles and removing even the Indian Medical Service crest on his cap. Mumtaz found this demoralising, as it took away his pride in being properly turned out, and it came alongside stark warnings on everyday risks: he must check for snakes before putting on shoes, and remain under his mosquito net throughout the night, until his orderly arrived each morning.

His work as the unit's medical officer began with the morning 'sick parade', when he would assess which men required treatment and possibly even evacuation. The troops were all Indian and regarded him with interest; he was the first officer they had had who looked like them, and this was in addition to his special status as their medic. 'I was told of the mixture of awe and respect with which a doctor was looked upon by the unit,' Mumtaz said. 'He could prescribe rest or have you disciplined for malingering, but most importantly he was a means to life-saving measures during battle. A soldier in combat faces a bullet more readily if he has confidence in his arms and leadership and secondly, a reassurance of support in case of injury.'

Sanitation and hygiene were also his responsibility and this involved a daily round of the camp, from barracks to kitchens and latrines, accompanied by two soldiers taking notes on anything he was unhappy with. He discovered that these notes were read daily by the unit's commander, and when I read General Slim's memoir I was able to put Mumtaz's work into the context of a major shift in military thinking. After the disastrous period Shahid had witnessed in Burma, when troops were being lost to sickness as well as enemy fire, a new determination to maintain the Army's health had taken hold. The emphasis on disease prevention and control became so strict that officers could be sacked if the men under their command became ill and were found not to have taken anti-malaria pills or kept up vaccinations. By the time the Allies moved into Burma again all of this would pay off.[111]

※❧❦

On the odd weekend off Mumtaz went to see Abid, Jimmy and Riffat, who were all training at Poona, south-east of Bombay. When he complained about living in a tent there was no sympathy: they were sleeping in dormitories in their barracks and thought his conditions didn't sound so bad. 'Count your blessings, old boy,' they said. 'Just think what it will be like if we get to Burma.'

Mumtaz soon had a greater taste of what that might be like, as his unit struck camp and moved deeper into the Ghats, travelling on foot with mules carrying their supplies. The weather added to his misery: the monsoons had come and it seemed to rain all day and all night, so that it was no drier under the shelters they put up than it was outside. The day was spent in wet clothes and squelching boots, with possessions coated in a layer of moss, and food completely unappetising; any salt, pepper or sugar sprinkled on top turned immediately to liquid.

He is honest enough in his memoir to say that he continued to dread the real version of what he was training for, especially the responsibility for setting up aid posts close to forward positions, where the only available cover might be a single tree or hastily dug trench. When he was called in to see his Adjutant he therefore braced for the worst, certain that the moment of being deployed to the front had come. Instead, the news was unexpected: he was being transferred out of the Army and into the Royal Air Force, in line, he was told, with his expressed preference. A faint memory came back: when he and his friends first signed on and were filling out forms, there had been a question about the various services and they had ticked the Air Force box, thinking it sounded glamorous. They never expected anything to come of it, not least because the air arm was a relatively small operation compared to the Army. Now, though, it was expanding, again as part of preparations for a return to Burma.[112]

Mumtaz could barely believe his luck: at the very least he was escaping camp and field life. He fired off a telegram to Mary and discovered that Abid, Jimmy and Riffat had all had the same news. From dismissing the Air Force as 'Brylcreem Boys', as the Army generally did, they were about to enter those very ranks.

❧❦❧

This new stage of life involved registering for duty in Lahore, and the proximity to Multan prompted him to make a trip home, in the hope that tempers over Mary had cooled. He discovered that, in a way, they had. His parents were no longer asking him to give her up, but the new path they proposed, again in front of his aunts and uncles, was almost as enraging. Islam permitted more than one wife, they said, and therefore he should take Rahima as his second and fulfil his father's promise to hers.

Mumtaz was repulsed. He had made his own promises – to Mary, and to the nuns at St Joseph's, assuring them that this Muslim husband would never take another wife. He was also well schooled in his faith and he knew there were parameters to polygamy in Islam. The practice in pre-Islamic Arabia had been of unrestricted numbers of wives, and the Qur'an rooted what it said about marriage in the social reality of early Muslims in the seventh century, when there were many orphans and war widows. 'Two, or three, or four' were only permitted if a man was capable of treating them justly, otherwise, the text said, it should be one.[113]

They argued late into the night. Mumtaz's father told him that the family's honour was being rubbed into the dust, and that his only remaining option was to assume responsibility for Rahima himself: she would remain under his protection, in the family home, and never marry at all. Mumtaz remembered that there were cases in Multan where families said their daughters were 'married to the Qur'an', usually a ploy to keep an inheritance undivided. In a conciliatory gesture he said that after his father's lifetime he would continue to support Rahima financially: she was, after all, his cousin.

Years later he discovered that this was not the way the family portrayed Rahima's position. When marriage proposals later came for her, they were refused on the basis that she was married to him, and this became the accepted version of events in Multan.

Rahima outlived Mary by many years, and I know that when she died in 2004 Mumtaz travelled from Karachi to Multan for the burial. I do not know what went through his mind as he stood at the graveside, but I am certain he never blamed her for the pressure he had been placed under, nor for the years it took for Mary to be accepted. Rahima had been a victim, he felt, of his family 'sacrificing the life of an innocent girl on the altar of a promise'.

9

Auchinleck

Shahid and Tahirah's second child Shahnaz was born in July 1942, soon after his return from Burma. The family would spend much of the rest of the war in Quetta, out in the far west and today the capital of the Pakistani province of Balochistan. It was the home of the Indian Army's Command and Staff College, founded by Kitchener, and the place where mid-career officers earmarked for promotion were sent. Shahid must have been pleased to be selected, but Tahirah was simply relieved. 'Such a posting was an absolute treat because you knew you were secure for a certain length of time,' she said, meaning secure from being deployed to a front line.

Over a three-year period Shahid would be both student and instructor at Quetta, and a third child, my mother Shama, was born there during an especially cold Balochistan winter. In between the two stints the Hamids had a posting in Calcutta, by then a significant base for Burma operations. It meant an epic journey by train across the entire breadth of India and, for Tahirah, immersion in a new part of the country. 'I'd never seen Calcutta, or the sea, or been anywhere near a port,' she says on tape. 'There'd been no reason to do that.' Now, this capital of the historic and cultured province of Bengal was her home, though she knew the experience would come to an

abrupt end if Shahid was sent on into Burma. By then he was not the only serviceman in her life: her younger brother Mahmood had joined the Air Force in 1941 when he was only nineteen, and was already further east, flying Hawker Hurricanes out of the airfield at Cox's Bazar.[114]

Despite Calcutta's war footing it was still possible to socialise, to be entertained and to soak up what the city had to offer. Compared to Quetta, where life was largely restricted to their Army circle, both British and Indian, here there were many Aligarh and Lucknow connections. 'It was a happy happy time,' Tahirah said. 'We were young, and I think the world is kind to the young.' They had evenings at the original hotel of what became the Oberoi chain, and outings to the races, about which Tahirah was initially apprehensive. 'When Shahid said "Come to the races" I was petrified,' she remembered. 'He only had his pay to live on and I worried about what would happen to us if he started to place bets.' She knew he had an uncle who had lost his money that way, and Shahid understood her fear. 'Don't worry,' he said, explaining that he lived by his father's maxim: to only ever

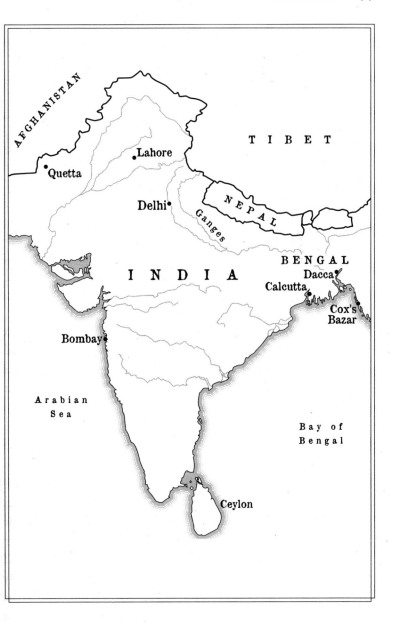

gamble what you could afford to lose. His bets were therefore never more than 15 rupees, and he gave any winnings to Tahirah.

For Shahid Calcutta's historic link with Lucknow was also resonant: this was where Wajid, the last Nawab of Avadh, had come in 1856 when his territory was being annexed by the British, and where he had died. In the neighbourhood where he had made his home in exile there were still businesses that could trace their origins to his court, staffed by descendants of artisans, cooks, tailors and grooms who had followed him out of Lucknow.[115]

❧

During their time in Calcutta, Shahid and Tahirah witnessed part of a dark chapter, the Bengal famine of 1943. It was a humanitarian disaster many months in the making, to which the authorities woke up too late, and Shahid's men were among those deployed to help. 'We were detailed to carry food and remove the casualties,' he wrote. 'It was a heart-rending task and shook us to the core. My unit decided to forgo a third of their rations and we carried cooked food for the populace.'

Multiple factors had combined to devastating effect, many of them linked to the war and its effect on the economy of eastern India. There had been a cyclone affecting the rice harvest in 1942, but beyond that the causes were man-made. Rice imports were no longer coming in from occupied Burma, fishing boats had been seized for fear they would fall into Japanese hands, and huge amounts of food were being bought for and consumed by Indian and other Allied troops, including American GIs. In Britain, rationing was in place in the face of the wartime challenge to food supplies, but India's relative poverty meant people were already malnourished before the conflict: as the availability of food decreased and prices went up, their situation became perilous. At the same time some food was being exported *from* India and neither the provincial government, led by the Muslim League, nor the Raj in Delhi seemed able to respond to the degree required.

One journalist had been trying to sound the alarm over conditions in Calcutta. In June 1943 Ian Stephens, editor of the English-language paper the *Statesman*, based in the city, warned that its problems were being ignored: food shortages, rocketing prices and rents, uncollected refuse, disease and a lack of clean water. 'Calcutta is full of troops of all nations, geography has made her an important war base,' his editorial read. 'The next few months are full of serious possibilities. If only for the sake of efficient prosecution of the war, the city's affairs should be put into tolerable order without delay.'[116]

They were not. 'Famine comes quietly,' Stephens wrote in his memoir. 'Even if you've been half-expecting it there's still no drama, nothing to hear, almost nothing characteristic at first to see, anyway, in a city like Calcutta, notorious for its swarms of pitiable poor living in squalor.' By August he was seeing desperate people staggering in from the surrounding areas, 'the humblest members of the outlying rural classes', who did not shout or create trouble. 'By the time they arrived they were mostly too weak to be rough. And they were strangers to the city, and generally to one another. Bewildered, finding no help, they squatted in the by-ways and grew feebler and lay down and after a while died.'[117]

Calcutta's mortality statistics edged up and Stephens could see that, while there were many causes of death, starvation was plainly one of them. 'Something factually indistinguishable from famine was beginning, and according to our information was doing so widely throughout rural Bengal,' he wrote. With newspapers in India under wartime censorship, his ability to cover the story was limited and he worried about giving 'propaganda points straight to Goebbels and the Japanese'. But he also knew that the *Statesman* had more scope to act than Indian-owned publications, and he wondered if using photographs rather than words was a way of getting around the rules.

Pictures taken by his team on the streets of Calcutta ran on Sunday 22 August 1943 and again a week later: images of emaciated men, women and children, in a state of collapse, dying or dead.

One of the most searing is of a woman sitting on her haunches in the street, her hand resting on the neck of a skeletal child flat on the ground, possibly no longer alive. These were the more palatable images, Stephens said; there were others which he considered 'utterly unpublishable'.[118]

That summer, the future Nobel economics laureate Amartya Sen was a young boy growing up in Bengal and a witness to famine's social and psychological as well as physical effects. Feeding stations in Calcutta all opened at the same time to prevent people going from one to the other and getting multiple rations, and he observed the long lines that formed. 'The starving fought with each other to get a place in the queue before the cut-off number was reached,' he wrote. 'The jostling to get ahead of others was hard to watch. But even as a ten-year-old child I could understand this was inescapable given the circumstances.' His grandmother told him of a woman she had seen who had managed to source some food; rather than give it to the desperate child on her lap, she was eating it herself. 'We are no longer human beings, we have become animals,' she told him.[119]

Further east in Dhaka, Rafiqul Islam, later a celebrated Bangladeshi writer and educator, also saw the famine. His father's work on the railways entitled the family to some rations, but he remembered how less fortunate people staggered through the city in search of food. As in Calcutta, they had often come in from rural areas, disproportionately impacted because they remained on fixed, low incomes while wages elsewhere rose in line with demand for war-related labour.[120] 'Whenever I think of those days, I am lost,' he told the BBC in 2015. 'It was not a natural disaster, it was a man-made disaster.'[121]

The famine was later estimated to have killed between two and three million people, and it was in September 1943, after Ian Stephens' work, that there was finally evidence of a real focus on it. By then, a significant change of leadership was taking place in India, as Wavell became the new Viceroy and Claude Auchinleck – for whom Shahid would later work – became the Indian Army Chief, a post he had held before wartime commands elsewhere. An emergency scheme using Army resources to transport and distribute food began, but many Bengalis remained in a fragile position through that winter. As late as March 1944, Wavell wondered if he might have to resign for the British government to understand the continuing pressure on supplies.[122]

✻✻✻

Auchinleck would become central to my mother's family for the last eighteen months of their life in India, and she and her siblings speak fondly to this day of the man they knew as 'the Auk'. Shahid felt strongly that Auchinleck's own country never sufficiently appreciated him, but when I began my research I felt I needed to form my own impression of this man, in as objective a way as possible. It was not easy: Auchinleck never wrote a memoir and rarely talked publicly about the war, or India, or anything else after 1947.

His return to India as Army Chief came after a difficult period in his professional life, when Churchill had removed him from command in North Africa. For this reason, I had assumed that the legendary Prime Minister did not think much of this particular general. But then, within the pages of an Auchinleck biography I had bought second-hand, I saw something that made me think again: a carefully glued-in copy of a letter to a newspaper in 1981. 'Sir,' it began. 'A memorial service is being held today for Field-Marshal Sir Claude Auchinleck. Much has been written and said about the relationship between Sir Winston Churchill and the Field Marshal ... For his part I don't think Sir Winston ever told the whole story. Now is the right moment to say one thing more which, as far as I am aware, has never been told.' The writer was a Conservative MP, Sir John Langford-Holt, who related a 1948 conversation with Churchill during which he had asked him who he would call the greatest British general of the war. 'There are many candidates whose names occur to each one of us,' said Langford-Holt. 'Sir Winston Churchill's answer was immediate and definite – Auchinleck.'

The person who secured this letter in the book must have felt about its subject as Shahid did, I thought, and loose within the pages there was also a miniature copy of a painting of Auchinleck. I remembered that in the Rawalpindi house, there was a framed photograph of the Auk in the living room, and I opened Shahid's 1986 book about their time together to check the dedication. Sure enough, it was to the memory of his old boss: 'The Last Commander-in-Chief in India'.

❧

Auchinleck was born in 1884 and lived in India as a small child before his family returned to England. His soldier father died when he was eight years old, after which his mother struggled to support her four children. Money remained very tight throughout his adolescence, and this was the reason he later opted for the Indian rather than the British Army after Sandhurst: in England he would have needed a private income to supplement his pay.

Once commissioned and back in India he developed his knowledge of the country and its languages before serving in Mesopotamia in the First World War. In the Second, he was appointed to lead the armies in the Middle East in June 1941, as the feared German general Erwin Rommel and his Afrika Korps were building up their presence and progress through North Africa. By the end of 1941 he had had some success against Rommel, but early in 1942 the Germans advanced again.

If you travel by road between Egypt and Libya, as I did in 2011 to cover the Arab uprisings of that year, you can see evidence of the long battle for control of that territory, in the graveyards of soldiers lost on both sides. In Tobruk, despite the instability of Libya at that time, I saw pots of small shrubs carefully lined up in the Commonwealth cemetery, kept well watered until they could be planted, and a German cemetery built like a desert fortress, with the remains in mass graves within the high walls. Those contrasting styles are replicated in the cemeteries further east, at El Alamein in Egypt, where the rows of Commonwealth graves stretch out along a large expanse of desert. As I watched the wind whip up and shift the surrounding sand, I found myself wondering how many people, or parts of people, were never recovered.

This was the inhospitable area where Auchinleck took personal command of the fight against Rommel in 1942, basing himself at the front, away from the comfort of his Cairo headquarters. It was a perilous moment: the Germans looked set to complete their advance through North Africa just as the Japanese had moved through Asia in the preceding weeks, and Churchill faced questions and a vote in the House of Commons on the direction of the war.[123]

It was Auchinleck who stopped Rommel's advance, at the first battle of El Alamein in July 1942, but he then found himself clashing with the Prime Minister over what should happen next. Churchill was unhappy with plans to temporarily assume a defensive position, allowing for reinforcements to arrive and further preparations to be made: Auchinleck was sacked and General Bernard Montgomery led the second, decisive, battle at El Alamein between October and November.[124]

Auchinleck was not a man to make a public fuss about things and, in a rare 1970s TV interview with David Dimbleby, he spoke of his great respect for Churchill. 'His job was to instil into everyone the certainty of winning and the necessity of fighting, which he did do,' he said. But in a large and complex military operation such as the one in Egypt, Auchinleck believed the commander in the field, not the Prime Minister, was best placed to know what could be done, particularly as new troops came in. 'Fighting in the desert was quite different to anything they'd been trained for. I think that's what the non-professional mind, the civilian, like Churchill – although he had been a soldier – failed to understand. And the prodding to attack before you're ready, before the troops are trained, risking everything, that was dangerous.'[125]

In 1946, when Tahirah met Auchinleck, she felt he was still suffering from the long tail of events in North Africa. 'At that time in

India he had been deeply hurt,' she says on tape, 'removed from the Middle East at a time when he had planned everything. The victory that came was according to what he had worked out.' But Auchinleck found his 1942 achievement completely eclipsed after Montgomery took full credit for the campaign and made 'Alamein' part of his title when he became a viscount.[126]

For a time Auchinleck was without a command, but when he returned to India in 1943 he threw himself into supporting the forces under General Slim, as they prepared for and then engaged in a new battle for Burma. 'It was a good day for us when he took command of India, our main base, recruiting area and training ground,' Slim wrote. 'Without him and what he and the Army in India did for us, we could not have existed, let alone conquered.'[127]

In May 1945, Auchinleck was in London when the war in Europe came to an end, and walked among the crowds celebrating VE Day. No one recognised the man without whom 1942 could have been the year of a spiral into complete Allied decline.[128] Once back in Delhi he broadcast a message to Indian forces, thanking them for their service but acknowledging what still remained. 'The task of cleansing the world of the enemies of peace and freedom is only half done', he said, and few would have needed to be reminded of it. At that point, the surrender of Nazi Germany made little difference to the pressures on Shahid, Mumtaz and military personnel and families across India.[129]

⊰⊱

As areas in Burma and elsewhere in Asia came back under Allied control in 1945, a new problem emerged to challenge Auchinleck: the Indian soldiers who had changed sides and fought with the Japanese, and who were now being taken prisoner. Initially this was seen as an issue for the Army alone, but as moves towards India's independence progressed fast after the war, the fate of these men soon became political.

At Headquarters in Delhi they were referred to as JIFs – Japanese Indian Forces – but they were commonly known by the name they had given themselves, the Indian National Army, or INA. Some had deserted the British amid desperate times in Malaya in early 1942, when they faced being overrun and felt they had been left unsupported. Others had been swayed by Japanese promises after the surrender at Singapore, or switched sides in order to get better rations and conditions than they would have as prisoners of war. Later, there were accounts of their involvement in the mistreatment of former colleagues, the Allied POWs. 'Taking their cue from the Kempatai,' Shahid said, referring to the Japanese military police, 'the INA committed atrocious crimes in the name of patriotism against their own comrades. These are considered among the most degrading crimes in the history of soldiering.'[130]

Set against this were examples of those who had made different choices, like Captain Mateen Ansari, taken prisoner at the fall of Hong Kong in 1941 and badly tortured when he refused to disown the British. He was beheaded in 1943, at the age of twenty-six, and was posthumously awarded the George Cross.[131] Elsewhere, thousands of Indians deemed particularly resistant to the Japanese had been sent to the Pacific islands of New Guinea and New Britain, where they lived without medicine, clothes, sheets or basic amenities, had little or no contact with the Red Cross, suffered violence and degradation and were reduced to foraging to survive.[132]

In 1945 Auchinleck had to work out how to deal with thousands of captured INA men, distinguishing between the misguided or coerced and those who had committed acts of brutality. Unlike many of his peers, he did not consider the mere desire for India to be free as a suspect or wrong position. 'Our ultimate object is to build up in this country a really national army of the country and for the country,' he wrote in one memo. 'The great majority of Indian officers are "nationalists". I for one should have little respect for them if they were not, and nor would most of the British officers of the Army.'[133]

As the process of interrogating prisoners and working through files got under way that summer, a new political era was also beginning. In Britain, Labour won the general election, on a manifesto that included progress towards Indian self-government, while in India, detained Congress leaders were released and invited into talks with the Viceroy. The party would soon become deeply involved with the INA cause, especially since the men were in need of a champion: their leader Subhas Chandra Bose had been killed in a plane crash at the end of the war.*

When the first INA trial took place in the autumn, the flaws in the system Auchinleck had devised were immediately apparent. He had wanted to avoid any perception of justice being carried out in secret, and so the accused were brought to Delhi, to be held and tried in the Red Fort. But this had been the seat of the Mughals, and the place where Bahadur Shah Zafar, the last of the line, had been held after the Mutiny. That added a powerful resonance to the proceedings, as did the identity of the initial defendants. In order to demonstrate an even-handedness between the communities, the first three were a Muslim, a Hindu and a Sikh. The choice backfired, as it meant all three communities had a vested interest in the trial. Placards proclaiming 'Patriots Not Traitors' were waved outside the Fort, and Nehru himself was part of the Congress-organised defence team.

Shahid was not based in Delhi at the time, but he thought the arrangements were ill-conceived, both by Auchinleck and by the new government in London. They did not realise, he said, that far from being a version of the Nuremberg trials, the process in India was politicised and 'a show of strength between them and the Congress'.

It was a battle Congress won. Having set itself at a distance from the war and therefore from fighting men over the previous six years – some of whom had disapproved of 'Quit India' being launched at a time of danger from Japan – the party gained a new standing.

---

*Bose had been a senior Congress politician until 1939. During the war he evaded house arrest in India and travelled to Germany, where he toured POW camps to recruit Indians to his anti-British legion. Shahid's brother-in-law Anis was among those who refused him.

Auchinleck was soon conscious that the mood within the armed forces was shifting: anger at INA brutalities was becoming muted and the trials were being seen as the British punishing patriotism in India, while applauding it elsewhere.[134]

❧❦❧

The first case concluded with all three defendants found guilty of waging war against the King, and one also convicted of inciting or encouraging murder.[135] The verdicts were sent to the Chief for confirmation, but in January 1946 Auchinleck announced that he was reducing the sentences. Joining the INA was a crime that the state could not ignore, he said, but he wanted to act in a way that would 'leave the least amount of bitterness and racial feeling in the minds of the people of India and Britain'. He also made a point of saying that the particular circumstances of the time in South-East Asia were relevant: 'These same men, up to the time of the British surrender to the Japanese, had been fighting gallantly enough in most adverse circumstances, and would certainly have continued so to fight had they not been involved in disaster.'[136]

He then wrote privately to British commanders, and it was reading this communication, preserved in the papers he left to the University of Manchester, which made me feel I understood why Shahid and Tahirah held him in such high regard. The Chief they knew was a man deeply interested in people and character, and in this memo he also demonstrated an attitude to race that was ahead of his time, as he asked officers to search their consciences about the experiences of Indians in the armed forces. There had been discrimination, he said, from the start of the Indianisation programme, 'discourteous, contemptuous treatment' of Indian officers by British peers and seniors, who should have known better. Between the wars the issues continued, he said, and some of the white officers hoped Indianisation would fail. He cited segregation, differential rates of pay and, in some cases, indefensible behaviour by British officers' wives towards Indian wives. This assessment was not for quoting or public consumption, he said, but he wanted commanders to think about how bitterness 'prepared the ground for disloyalty when the opportunity came'.[137]

Only a few more INA trials took place before Auchinleck decided in April 1946 to halt further proceedings. Nehru wrote to thank him, saying the decision would 'help in producing an atmosphere which we all desire'.[138] But echoes of the INA affair rumbled on. A month before independence in 1947 Auchinleck received a letter from Edwina Mountbatten, by then the Viceroy's wife, enclosing one she had received from the wife of an ex-INA man pleading for him to be allowed back into the Army. The Chief was polite but firm. 'One cannot help feeling some sympathy for those misguided men, but they were lightly punished,' he wrote back. Reinstating them would be wrong and would risk strife and misery among innocent and loyal men. It was also inappropriate, he said, for the 'dying Government' of the Raj to do that. The woman's letter was returned to Lady Mountbatten with his reply.[139]

10

To Delhi

Mumtaz and Mary spent the final two years of the war on a series of short postings at Air Force bases in the east and south of India, with their family growing fast; a second son, Ejaz, was born in 1944 and a third, Niaz, in 1945.

Much of Mumtaz's memoir for this period is about his struggle for housing: he was still below the age at which officers were allowed to marry and thus had no right to anything other than a mess room. In each location he hoped for a sympathetic senior officer to make an exception for his family, or to find some cheap private lodgings. Surprisingly, he was successful most of the time: I think the pressures of war made his seniors keen to find a compromise rather than risk losing a doctor.

Service life brought opportunities to see more of his country and he was captivated by the range of landscapes, climates and languages he discovered. One early posting took him to RAF Vizagapatnam, close to Mary's home, which was not much of a flying station but oversaw a number of radar outposts along the coast, keeping watch for Japanese planes. The health of the British personnel manning these had to be monitored in line with other servicemen, and Mumtaz would travel to see them, often hearing complaints that they felt like 'poor forgotten bastards, rotting away in God-forsaken holes'. He knew much of this was performative: these were luxury postings in a time of war and there was a fair bit of swimming and sunbathing going on. 'Boredom and sagging morale,' he concluded, 'were the main problems.'

Later, in Calcutta, he was assigned to another small base, at Red Road in the heart of the city, a major boulevard that had been turned into a wartime landing strip and repair unit. This was not a prestige posting, as there was little to do other than ensure ambulance cover for the aircraft flying in and out, but he gained valuable experience at the inpatient facilities run by the RAF. Here he encountered a new set of medical issues: injuries from brawls, usually between British troops and American GIs. These were almost always over women, he said, as the Americans tempted away the British soldiers' girlfriends in an echo of the 'overpaid, oversexed and over here' complaints about GIs in the UK.

Calcutta was close enough to Anakapalle for Mary's family to come and stay, and for the nuns to visit them, and when Mumtaz introduced Anne to his medical colleagues during one trip she decided to stay and complete her nursing training there. With his own family there was little contact. He wrote from time to time and sent pictures of the children, and he made one trip home, alone, for his sister's wedding. Sakina married their cousin Majeed, Rahima's brother, and Mumtaz felt his own actions had informed her decision. 'I think Sakina was not quite happy,' he wrote, 'but went along with the marriage because she felt strongly that with me having wandered off, it was her duty to stay in the house and look after the ageing parents.'

❦

By Christmas 1945 he and Mary were living in Cochin, on the southwestern coast, where he had become the sole doctor for an entirely British unit. He had been apprehensive about it at first. What if he made a mistake, at a time when Indian doctors could still be

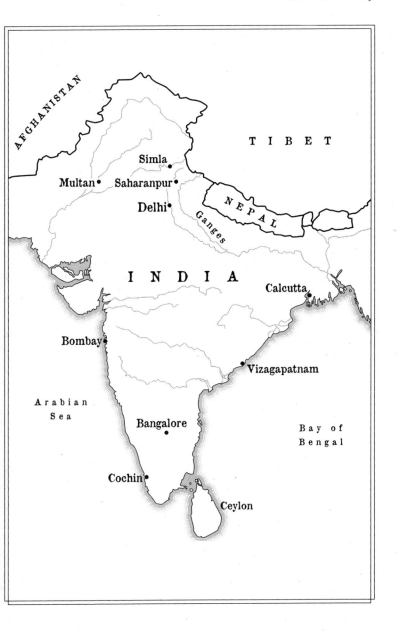

perceived as inferior to their white counterparts? 'I managed to put such qualms to rest with the belief that, after all, I was the qualified person to take decisions,' he wrote. 'I gradually matured from a raw, not altogether self-reliant individual into a confident medical officer responsive to all situations.'

The base was on an area of reclaimed land just offshore and after a period of commuting (putting his bicycle on a ferry), he and Mary managed to turn a couple of vacant huts on the base itself into a home. They put in the beginnings of a garden – jasmine and bougainvillea grew quickly thanks to the fertile soil and frequent rain – and found that Christmas a joyous affair, the first peacetime one for six years. Decorations went up on every hut, and Mumtaz was amused to see the determination of his Sick Quarters staff to play their part. Raiding the medical stores for the condoms freely issued to troops, they inflated them, dipped them into paint and strung them up as makeshift balloons. It was fine for a day or two, Mumtaz said, until the condoms slowly deflated, and then there was no mistaking what they were.

Once a week, he would take Mary back onto the mainland for Mass, where, as ever when they moved to a new place, they were a curiosity. 'How does he treat you?' she would be asked, and Mumtaz rather enjoyed the attention and the compliments that followed.

It was around this time that he began to be aware of new political sentiments in the air, particularly the word 'Pakistan', which seems to have come as a shock to him. Wartime censorship had affected everyone's access to news, but those in the armed forces had been especially insulated from debate, with rules preventing contact with political figures, reading 'partisan' newspapers and even listening to broadcasts in vernacular languages on All India Radio. 'Incidents were quite frequent in the officers' messes,' Mumtaz said, 'when a British officer would turn the channel off if any Indian officer had dared to listen to a "wog" music or news broadcast.'

Even as the war came to an end, he seemed not to envisage any change to the old order: 'For us, in uniform, the British Raj was indestructible and there to stay for all time.' Then, on a train journey up to Delhi, to apply for his emergency commission to become a permanent one, he heard slogans shouted out as he passed through areas of the United Provinces with significant Muslim populations. 'Pakistan Zindabad!' – Long Live Pakistan! – was heard repeatedly, alongside cries about building the country one brick at a time. A British officer travelling in the same compartment became increasingly annoyed and wanted the shutters closed against the 'awful noise', but Mumtaz realised that while he had been closeted in a military–medical circle, a new India had been developing.

Even in Cochin, where Muslims were present in tiny numbers, he heard 'Pakistan Zindabad!' ring out from the mosque near their home at the end of evening prayers. It puzzled him. A homeland based on areas where Muslims were in the majority – which meant the north-west and the east of India – would never include Cochin. Its Muslims were unlikely even to have travelled to such places, let alone to contemplate moving there. One day he asked a Muslim shopkeeper about this: 'If there is to be a Pakistan, will you leave and go there?' The man looked baffled. 'No, sahib, we are for the basic idea, but we will stay here. Where would we go?' Mumtaz understood then that the idea of Pakistan was conferring a sense of agency on Muslims spread out across India, and that for those living as minority populations it was being seen as a form of security and protection of their interests.

By this time many of the smaller RAF bases were in the process of winding down, or at least demobilising and sending home personnel drafted in during the war. At a posting in Bangalore he found much of the work was administrative, as servicemen were assessed against the criteria for different kinds of pensions and benefits. Then came a call asking him to come and do a similar job at Air Headquarters in Delhi. It was an honour, as a more prestigious posting could not be imagined, but Delhi was notorious for its lack of family accommodation and it would mean being apart. He wavered, but Mary felt this was an opportunity that could not be passed up.

She would take the children to Anakapalle, and they would hope for a reunion at the earliest opportunity.

❦

For Shahid, the end of the war had come at a difficult time in his life, with the sudden death in Lucknow of his father Hamid. He was only sixty, and Shahid was devastated to receive the news, while he was far away in Quetta. When I found the telegrams the family exchanged at that time, flimsy slips of Indian Posts and Telegraphs Department paper, I could almost hear how broken he was, as he told his sister he was on his way home to be with their mother: 'Reaching Monday. Tell Bee she has to live for my sake. My life depends on her.'

He was thirty-three and conscious of a new responsibility. As the eldest son of the family he had to step into his father's shoes and take care of a household that also included his grandmother, his widowed aunt and his two youngest sisters, Aziza and Saeeda. He asked for a posting on compassionate grounds so that he could be with the family in Lucknow, and then by early 1946 he had a new assignment at Saharanpur, north of Delhi. It was there that his senior officer called him in one day, puzzled by a cable saying that Shahid Hamid was required immediately in Delhi, for an appointment at General Headquarters, where the Army's top brass were based.

The summons was unnerving for them both, but Shahid was in Delhi by the next morning. His meeting with a senior general was odd – he was not told why he was there, and after little more than small talk he was sent on to a second general, and then a third. 'Wherever I was ordered or guided to I found people scrutinising me more in meaningful silence than through overt questioning,' he said, bewildered by the sense that he was on display. Finally, he asked if he was free to have lunch with the Chief himself, which of course he was, and by this point he had worked out that the process was a job interview. Lunch was at Auchinleck's residence, Flagstaff House, and was a relaxed affair, as the two of them spoke mostly about gardens and tree-planting.[140]

The only other person present was the Chief's sister, Cherry Jackson, who had come to live with him and act as his hostess after the end of his marriage. Shahid would learn later about this crisis in Auchinleck's personal life, which had occurred not long after the professional turmoil that arose in North Africa. His wife Jessie had fallen in love with a friend and fellow officer in Delhi, and Auchinleck had not picked up on what seemed obvious to many others. There were no children and by the time Shahid met him the divorce had come through and Jessie's possessions were being packed up and sent to her in England. 'I have been told she could never reconcile herself to the composed and sedate life expected of her,' Shahid said. 'She found Auk's long office hours and dedication to work tiresome.'

Once he was back in Saharanpur a letter came in confirming what was going on: Auchinleck's Private Secretary, a British officer, was being demobilised and was going home. 'His Excellency desires to appoint an Indian Army Officer to this post and has instructed me to ask whether you are willing to accept it,' wrote one of the generals he met. 'I need not, I am sure, emphasise what an important post it is in the working of GHQ.'

By this time Indians had already served as aides-de-camp to Auchinleck, but a private secretary was part of the inner office, with access to the Chief's paperwork, including confidential information. 'It was commonly believed that a "native" would never be appointed to such a sensitive post,' Shahid said. From Lucknow his mother wrote, happy but also reminding him to be humble: 'Remember, the more a bough is laden with fruit,' she said, 'the more it bends to the ground.'

❧❧❧

It was March 1946 and Shahid was to start at once. He was conscious from the outset not only of the access he would have but of the pivotal moment at which he was taking up the job: India's first elections in nine years had just taken place, and the political changes in the UK suggested swift progress towards independence. 'The days that lie ahead will become an important part in our history, too important to be consigned to the frailties of human memory,' he wrote in the first entry of the diary he now resolved to keep. 'I have decided to record them fresh, and preserve them.'[141]

The office he inherited was shared with an ADC and a stenographer and he described it as a virtual madhouse. 'People keep popping in and out endlessly,' he said. 'There is a battery of four telephones on my desk which ring incessantly.' His daily responsibility would be to take care of all the paperwork, files on every possible subject that had to be marked up and sent in to the Chief, for approval or otherwise.

Auchinleck was away in England during Shahid's first weeks in the job which meant that he began his assignment working for the senior Air officer who was standing in. He found that files were returned unsigned, even after he sent them in a second time. When he finally asked why, the Air Marshal said he should decide himself on the actions to be taken. 'This has really shaken me,' Shahid wrote in his diary. 'He is a gentleman and a distinguished airman but hates office work. However, his method is doing me immense good. I have to study each file in depth and am gradually picking up the working of the War Department and GHQ. It is also giving me confidence which as a novice I badly need.'

Once Auchinleck returned, Shahid was able to observe the way he operated, and he liked it: the Chief was pleasant and down to earth, arriving at the office without an escort and in what Shahid considered to be a very ordinary vehicle. 'It is a great honour to serve this distinguished Commander, the first to inflict a defeat on the Germans in the midst of their astounding military successes,' he wrote. 'He does not talk down to me, despite being the head of the mighty military machine.'

The Chief's sister was much trickier. 'I did not like your predecessor and I wonder whether I will like you,' she said when they met for the first time after he started work. 'I also wonder whether you will last in this job.' Shahid thought her eccentric, trailed everywhere by six dogs and with an 'odd selection of friends' whom her brother did not particularly like. 'At this time,' he concluded, 'the atmosphere at the C-in-C's house is heavy with a brother's personal misery and a sister's social oddities.'

His own assigned house was close by, a white-washed villa in a street called Willingdon Crescent, within the precinct laid out by Lutyens as New Delhi. It had a lawn to the rear and several bedrooms, more than enough for a family of five, Shahid said, and soon they were all forming their own bonds with Auchinleck.[142] 'He was living in a vacuum as far as his personal life was concerned,' Tahirah remembered, and perhaps for this reason he took them to his heart. 'The Auk gradually became a father figure in our lives,' she said. 'Apart from Shahid working for him we grew to know him and love him for so much that he possessed: his sense of values, his integrity, his great ability.'

To five-year-old Hassan and four-year-old Shahnaz, Auchinleck was 'Chiefi' and he would regularly send his ADC to collect them for an hour's play in the gardens of the big house, while he tended to his plants in the early evening. 'I think he just loved to be with them,' Tahirah said, remembering the set of miniature tools kept for the children. 'It took away the strain of the day's work.'

❦

Shahid's own work would place him at Auchinleck's side on ceremonial occasions as well as day to day in the office, and early on they went together to the Victory Parade in Delhi, the Indian Army's commemoration of the conflict that had ended the previous year. There, Shahid saw the Viceroy for the first time. 'Wavell stood there like the great Commander which he is,' he observed. 'His face reflected the pride and satisfaction which he must have felt.'

The parade was a two-hour display of men, weapons, vehicles and animals, but with the INA issue still bubbling it was affected by political realities. Congress representatives were not present. 'Not only did they boycott the Parade but [they] also staged demonstrations in the city,' Shahid said. 'Violence broke out.'

By then the election results were in, confirming Congress and the Muslim League as the two dominant players in Indian politics. On a still limited franchise, the League won three-quarters of the votes cast by Muslims, a significantly better showing than it had managed in 1937, and formed governments in two provinces, Bengal and Sindh.[143] As it had placed a demand for Pakistan at the centre of its election campaign – hence the shouts heard by Mumtaz on his train journey to Delhi – the result was interpreted as a mandate. But the term 'Pakistan' continued to lack a precise definition. For some it meant an autonomous sovereign state, while others could imagine it as part of a federation. And as Mumtaz saw in Cochin, 'Pakistan' could also symbolise a demand for religious equality and minority rights.[144]

In London, the Attlee government was keen to move forward with its stated aim of full self-government for India, and in March 1946 a delegation tasked with this arrived in Delhi. It was a three-man 'Cabinet Mission': the Secretary of State for India, the First Lord of the Admiralty and, once again, Stafford Cripps.[145] 'No one is quite certain whether they are coming with any definite proposals or are just on a fact-finding mission, making up their minds later,'

Shahid recorded in his diary, and he wondered if Cripps' associations with Congress figures would adversely affect his perception of the Muslim League.

The Mission spent several weeks in India, working out of the Viceroy's House but living at 2 Willingdon Crescent, not far from the Hamids at no. 12. The main issue for the 'Three Wise Men', as they became known, was to find common ground between the two principal parties on how power could be transferred – a system that could deliver a new Constitution and representative institutions. They held an exhaustive series of meetings, not only with Congress and the Muslim League but with representatives of communities such as the Sikhs, other minorities, and rulers of princely states.

When they were ultimately unable to find enough landing ground for an agreement, they went public with their own blueprint, in May 1946. That plan was for a union of British India and the states, where most powers would be exercised at the provincial level but there would be a central executive and legislature which would deal with other matters, notably defence and foreign affairs.[146]

The Misson said they had heard the 'very genuine and acute anxiety of the Muslims lest they should find themselves subjected to a perpetual Hindu majority rule', but they could not recommend dividing India. The demographics were too complex, they said, as were the administrative, military and economic considerations. However, their plan included one element that could be of use to Muslim-majority areas with common interests, as they allowed for provinces to group together on particular issues.

Given the trio's rejection of Pakistan, the Viceroy was braced for Jinnah to come out against the plan.[147] Instead, in early June, the Muslim League council voted to accept, and Jinnah moved on to talking to Wavell about names and portfolios for the interim government also set out in the proposals.[148]

Meanwhile, on the Congress side, there were grave concerns about the idea of provinces being able to group together, and also about the princely states being left intact. But in late June 1946 it, too, issued a qualified acceptance of the Cabinet Mission plan, in what the party's President Abul Kalam Azad called 'a glorious event in the history of the freedom movement in India'.[149]

It was not to last. Azad was in the process of handing over his role to Nehru, whose public school and Cambridge background made him well placed, Gandhi believed, for the coming negotiations with Englishmen.[150] Within weeks Nehru had publicly expressed his doubts about the Cabinet Mission plan, saying that the proposals could be modified and that some aspects, including the grouping of provinces, were unlikely to happen.[151] Jinnah was furious. It was proof, he said, that Muslims could not trust Congress, and he paused the League's participation in the interim government in protest.[152]

❦

Reading about this period in pre-independence history enveloped me in thoughts about alternative realities: what if this 1946 path towards an independent, united India had remained? It was a narrow path, to be sure, but different personalities at the helm of affairs, able to have some degree of trust in each other, could perhaps have found a way to proceed. By then, Gandhi was seventy-five and more of a father-figure to Congress than in an active everyday leadership role. Had that not been the case, he and Jinnah might have been able to produce a different outcome. Their relationship was not without its tensions but there does seem to have been a mutual respect, and, according to Jinnah's daughter Dina, Gandhi was someone her father liked.[153]

On the British side Wavell and Auchinleck were working as a team. The Viceroy made sure that the Chief was kept informed of the Cabinet Mission's thinking, and once the proposals were announced Auchinleck went on the radio to explain them to the armed forces, in Urdu. There would now be a temporary government, he said, and he himself would be reporting to a civilian Indian, 'just as the Commanders in Britain serve under civilian Ministers'. Although it was a time of change, he asked service personnel to remember how they had long lived and worked together, notwithstanding their diverse backgrounds. 'I trust you to go on setting this example and to do your duty,' he said, 'as you have always done it, in war and peace.'[154]

Publicly, Auchinleck sounded sanguine, but in his diary Shahid recorded the nervousness in Army circles, especially among the British officers, about the changes to come, including the Chief's new reporting line. Increasingly, politics had become part of everyday discourse, in a way unimaginable a year before, when it was still wartime.

By now, he and Tahirah had placed their trust in Jinnah, who was becoming known as 'Quaid-e-Azam', meaning the great guide, or leader. This support for the Quaid – as they called him – was not, however, a settled view across their families. Shahid's most politically active sibling was his sister Jamila, who had been a committed leftist and Communist, but the Muslim League's 1946 election success had made her want to know more about its leader. Shahid agreed to take her to see Jinnah, and they went together to his large house on Aurangzeb Road in New Delhi.

As they sat together and Shahid heard the tone of his sister's questions, he almost regretted agreeing to the visit: Jamila seemed to him far too direct and not at all tactful. He tried to stop her, but Jinnah interrupted him and continued to address her points, for what seemed a very long time. Finally, Jamila stood up and they took their leave. 'She kissed his hand and said she had been converted to his way of thinking,' Shahid wrote. The Quaid smiled at him. 'Look, my boy, I have not wasted my time,' he said. 'I have gained a worker.'

It was an account strikingly similar to another I read, from Shaista Ikramullah, who would have been about the same age as Jamila when she met Jinnah in 1940. In her case her father had suggested she accompany him to a meeting with Jinnah, and she had been reluctant. 'I believe he is very rude and snubs everybody,' she protested. 'And then, before I knew what I was doing,' she wrote, 'I was asking the Quaid questions and he was answering them, not impatiently or brusquely but kindly and in great detail … It was not that he overruled you, it was not that he did not reply to your argument, but that he was so thoroughly, so single-mindedly, so intensely convinced of the truth of his point of view that you could not help but be convinced also.'[155]

After her 1946 meeting, Jamila might well have thrown herself into Muslim League politics, but her health failed: she died of cancer less than a year later, leaving behind three children under the age of ten. Shaista, however, did become active in the party and was an eyewitness to key events, including the moment in June 1946 when Jinnah told the League he was accepting the Cabinet Mission plan. At the end of his speech, she remembered, he smiled. 'They say that at last reason has dawned upon me,' he said. 'Well, that is a very good thing. I only hope reason will also dawn on the leaders of Congress.'[156]

❦

That month Shahid was due to travel with the Chief to the post-war Victory Parade in London. Shortly before their departure he picked up a cable that came into the office in Delhi. It was wonderful news: His Majesty was making Auchinleck a field marshal. 'Shahid, don't be funny,' was the Chief's response when he told him, but the announcement was well timed. Within days he had been presented with his baton at Buckingham Palace.

Shahid and the ADC, a young Hindu officer called Govind Singh, both travelled with him to England and they went together to see the Indian troops who had come earlier, by sea. Ahead of the parade they were camped in Kensington Gardens, where they had become a major attraction. 'There were so many visitors and onlookers that a perimeter wire had to be erected to keep them away and afford the troops some privacy,' Shahid wrote in his diary. 'The members of the contingent are feasted constantly and are shown around the sights of London by the retired British officers of their units.'

On the day of the parade, he and Govind had seats opposite the saluting base on the Mall, and when I looked up the archive footage I understood what a wonderful vantage point it must have been. They

Govind with the feather in his cap, Shahid in beret in foreground

would have been looking directly at the King and Queen, the two Princesses and Queen Mary, Churchill and Attlee, and an extraordinary international roll call of those who served, 'whose deeds will be remembered as long as stories of bravery are told', as the British Pathé commentary put it. 'All eyes were on Churchill,' said Shahid, 'who made the victory possible,' but he and Govind were also gratified to hear a murmur of approval as their own boss drove past: 'Look, there is the Auk.'[157]

Shahid would travel frequently with the Chief, and ahead of the longer foreign trips there was a tradition that Auchinleck's team would drop in with their wives the night before a departure, to say goodbye. That was how one trip involving Tahirah came about, her first journey out of the country. It was in July 1946 and she had walked up to Flagstaff House with Shahid and joined a group sitting together on the terrace, given the warm summer evening. Auchinleck turned to her and addressed her formally. 'Begum Sahiba,' he said. 'Half of GHQ wants to be on one of these trips abroad. But you have never asked to go.' Tahirah says in her tapes that she had never thought of tagging along, and at that moment, she wondered why not. 'I think I will come with you this time,' she said slowly, surprising not only Auchinleck but Shahid, too. There was just enough time to make arrangements for the children to go to Lucknow, and the next morning she was airborne with the entourage. What no one had considered was documents, and it was only when the plane stopped in Karachi and Tahirah was asked for her passport that she realised she should have had one. All that could be done was to pin a badge on her sari and pass her off as part of the delegation.

She enjoyed her first sight of London, but when they stopped in Germany and Austria on the way home –Auchinleck wanted to visit a regiment stationed at Klagenfurt – she was unprepared for the post-war poverty she witnessed. They drove through towns and cities in ruins, and when she carelessly threw a cigarette butt out of the car window she saw three people scramble to retrieve it. She thought of Berlin and the family her father had lodged with in the 1920s, whose faces she would have recognised because she had grown up with their portraits in the Aligarh house. It was never possible to discover what had become of them.

❧❦❧

After this Delhi would remain the Hamids' home for another full year, until the summer of 1947. The city was also home to my father's family in the run-up to independence because, almost miraculously, Mumtaz did manage to find family accommodation.

He had arrived, as agreed with Mary, on his own and found the environment a shock at first, not the work but the extent to which he was immediately immersed in questions of politics, religion and identity. All of this was the subject of live debate in a way he had not experienced in the less restive south of India, nor had he thought much about the rights of the various communities and their relationships with each other. He had grown up a Muslim, in a Muslim-majority area, and while he had faced some prejudice – including a Hindu landlord in Bangalore not wanting to let to him – his only faith-related battle had been in finding a way to share his life with Mary. Now, he heard intense discussions on the future of his community, especially when he was with Abid's relatives, who were natives of Delhi and closely following developments. Mumtaz saw he had a lot to catch up on, and felt privileged to be in the nation's capital at that moment, likening it to 'enriching oneself in emerging history'.

At Air Headquarters he discovered that the top British officer in the medical branch was only nominally in charge, and mostly playing golf ahead of his return to England. The main man was his Indian deputy, Group Captain Madhu Shrinagesh. His manner impressed Mumtaz from the moment of their meeting, when he got up from behind his desk and crossed the room with an outstretched hand and a warm 'Welcome aboard, Mumtaz' – rarely the way junior officers were treated.[158] Precision was the key trait he wanted to see from Mumtaz, Shrinagesh said, as he worked on assessing servicemen's eligibility for benefits; the military finance department was known for taking issue with slapdash annotation on files and refusing to process what the medics had recommended.

Mumtaz did well. 'They started saying they found it difficult to shoot down the concise reasoning in my noting on the files,' he said with pride, and when Shrinagesh quickly promoted him to squadron leader he was thrilled: it was a step up in every way, including on housing waiting lists. An option was put to him – not a house or a flat but a set of rooms in a mess – and he went for it, conscious that a fourth baby was on the way and Mary would soon be unable to travel.

Early in 1947, she and the three little boys arrived in Delhi, and she fitted with ease into a new social circle, a diverse group consisting mostly of Air Headquarters officers and their wives. Mumtaz and Abid were the only Muslims and soon understood that even among friends, the topic of Pakistan needed to be treated with care. Their boss's wife Jaya Shrinagesh had a keen interest in current affairs and was great company, especially as she was oblivious to differences in rank between them and her husband. But she was shocked to discover that Mumtaz and Abid did not share the dim view she took of a Muslim homeland. 'How can an utterly unviable proposal like that find supporters among intelligent and politically aware people like you?' she asked them one evening.

They resolved to avoid the subject in future but, as the weeks went on, it inevitably resurfaced. One evening, when Jaya asked Mumtaz directly about 'the Pakistan business', she brought Mary into the conversation. Had he thought of what her fate could be, she asked, 'in a bigoted place like that'? By then, violence between the communities had set in and Mumtaz thought to himself that bigotry was evident everywhere, with Muslims, Hindus and Sikhs victims as well as perpetrators. Jaya also turned to Mary, asking what she thought. 'I will, naturally, follow what Mumtaz does and I am not concerned by anything else, as long as we are together,' Mary replied. To her, marriage was a sacrament, a promise for life, and she had made her choice back in 1942.

❧

Delhi had brought the Husains much closer to Multan than they had been during the postings in Bangalore, Cochin and Calcutta, and when Mumtaz's parents learned where they were, they told him they were coming to visit. It was not a happy prospect for him: he knew their opinions on his marriage had not changed. 'I was not sure of the kind of storm they would raise and the animosity they would show to Mary,' he said, although he knew their primary purpose would be seeing their grandchildren for the first time.

Mohammed Ali and Sardar Begum must have travelled on an overnight train, for they arrived at the mess in Delhi in the early morning, when the family was barely dressed. 'I did some perfunctory introductions and Mary said *salaam* to them in the demure way that came to her so naturally,' Mumtaz remembered. There wasn't much of a reaction. 'My parents looked her up and down with nary a polite gesture or response to her salutation and rushed past her to the next room.' This was where the boys were, but as they knew only of two grandsons, Mumtaz heard his mother exclaim as she spotted eighteen-month-old Niaz: 'There is a third one also!'

'The poor little children were bewildered to see utter strangers – in appearance and dress – suddenly among them,' Mumtaz said, but they acquiesced to being picked up, one after another. It was a Sunday, which meant he could be at home, which must have been a relief to Mary. 'I was grateful for no bitter outpouring or unsavoury scenes at this encounter,' Mumtaz said, but he could also see that his parents still regarded Mary as the woman who had destroyed their plans. He watched his father look at the breakfast on offer with 'polite disdain' and Sardar Begum busy herself with the children, barely looking at their mother. 'Having a decent word with Mary was not in their thoughts,' he said. 'I admired her aplomb, showing no reaction to this apparent rudeness and indifference.'

After they had left, he apologised to Mary, but she brushed it aside, saying the experience was no worse than she had expected. 'In fact, you should have tried me way back in Lahore,' she said, taking him back to 1943 and the time he had spirited her away rather than allow the two parts of his life to come together.

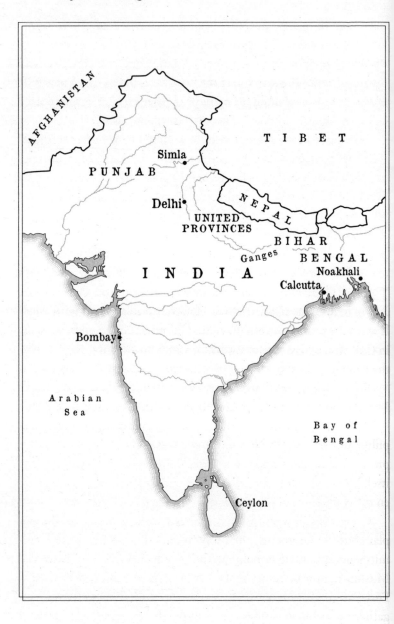

11

Dividing Lines

B y the spring of 1947, communal tension had turned into violence in many places, from urban neighbourhoods to remote villages. It was a depressing pattern that could be traced back to August 1946 in Calcutta, where several days of brutality sparked reprisals and set the worst of tones for the months ahead.

Politically, the background at that time was the failed Cabinet Mission, and the Muslim League's anger that proposals it accepted – despite their explicit rejection of a separate homeland – were being publicly questioned by Nehru. This seemed to roll back on his party's previous statements, and the suggestion that Congress would regard itself as 'completely unfettered by agreements' had, Jinnah said, 'shaken the confidence of Muslim India'.[159]

Congress still wanted to push ahead with parts of the Mission plan, but the League sought a way to underline its point that commitments should be honoured. The time had come, it said, 'for the Muslim nation to resort to Direct Action to achieve Pakistan'.[160] Friday 16 August 1946 was set as a day for Muslims to stop work and gather for public meetings across India, in what the League hoped would demonstrate popular support for its position.[161] But amid the uncertainty of the time, the potential for serious trouble was clear.

❧❦❧

Ahead of Direct Action Day Francis Tuker, the British general in charge of the region around Calcutta, was apprehensive and ordered more troops into the city, although he was told by local police that they could handle any incidents. Early on that Friday morning Tuker heard that Hindus had erected barricades on two bridges to try and prevent Muslims coming into the city centre from the surrounding areas. Large crowds nevertheless assembled for the main meeting, but as it came to an end Army intelligence spotted a number of known Muslim *goondas* – thugs or criminal gang members – heading towards the commercial areas of Calcutta, 'where they at once set to work to loot and burn Hindu shops and houses.'[162]

The nexus of political tension, insecurity and criminality was potent, and Calcutta also had Hindu militias who were ready for the moment. 'I called all my boys and said this is the time when you have to retaliate,' the leader of one such group said later. 'You have to answer brutality with brutality. If you come to know that one murder has taken place, you commit ten murders.' Weapons were readily at hand: not only knives and rods but guns, some of them obtained from US servicemen stationed in Calcutta during the war: in return for a bottle of whisky they would hand over a pistol and 100 cartridges.[163]

The scale of what unfolded was far beyond what Tuker had anticipated. When troops went out to enforce the curfew that was declared in riot-hit districts they described fires raging in every street, as if 'an armoured division had swept through on the tail of a heavy bombardment'. It was unbridled savagery, he wrote, as the Calcutta underworld took over, and two days later people armed with guns, swords and iron bars were still roaming around. In their wake were victims so numerous that one British officer called Calcutta a place of the dead. 'Handcarts were piled high with bodies and had been left abandoned at the kerbside,' he said, 'the arms and legs sticking out grotesquely like a load of large, broken dolls.' His men were tasked with removing these bodies, helped by sweepers from the Dom caste of Hinduism, so poor that they would often ask if they could take and keep the clothing from corpses. Those identified as Hindu would be taken to cremation grounds and the others to Muslim graveyards. On arrival at one of these, with a truckload of bodies, an officer was told to wait: hundreds were already piled up on other vehicles or in open graves.[164]

In all, the rioting lasted for five days and nights and was later estimated to have killed 4,000 people. Both Indian and British units were used to restore order, but the calm that finally came was, Shahid said, 'mainly due to the presence of the British troops. The public had full confidence in their impartiality.'

The worst violence had taken place in the poorest slum areas, and Shaista Ikramullah saw its aftermath, as a college near her house became a makeshift refugee centre for people who had been burned out of their homes. 'None of them possessed anything but the clothes they stood up in,' she wrote. 'I was later to see many more such people, to get used to them almost,' she added, thinking of partition a year later. 'But at this moment it was still unfamiliar enough to be an appalling shock.'[165]

⊰⊱

For Wavell the Calcutta violence was not only horrifying but an added obstacle to his efforts to get Congress and the Muslim League working together on at least some elements of government that summer. Then came copycat attacks and reprisals, further east in Bengal, in the province of Bihar, and in Bombay. Hindus or Muslims would be targeted where they were in a minority, and small communities in more isolated places were particularly vulnerable. In Noakhali, a Muslim-majority area now in Bangladesh, there were incidents of Hindu girls being abducted and men forced to convert to Islam, while in Bihar, the British Governor reported 'roving Hindu mobs' trying to exterminate Muslims.[166] The violence was not always entirely motivated by religion: economic disparities and even personal grudges could play a role, as people seized opportunities to improve their lot or found an outlet for their grievances.

With all of this unfolding, it was a considerable achievement on the Viceroy's part that, later in the autumn of 1946, both the Muslim League and Congress were represented in a new interim government. Congress had come in first, with Nehru taking the Foreign Affairs role, and the Sikh leader Baldev Singh became the Defence member. When the Muslim League joined, Jinnah did not take a position himself and his party's most significant portfolio was Finance, accepted by Liaquat Ali Khan.

There was then a joint effort to curb the communal violence, and Shahid recorded in his diary a Muslim League–Congress trip to riot-hit Bihar that November. 'There appears to be a competition in murders and brutalities,' he heard Nehru say, and violence came close to Delhi too, when Muslims were killed in Garhmukteshwar, east of the city.[167] All of this affected the atmosphere when the interim government met, even with the neutral figure of the Viceroy chairing them. At the same time, important questions about future constitutional arrangements and about how power could be transferred from British to Indian hands remained unresolved.

❧❦❧

With little sign of agreement on these crucial matters, Wavell took a small group of politicians with him to London in December, in an effort to focus minds. Both Nehru and Jinnah were included, but the discussions made no progress. At a Buckingham Palace lunch the King spoke to Jinnah at length but found Nehru uncommunicative. 'The leaders of the 2 parties I feel will never agree,' he wrote in his diary. 'We have gone too fast for them.'[168]

Wavell felt the best hope lay in a concerted bid to revive the Cabinet Mission plan, one which kept India united and in which, at various times and in various ways, both parties had seen merit. All the alternative paths to self-rule had problems: a fresh attempt at negotiation would probably involve dividing India, which Congress would not like, or Britain could 'surrender' to Congress as the largest party, which he thought unwise. Other than that, the only option would be for Britain to withdraw unilaterally, province by province.[169]

Wavell did not appreciate the extent to which he himself was, by then, being regarded by the Attlee government as a problem. By mid-December 1946 the Prime Minister had not only resolved to replace him but had already identified a successor, Louis Mountbatten, who had been Supreme Commander South-East Asia during the war. 'I thought of Mountbatten ... an extremely lively, exciting personality,' Attlee later explained. 'He had an extraordinary faculty for getting on with all kinds of people.'[170]

He discussed his choice with the King, delicately at first, conscious that Mountbatten was George VI's cousin, and thus it was a family as well as a state matter. 'Wavell has done very good work up to now,' the King wrote in his diary, 'but Attlee doubts whether he has the finesse to negotiate the next steps when we must keep the 2 Indian parties friendly to us all the time.'[171]

It was only in 1942, through a conversation with Churchill, that George VI realised he might never have the chance to visit India as King-Emperor. Told that all three of the main parties in Parliament were prepared to give India up after the war, he recorded his reaction. 'Cripps, the press & US public opinion have all contributed to make their minds up that our rule in India is wrong & has always been wrong for India. I disagree & have always said India has got to be governed, & this will have to be our policy.'[172] But the following year, when the question of a new viceroy came up, he was against Churchill's choice for Foreign Secretary, Anthony Eden. The King acknowledged that someone of Eden's calibre was needed, as 'India is in a bad state,' but he felt his skills were required at home. 'We must not lose India by keeping our best people here, but I do not feel that Eden can be spared at present,' he wrote. The job went to Wavell.[173]

In 1946, when his own cousin was the choice of another Prime Minister, the King approved, though he wanted to make sure that, unlike Wavell, Mountbatten was properly supported. He needed 'concrete orders', the King wrote. 'Is he to lead the retreat out of India or is he to work for the reconciliation of Hindus and Moslems?'[174]

❦❦❦

As 1947 began, Wavell was still in post as Viceroy but exchanging increasingly tense messages with the Prime Minister. Then, Attlee told him he was being removed. In response, Wavell attacked what he saw as the government's lack of policy on India, and he was stung at being told he needed to leave Delhi within a month; the usual notice period for a viceroy was six months.[175] 'I have been dismissed as if I were a cook,' was the way he put it to Auchinleck. It was, Shahid thought, 'a shabby way of treating a great man ... The more I have seen of Wavell the more I admire him. He has stood like a rock between order and chaos. The Auk is very upset over this.'[176]

On 20 February the Viceregal news was made public, alongside a statement of policy on India, which came after discussions between Attlee and Mountbatten. Within the government, Cripps was the only other person to have a say on India policy, and the Prime Minister had become convinced that the key was to set a firm British withdrawal date, believing that it would force Indian leaders into an agreement.[177]

It was an approach in line with Mountbatten's own thinking. While the statement said His Majesty's Government still hoped for the parties to agree a constitution in accordance with the Cabinet Mission plan, it also set out 'the definite intention' for power to be transferred 'into responsible Indian hands' no later than June 1948. It allowed for there to be more than one set of such hands: power could be handed over 'as a whole to some form of Central Government for British India or in some areas to the existing Provincial Governments, or in such other way as may seem most reasonable and in the best interests of the Indian people'.[178]

When Shahid heard these words he felt sure Pakistan would come into being: no longer was the idea overtly dismissed, as it had been by the Cabinet Mission less than a year before. His mind went back to Sir Syed, the founder of his alma mater of Aligarh and the man who had organised and energised India's Muslims in the previous century: that was the work, he felt, that had laid the ground for a separate homeland.

Among British officials in India were some who could not understand the Attlee–Mountbatten strategy, and the Governor of Punjab's view was relayed to London. What incentive was there for the parties to agree a compromise, he said, when power would be transferred in any event in seventeen months' time? This was a plan, he wrote, that rewarded digging in and maintaining control of territory, so as to be in de facto charge the following year.[179]

In both Shahid's written accounts and in Tahirah's tapes, I looked for references to any of their own discussions, weighing up Pakistan or India as their future country. I found none. Both had ageing parents and family homes in areas that were Hindu-majority and would never be part of a Muslim state, but they had also placed their trust in Jinnah, a man head and shoulders above any other Muslim leader they had seen. It is possible that they did not linger much on their choice, possibly because it did not seem as consequential as later turned out to be the case. I don't believe they contemplated the possibility of enmity between the two nations, and what that would mean for people like them: links severed, property lost and friendships fading away.

❦

Auchinleck was among those who put his reservations about the new policy on the record, writing to the India Office in London. June 1948 was too soon, he said. Most people in India had thought the process would be slower, and the way the statement was phrased was unsettling for the armed forces, both officers and troops. 'The lack of definition in the announcement concerning the party or parties to whom responsibility is to be handed over is causing the greatest uneasiness in practically everyone's mind,' he wrote.[180]

Whatever happened, he would not be facing it with Wavell, who was preparing in March 1947 to leave India. Auchinleck offered to host a farewell banquet, but Wavell refused. Instead, there was a dinner at Flagstaff House, the smallest Shahid ever saw take place there: only the Wavells, Auchinleck and his sister, and the two Hamids. Given the circumstances the outgoing Viceroy was on better form than Shahid had expected, and after dinner they sat around a low table for a series of games including one that involved the loser putting their face into a tower of flour to retrieve a ring. 'He was a man full of humour, who could be the life and soul of the party,' Shahid wrote of Wavell. 'It was one side of his character that few people knew about or even thought he possessed.'[181]

Wavell left a memo for his successor, describing the experience of presiding over an 'unreal coalition' of Indian leaders. 'Though neither side shows any sign of wanting to leave the Government, and though Cabinet meetings are carried on in a superficially friendly atmosphere,' he wrote, 'it is almost impossible to get members of the opposing groups to discuss things amongst themselves and they seldom meet except in my presence.'[182] He left after a final broadcast on All India Radio, paying tribute to the country and the people he had first known as a small boy in 1888 and then as a soldier from 1903. 'God be with you,' he said, adding that the words came from his heart, 'for I owe much to India'.

❦

By the time the change of Viceroy came in 1947, Gandhi had been working for months to try and calm the tensions that had spilled over into violence between communities. His method was to travel, to spend time in the affected places, and to attempt to ease the fury and fear through the power of his presence. In the autumn of 1946 he had visited areas where Hindus had been attacked in east Bengal and in 1947 he did the same with Muslims in Bihar: going to riot-affected districts, holding prayer meetings and seeking to discover exactly what had happened. If officials told him there had been no trouble, he set that against the accounts of local people, even having wells opened up to reveal decaying corpses.[183]

As he travelled he took Hindu and Muslim children with him in a living symbol of unity, and one of those who had this experience was eleven-year old Eqbal Ahmad, later a prominent Pakistani political scientist and thinker. Born to Congress-supporting Muslim parents in a small village in Bihar, he had witnessed his father's murder as a three-year-old, after a dispute that was partly political and partly about land. His elder brothers later turned to the Muslim League and when Gandhi came to their area they were unwilling at first to let Eqbal walk with him. But when he did, he saw the extraordinary effect Gandhi had on people, 'the continuous, almost infectious love' he inspired.[184]

Only four months later, Eqbal would be setting off from his village with his brothers and walking more than a thousand miles west to Pakistan, as independence took place. Their mother, believing that it was the wrong decision, refused to go with them, and Eqbal saw her only once more before she died. Then, in the 1990s, he went back to Bihar with a BBC TV crew, searching for the spot where his father had been buried and finding people who still remembered his family. Watching him reminisce on film about the coexistence in his village, how Hindus would wait to greet Muslims as they emerged from the mosque after Eid prayers, reminded me of my grandfather Mumtaz's description of old Multan. 'There were tensions in this relationship, as there are in all relationships,' Eqbal acknowledged, but he puzzled over how the long-established reality of communities living side by side had come to be challenged so hard and so fast in the mid-twentieth century. The answer, he concluded, was that a generation of leaders had chosen nationalism as the replacement for imperialism: 'Nationalism is an ideology of difference.'[185]

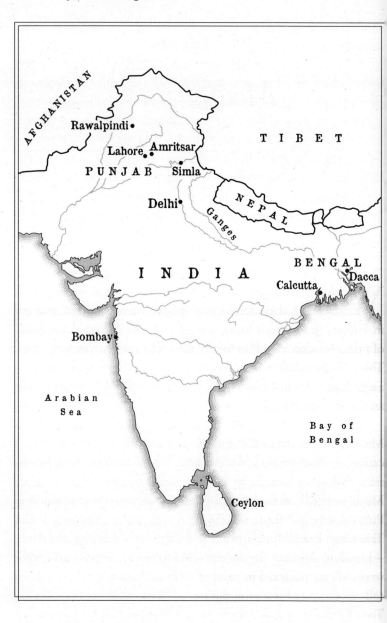

12

Mountbatten

Within a fortnight of the British government's new policy statement, there were clear signs of serious trouble brewing in Punjab, in northern India, a region which contained a number of princely states as well as the British-ruled province of that name. This had a population which was majority Muslim overall, alongside a significant Hindu minority and a Sikh community, for whom it was an ancestral heartland.[186]

Some of the holiest places of the Sikh faith lay in the western, Muslim-dominated part of Punjab, and as India digested the implications of what Britain had set out, Sikhs realised that these precious sites, and other areas, were likely to become part of an emerging Muslim state.[187] Shahid recorded in his diary a large procession in Punjab's capital Lahore on 4 March 1947, led by the Sikh leader Tara Singh brandishing a sword and shouting 'Pakistan Murdabad!' – Death to Pakistan! In the days that followed, Hindus and Sikhs were violently targeted in parts of western Punjab, where the death toll was estimated at several thousand.[188] Accounts from one village, Thoa Khalsa, near Rawalpindi, became emblematic of the impact on entire communities: after a siege and the killing of some of the men, scores of Sikh women took their own lives, jumping into a well to avoid the risk of rape, abduction or other forms of dishonour.[189] In Amritsar, Sikhs retaliated, burning down the Muslim bazaar. 'The administration took no action to control the mob,' Shahid wrote, 'which ransacked what it could for twenty-four hours.'

If there was to be a Pakistan, the Muslim League had long been set on it including both Punjab and Bengal, another province with an overall Muslim majority. Both were economically more developed than other regions which were part of the 'demand for Pakistan', and they were also prized for their cultural and historic resonance. But in the spring of 1947 some Congress leaders were noting the more detailed demography of the two provinces, and how Muslims were greater in number in the west of Punjab and the east of Bengal. If Pakistan was going to happen – and being rid of Jinnah and the League was not entirely unattractive – then perhaps Muslim-majority *areas* could be separated from others. It was an approach that did not take into account the way people of different faiths had bonds such as common languages and shared identities as Bengalis and Punjabis, but a readiness to concede a version of Pakistan took hold. Without telling Gandhi, the party put out a statement on the possibility of dividing Punjab and Bengal because, it said, 'there can be no settlement of the problem by violence and coercion'.[190]

❧

On 22 March 1947 the new Viceroy and his wife flew into Delhi, and Shahid was with Auchinleck in the large party waiting to receive them at the airport. Two days later the Mountbattens were inaugurated, in a ceremony which everyone present knew was the last of its kind. Again, Shahid was there, but I found a much more vivid description in the account of another guest, the wife of a British general who had arrived in Delhi in 1945, after five years as a German prisoner of war.[191] By 1947 Henry Swinburn was Auchinleck's Military Secretary and his wife Barbara's detailed and previously unpublished letters to her mother in England were shared with me by her family.[192]

As they took their seats in the Durbar Hall of the Viceroy's House the scene before the Swinburns was one of splendour. In what is now the official residence of India's President, two thrones were draped in red velvet and surrounded by the Viceroy's ceremonial bodyguard, men in scarlet tunics and gold turbans. Alongside the thrones sat Indian princes and members of the government, and the Mountbattens entered to a fanfare of trumpets, with their entourage processing ahead of them.

'Slowly and majestically, they walked through the centre of the Durbar Hall to their thrones, where they turned and stood facing the assembled guests,' Barbara told her mother. 'A wonderfully imposing couple.' The new Viceroy held the Bible in his hand as he was sworn in and then came the opening bars of 'God Save the King', played by the band outside. 'Those of us lucky enough to be present on this historic occasion realise that Lord Mountbatten has a stupendous task ahead, that of winding up the old order, preparatory to giving India her own self-government,' Barbara wrote. 'There was a feeling of sadness that we as Britishers were going to leave this land where for so many years now we have lived, worked, played and enjoyed ourselves.'

Mountbatten made a speech, in which he said he hoped all leaders would work together for India's good, and then Barbara watched as the couple 'slowly walked out with their staff, through the assembled throng, to take up their positions in the long drawing room, where they shook hands with everyone as they filed past, bowing and curtseying'. Every viceroy was a representative of the British sovereign, but the blood relationship between this one and the royal family added an extra aura to the ceremony, a link which Mountbatten cultivated; later in life he was well known for dropping the words 'My niece, the Queen' into conversation.[193]

❧❧

Mountbatten was only forty-seven and still a serving naval officer, with ambitions to rise higher in that service. The high-profile role in

Delhi was therefore not the culmination of his public life, as it had been for most previous incumbents, but an interlude: he had made it clear he wanted to return to the Navy as soon as possible. He also knew enough about Wavell's difficulties to insist on greater powers and an expanded staff, including a press attaché.[194]

Ahead of the new Viceroy's arrival, Delhi was awash with rumours. 'According to common gossip Mountbatten has come to partition India as quickly as possible, irrespective of the consequences,' Shahid wrote in his diary. The plan was to 'sort out the Princes; take all possible measures to keep the two countries in the Commonwealth; ensure that Britain's strategic and mercantile interests in south Asia are not jeopardised and, finally, keep the Indian leaders under pressure and give them no time to think'. He also heard that Mountbatten was coming with plenipotentiary powers, allowing him to act independently of London. This was indeed the case. 'I don't want to be under the Secretary of State for India or under the Cabinet,' was the way Mountbatten later explained what he had said to Attlee. 'I want to do the negotiations myself and you will have to do what I say.' The Prime Minister agreed.[195]

Both men were aligned in their belief in a fixed withdrawal date but Mountbatten had pushed for the original plan – for independence in the second half of 1948 – to mean June rather than December. He had also insisted on a set of written instructions. In these Attlee told him that the preferred objective was to hand power to a single, unitary government of India. If there was no prospect of this by October 1947, he was to report back to London and advise on alternatives. This gave Mountbatten six full months from his arrival in Delhi to work on a united India. Instead, within five months, the country was divided.[196]

❦

Given his role at Auchinleck's side, Shahid was soon able to form a personal impression of the new Viceroy. Mountbatten was clearly a man of energy, he thought, but the degree of haste that appeared to accompany him in every endeavour seemed unsuited to the complexities of India. 'Nothing happens here in a hurry, because of the intricate inter-racial, religious and political currents,' he wrote. He wondered why Mountbatten had been chosen for such a consequential task, especially given his lack of prior knowledge of the issues, or experience of diplomacy and governance. 'To my mind,' he concluded, 'his whole image and career has been built up because he is a member of the Royal Family.'

Shahid worried, too, that the previous sense of teamwork between Viceroy's House and Army Headquarters had evaporated. Early on he saw Auchinleck and Mountbatten disagree on whether British or Indian troops should be used when civil authorities asked for Army support. Communal violence had made such call-outs more frequent, and Mountbatten believed Indian troops should be used. But Auchinleck was deeply apprehensive about soldiers being repeatedly exposed to scenes which might well involve the targeting of their own community. India's police forces had already become partisan, too often interested in protecting only their co-religionists, and he did not want the same to happen to the Army.[197]

'In many ways Mountbatten has increased the Auk's problems,' Shahid recorded on 31 March. 'He is of no help to him and seldom accepts his advice.' A lack of trust between military and political circles was setting in: where Army officers used to refer to Mountbatten as 'Pretty Dickie', on account of his looks, he was now more likely to be called 'Tricky Dickie'.[198]

❧❧

While Auchinleck had asked Shahid not to write anything about him during his lifetime, Mountbatten's perspective on events in India and elsewhere was well circulated while he was alive. The memoir of his Press Attaché was published in 1951 and in the late 1960s Mountbatten himself fronted a lavish twelve-part TV series on his life and times. After his assassination by the IRA in 1979, access granted by his family to his papers resulted in an official biography by Philip Ziegler. Mountbatten was a great man, Ziegler concluded, but his version of events was not always reliable: 'The truth, in his hands, was swiftly converted from what it was to what it should have been. He sought to rewrite history with cavalier indifference to the facts to magnify his own achievements.'[199]

He had begun work as Viceroy with a series of meetings with key Indian leaders, and from the outset very different tones were set. 'I want you to regard me not as the last Viceroy winding up the British Raj but as the first to lead the way to the new India,' he said to Nehru, leaving the Congress leader visibly moved. It took another ten days for a corresponding meeting with Jinnah to take place, but Mountbatten did not enjoy his company in the same way, asking his aides to delay a scheduled dinner and describing the Muslim League leader as cold.[200] None of this should have mattered in the face of the crucial business at hand, but the Mountbattens soon became very close to Nehru, which meant he had their ear and greater access to put his point of view across in convivial settings.

Gandhi also came to see the new Viceroy. With searing accounts of events in Punjab fuelling fraught community relations elsewhere, he used the opportunity to put forward a novel idea. Wishing to avoid the division of Punjab and Bengal and the creation of Pakistan, he suggested that Jinnah be invited to form a government, which Congress would support: a grand gesture to set a conciliatory tone and act as a symbol of unity at the highest levels. Mountbatten was taken aback, as were senior Congressmen, who told the Viceroy they could not endorse such a proposal. It was never formally put to Jinnah.[201]

Within a few weeks of arriving in India, Mountbatten became convinced that he needed to move even more quickly than envisaged. There was a fear of political collapse and of India ending up as China was at that moment, with a raging civil war. Dividing the country and creating Pakistan increasingly appeared to be a solution.[202] The Viceroy's team began to consider shorter time frames than June 1948, and his Chief of Staff Hastings Ismay produced several versions of partition plans. He told his wife it was difficult to get the Viceroy to go through them methodically: 'He is a grand chap in a thousand ways but precision of thought and writing is not his strong suit.'[203]

In early May Ismay took a draft plan to London, centred on the creation of two states, one predominantly Hindu, the other mainly Muslim. The western part of Punjab and the eastern part of Bengal would go to Pakistan and the remainder of the two provinces, including the economic prize of Calcutta and its port, to India. Beyond this, the exact frontiers would be the responsibility of a Boundary Commission.[204]

Some of those who had dreamed of – and worked for – a united, free India were by this point resigned to the direction of travel, but others tried to fight it. Abul Kalam Azad, the most senior Muslim in Congress, had pinned his hopes on Gandhi being able to keep the country together. As that aspiration faded away, he went to see Mountbatten. Begging him to exercise patience, Azad said that once the deed was done there would be no going back, and creating Pakistan in the current atmosphere could lead to yet more bloodshed.

'On this one question I shall give you complete assurance,' Mountbatten told him. 'Once partition is accepted in principle, I shall issue orders to see that there are no communal disturbances anywhere in the country. If there should be the slightest agitation, I shall adopt measures to nip the trouble in the bud.'[205]

Maintaining law and order in the way Mountbatten suggested would require every ounce of capability from India's armed forces, at a moment when they, too, would be in the process of being divided. Yet, according to Shahid, Mountbatten did not consult Auchinleck on the plan that was sent to London that May. 'He seems to have no confidence in the Commander-in-Chief and is doing his level best to keep him in the dark,' he wrote.[206]

Shahid himself may have been part of the reason for this secrecy. One day, soon after Mountbatten's arrival in Delhi, he had seen

Auchinleck very angry after returning from a meeting with him. Once his temper had cooled the Chief revealed that Mountbatten wanted him to sack Shahid, as he did not believe a Muslim should be serving as his Private Secretary. Mountbatten's own Private Secretaries were both British, although he did have a Hindu, the senior civil servant V. P. Menon, as his constitutional and political adviser; Menon seems not to have been regarded as a problem in the way Shahid was. Nothing came of the row, Shahid said, because Auchinleck told Mountbatten he could not interfere in his affairs.[207]

By this stage the Chief was having to confront a scenario he found personally difficult: giving independent India and Pakistan their own separate military capability meant breaking up British India's armed forces. This was a complex endeavour and one difficult to execute fairly, as resources did not exist in duplicate.

At the same time Auchinleck was preparing memos on the challenges the new country of Pakistan would face. It would be in two non-contiguous sections, separated by a 1,500-mile-wide expanse of India. The eastern part – present-day Bangladesh – had limited road and rail communications, few resources and wartime-era airfields that would need significant expenditure to maintain.[208] The western part – present-day Pakistan – had some wheat and cotton and a little oil, but no minerals or industry, except ship repair at Karachi. West Pakistan's border regions carried obvious risks: tribes on the Afghan frontier and the developing Cold War realities of Stalin's Soviet Union. There could be no corridor between the two sections and the possibility of a hostile independent India was yet another source of instability.[209]

❦

In May 1947 the Cabinet approved the partition plan brought to London by Ismay, making only a few presentational changes.[210] Mountbatten had envisaged putting it to the leaders at a conference in Delhi in the middle of that month, but his timetable ran into trouble when he showed a draft to Nehru. They had been together n Simla, where the Mountbattens had invited Nehru to stay, and he Viceroy had given him a copy one night before everyone retired o bed. The next morning Mountbatten found he had a crisis on his hands: Nehru said the plan amounted to a frightening picture of 'fragmentation and conflict and disorder'. He could not accept it.[211]

This was a genuine upset, for Mountbatten had thought the shape of the plan was understood. But now Nehru saw, in black and white, that princely states as well as provinces would have the right o become independent, as an alternative to joining one of the new nations. This, he said, would mean a 'balkanized' India.[212]

Changes would have to be made, which meant a delay to the planned timetable. For the Cabinet to conclude that the Viceroy had miscalculated or had failed to prepare the ground properly was not a good look, and Mountbatten flew to London to ensure control of the narrative there. He told the government that if power was transferred earlier than 1948 he believed he could get Congress o agree to India becoming a Dominion, and therefore remaining in the Commonwealth once independent.[213] This was an important and enticing proposition, for at the time only Jinnah was known o be keen on Commonwealth membership; Congress believed in India being a republic, without the British sovereign as head of state, which was at that time incompatible with being in the Commonwealth.*

Attlee praised Mountbatten for his 'remarkable skill and initiative', but there was still the question of legislation. A transfer of power in 1947 rather than 1948 required a bill to be passed quickly and that meant getting the opposition Conservatives on board.[214] This Mountbatten achieved personally, by going to see Churchill and explaining how dangerous India was becoming, with blood being shed through violence between communities. 'That's the result of

---

*This changed in 1949, when a London Declaration allowed republics to be part of the Commonwealth. India became a republic the following year.

what you're doing,' Churchill said, meaning the Mountbatten–Attlee plan. But the idea of India and Pakistan both being Dominions of the Empire did appeal, and his support was secured on that basis.[21]

✤✦✤

Shahid was away from Delhi for much of May 1947 as he had accompanied Auchinleck to England for a post-war military exercise. 'Everybody is on edge and talking in whispers,' he observed on their return. By then the partition plan was being referred to as the 'Menon Plan', after the civil servant widely known to have reworked it.[216] In addition to the faster timetable and the Commonwealth dimension, there was a change in relation to the princely states. Nominally, they would become independent, but they were advised to accede to either India or Pakistan.

For the Muslim League the biggest issue was the fate of the provinces of Punjab and Bengal, which it wanted in their entirety for Pakistan. Failing that, they should be independent, Jinnah had told Mountbatten, as a division could not be justified 'historically, economically, geographically, politically or morally ... the results will be disastrous for the life of these two provinces and all the communities concerned.'[217]

That was, however, precisely what the plan entailed, subject to voting in their provincial assemblies. Getting only part of Punjab and Bengal would mean a 'truncated or mutilated, moth-eaten Pakistan,' Jinnah had said, and Mountbatten could not be sure how he would react when the details were placed before him and other leaders, in the Viceroy's study on the morning of 2 June.[218] Timings for the next twenty-four hours had been carefully worked out, for an announcement would also need to be made in London, and when the leaders gathered again on 3 June Mountbatten went around the table asking each for their formal go-ahead. He said later that the moment he turned to Jinnah was the most anxious of his life. 'There was an awful pause and then he slowly put his head down, just the minimum, to indicate "yes".'[219]

❧❧❧

That evening the Viceroy went on All India Radio, followed by Nehru, Jinnah and Baldev Singh. Three of the four speeches are easily available online today and, as I listened back, I was struck by how difficult it would have been for listeners to get a full sense of what had been agreed. Jinnah sounds pleased to have the opportunity to speak directly to people, 'through the medium of this powerful instrument', and presents the plan not as a done deal but as one to be considered by his party. Nehru's tone meanwhile is downbeat, accepting the plan with 'no joy in my heart' because of the prospect of 'certain parts of India seceding'.

For his part Mountbatten emphasised that Punjab and Bengal would now decide their own future, although the way the voting of their legislators was being organised made the outcome a foregone conclusion. He did not say the word 'Pakistan', and nor did Attlee when he spoke in London. Timing was kept vague, apart from the government's plan to legislate for the transfer of power that same year.[220]

The next day there was a press conference in Delhi and the Viceroy was asked if he envisaged a mass movement of people as a result of partition. Only in a natural way, he replied, in that 'people would just cross the boundary or the Government may take steps to transfer population'.[221] The most important bit of news to come from the event emerged casually, almost as an afterthought: the date of independence would be 15 August 1947, just over two months away.

How this crucial date came to be fixed remains unclear: there is no record of it being agreed in advance with London, with Indian leaders or even within Mountbatten's team.[222] Shahid thought it deeply irresponsible to move so fast: 'Why this shock treatment? Has he got cold feet and is losing control or is he not prepared to shoulder the responsibilities? Why is he bulldozing everything and leaving no time for an organised handover?' He concluded that the Viceroy wanted to get out before insecurity and violence got even worse.

Auchinleck had not been involved in these momentous decisions and, by Shahid's account, was so frustrated that he considered resigning. 'On a few occasions he has stood up to Mountbatten and got his way but invariably he is dictated to by him,' he wrote. 'Mountbatten has the full support of the Cabinet and the Crown. In these circumstances the Auk can do little.'

❧❦❧

Mumtaz and Mary had not heard the leaders' 3 June broadcast themselves, but that evening they went to Abid's family home in Delhi's Lodhi Gardens and heard his father say with pride: 'We have got our Pakistan.' In the days that followed, forms began to be circulated at every military facility in India, asking officers, men and serving civilians to declare the Dominion they would be going to. For people like Mumtaz there was not much of a choice: if you were a Muslim born in a Muslim-majority area – such as his native Multan – you were expected to opt for Pakistan. It was only those from areas where Muslims were in a minority – Abid in Delhi or Shahid in Lucknow – who had a choice of India *or* Pakistan.*

By then the new baby had been born, in April 1947, another boy they named Saleem. There were now four children under four and when I think about the combination of pressures on Mary in this period it's hard to imagine their impact: a newborn, three other pre-school-age children, her own relatives hundreds of miles away and her country in a state of flux. Five years after marrying Mumtaz – and thinking that they had surmounted barriers of faith and background – she now had to face what the Pakistan–India question meant for their shared life. Hindu friends in their Delhi circle were worried for them, and in Mumtaz's memoir he details how Jaya Shrinagesh invited Mary for coffee and pleaded with her to

---

*The same principle applied in reverse to Hindus, Sikhs or those of other faiths whose homes in Muslim-majority areas were expected to fall to Pakistan.

think through going to Pakistan. It was likely to be a theocratic state, she said, where other communities would be persecuted and Mary unable to practise her religion or bring up the children in the way she wanted.

Mary reminded Jaya that Mumtaz's Multan origins meant that he did not have a choice of which country to serve, and that she was committed to being with him. It seems that Jaya then went back to her own husband and asked if there really was no way around the rules. The next thing Mumtaz knew was that Shrinagesh called him in with an offer: if he resigned his commission, he could be recommissioned on the spot in the new Indian Air Force, with the same seniority and other rights. He should give it serious consideration, Shrinagesh said, as Pakistan did not look like a viable state. It would be a narrow-minded place, he added, and in an inter-faith marriage, religious tensions had to be considered.

Mumtaz was deeply touched by the effort being made on his behalf. Although his instinct for Pakistan was unchanged, he did think hard about the new possibility. If the Air Force career didn't work out, he reasoned, they could move to Anakapalle and be of help to Mary's mother, who remained vulnerable to people trying to take advantage of her.

It was Mary who brought these thoughts to an end. They were 'wild dreams', she said. Mumtaz would never be able to deal with people in Anakapalle when he was unfamiliar with the language and customs. Nor did she believe that he could be happy there, after breaking off completely from his own people and roots. And, despite the way his family had treated her, she took them into account: 'Think of your old parents, being denied the support they must be looking forward to in their declining years.'

When Mumtaz sat down to write his memoir and all of this flooded back to him, he reflected on it with deep emotion. 'What a woman,' he wrote. 'To think of looking far into the future, rather than seek shortcuts. Such steadfastness and the ultimate in loyalty and devotion, to live with the choice she had made. Her own sentiments and attachment to her own moorings were, again, relegated to the back burner.'

He went back to Shrinagesh and thanked him, but said he was an only son and would be going to Pakistan.

In that period he was also due for promotion, and he heard that there had been an outburst when his service file and his Pakistan form appeared together in front of a senior Hindu officer at Air Headquarters. How could a promotion be given to someone about to transfer to Pakistan, he raged? News of this spread and soon reached Shrinagesh, who had the man reprimanded by the Chief for an 'unservice-like remark' and then took it upon himself to apologise to Mumtaz. Even at this most testing of times, there was a code of behaviour considered important to live by.

PART THREE

After Midnight

13

Freedom and Farewells

My mother's parents would also be going to Pakistan, although, looking carefully at Shahid's memoir, I wonder if that decision was more finely balanced than he later made out. His entry for 6 June 1947 records Auchinleck asking if he was interested in becoming the Military Attaché at the Indian Embassy in Washington. Rather than saying no, he was becoming a Pakistani, he replied that it was difficult to think of going overseas, with his mother and the family to consider. Auchinleck nevertheless put his name forward to Nehru, as Foreign Minister, who wrote on the file that he could not agree to the appointment.

Among Shahid and Tahirah's siblings and parents, almost everyone decided that summer to stay where they were, in India. Ataullah and Ameerunissa were not leaving the house they had built on Marris Road in Aligarh; their elder son Hameed was staying in Bombay, where he worked in the film industry; their daughter Negin and her family would remain in the same city, and the youngest, Mahmood would soon join the Indian Civil Service. India would still have millions of Muslims who deserved to be represented in officialdom and with the authorities, he told Tahirah: most were very poor and their existence too precarious to contemplate abandoning the little they

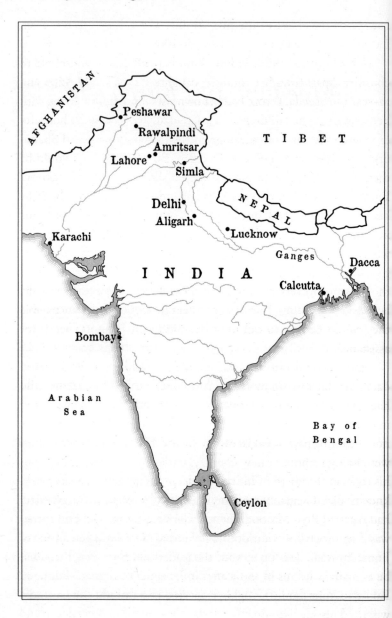

had. Only the eldest of the five, Amina, whose husband was from Lahore, would be making the same decision as Tahirah.

In Lucknow, Shahid's widowed mother had a large household to consider. Apart from her youngest daughters, 25-year-old Aziza and 22-year-old Saeeda, Feroze had her own sister and mother living with her, as well as the children of her late daughter Jamila. A houseful of women was far from ideal, given the insecure times, and Shahid urged his mother to come to Pakistan. Both of her sons would be there, he said, unable to provide help if she needed it in Lucknow. But Feroze could not contemplate abandoning the house built by her late husband and named 'Feroze Kothi' after her; nor could she imagine uprooting herself from the city and surrounding countryside where her family had generations of connections. 'We were not going to leave Lucknow,' Aziza told me when I interviewed her in 2007, on the sixtieth anniversary of independence, by which time she was the last surviving sibling. They felt confident that if there was any trouble they would be able to call upon Hamid's many Hindu friends for assistance.

Feroze would also have taken some comfort from her eldest daughter Razia's plan to stay in India with her husband Anis, who had rejoined the Indian Army after his five years as a prisoner of war in Germany. Like Tahirah, Anis was from Aligarh, which was clearly not becoming part of Pakistan, and he had felt torn. Fellow Muslims were going to build a new country, under Jinnah's leadership, but his roots in the north of India were deep: his father had been a well-known Vice-Chancellor of the university at Aligarh, Anis's sister had married Ross Masood, the founder's grandson, and his brother was a senior civil servant opting for India. He sought the advice of Jinnah himself. 'It is up to you,' the leader told him. 'But there will be as many Muslims in India after independence as there will be in Pakistan. Your family is highly respected and the Muslims of India will need people like you.'[223]

Jinnah's own arrangements involved selling his Delhi house but keeping his property in Bombay, the city where his only child, his daughter Dina, would continue to live. He was seventy years old and probably sensed he might not have much longer to live, as his health had been failing for several years. According to his sister Fatima he had never been especially strong physically, but a bad bout of pleurisy in 1940 and the demands of intensifying political activity had taken their toll. 'Despite the advice of his doctors and the pleading of a younger sister, he did not spare himself, refusing to take rest or respite,' she wrote. She saw him marshal his energies for public appearances and collapse into bed afterwards, in a pattern that continued daily. 'With the approach of dawn came fresh letters, fresh requests, new problems and weighty decisions to be made ... he kept up this feverish tempo of life for a number of years, in spite of the recurring bouts of fever that emaciated his body.' It was only in July 1948, shortly before Jinnah died, that he was diagnosed with tuberculosis, his doctors concluding that he had had it for at least two years.[224]

❦

In June 1947, after the leaders' broadcasts and Attlee's announcement from London, Barbara Swinburn had initially felt positive about the way independence would happen. Offering Dominion status had been a masterstroke by the Viceroy, she told her mother, and she suggested that the votes in Punjab and Bengal might yet keep the provinces intact: 'They now have to decide whether they want Pakistan or Hindustan or United India,' she wrote. 'The princes too have to decide whether to remain as Indian states or join in the new India.'[225]

By mid-July her mood was less upbeat. 'We've only got another month now till the handover of power,' she said. 'The Muslims are all out for our support. I've always liked Jinnah the best; Nehru doesn't like to ask the Britishers for anything in case he loses face. He and the Viceroy are great buddies and Dickie almost eats out of his hand.'[226] The Viceroy was 'all for Congress', she said, and the growing tensions were affecting social relations in Delhi. 'One can hardly have Hindus and Muslims to the same meal now,' she lamented. 'The Army is the only body who still live happily together and are miserable at being split.'

That division was an emotional wrench as well as a logistical challenge, as men were removed from regiments which they had seen as lifelong professional homes. The 19th Lancers, stationed in Peshawar and allocated to the Pakistan Army, was just one example: its Hindu and Sikh soldiers were having to leave, replaced by Muslims serving in the Poona Horse, which had been assigned to India.[227] Bonds which Auchinleck considered vital to discipline and operation were being severed, and that too at a time when insecurity was affecting law and order.

Meanwhile the Chief's differences with Mountbatten over the use of British units continued. They could not be called out in support of the civil authorities, the Viceroy said, as 'it might give the impression that His Majesty's Government is trying to re-establish its authority and prolong British rule'.[228] Auchinleck worried, too, about leadership gaps in the two new armies. In 1947 only one Indian had reached the rank of general and representation was not much better below: 5 per cent of brigadiers and 10 per cent of colonels. After independence both India and Pakistan would need British officers to stay on for a few years, but the prospect was looking less appealing by the day. Given the communal tensions it would be largely a policing job, many concluded, and nor did they feel especially welcome.[229]

In this period the division of physical military assets was also taking place, under the broad principle that one-third of everything was to go to Pakistan. For the Navy this meant thirty-two ships to India and sixteen to Pakistan, but complexities were apparent everywhere: aircraft could be similarly assigned but squadrons and maintenance crews had to be reorganised. Built assets were impossible to sort out equitably: few ordnance factories, military workshops or laboratories were in the less populated western – and less developed eastern – regions that were to become Pakistan.

Similar problems were arising in multiple spheres over the assets of what had been British India, from currency holdings to control of waterways, from power supplies to files and official records. All of this came under a Partition Council chaired by the Viceroy, but even starting principles were contested: Nehru's approach was that Pakistan was seceding, while Jinnah wanted the two countries treated as equals emerging out of the old India.[230] A row over printing presses was indicative of the prevailing atmosphere: when Pakistan asked for one of six government presses to be moved from Delhi to Karachi, Congress's Sardar Patel said none could be spared. 'No one asked Pakistan to secede. We do not mind their taking their property with them but we have no intention of allowing them to injure the work of the Government of the rest of India.'[231]

The process continued in offices and government buildings everywhere, as contents were itemised and then allocated: rugs and lamps, cupboards and screens, inkpots and calculators, right down to magnifying glasses and waste paper baskets.[232]

❦

By the middle of June it was clear that Punjab was a major, and growing, problem, particularly as the Sikh community faced the implications of partition. 'They feel themselves to be sacrificed on the altars of Moslem ambition and Hindu opportunism,' Mountbatten's Press Attaché wrote, while other members of the Viceroy's team had what felt like fruitless meetings with key Sikh leaders. 'We told them that if they resorted to violence, either before or after Partition, they would be very roughly handled,' Ismay said. 'But we did not feel our warnings had the slightest effect.'[233]

Shahid felt that Mountbatten's mood was darkening amid new realisations. One evening, as he and Tahirah attended a small dinner party around the pool at the Viceroy's House, he heard the wife of an American diplomat turn to Mountbatten. 'How is the partition getting on?' she asked. 'There was pin-drop silence,' said Shahid, 'and he only smiled in reply.'

Overall, he thought the Viceroy looked agitated. 'I asked one of his staff the reason and was told that Mountbatten wants to stay on as Governor-General of both Dominions, failing which he would resign.'[234] This issue seems to have been a major source of Mountbatten's subsequent, quite vicious, characterisation of Jinnah, whom he blamed for scuppering his plan to have an equal role across the two countries after independence. Nehru was preparing to become independent India's Prime Minister, and was happy for Mountbatten to take the more ceremonial Governor-General role; the Viceroy thought that there would be a fitting symmetry and ease of transition if he had the same position in Pakistan, where it was assumed Jinnah would lead the government.

Jinnah had other plans. Perhaps conscious of his failing health, he wanted Liaquat Ali Khan to be Pakistan's first Prime Minister. It was also hard to imagine Mountbatten being even-handed between India and Pakistan, given his demonstrable closeness to Nehru. When Jinnah told Mountbatten that he himself would be Governor-General, the Viceroy was furious, and tried to change his mind on the basis that without him, India would short-change Pakistan on assets. Jinnah accepted that, sadly, this was the likely result. Mountbatten was angry enough to storm out of the room and, in his next report to London, to describe Jinnah as a megalomaniac.[235] Shahid saw it differently. 'If Mountbatten was appointed a common Governor-General, where would he function from? It would obviously be Delhi,' he wrote. 'He would take the advice of the leaders of a bigger country.' In the circumstances, the fairest path might have been to bow out entirely on 15 August, but Mountbatten was conscious that this would look like a rejection of India's invitation. London thought it best for him to stay on, as Governor-General of India alone, despite the imbalance thus created in the relationship between the former colonial power and the two new countries.[236]

❧❧❧

Auchinleck's assigned role after independence did span both Dominions – as 'Supreme Commander' he was to oversee the withdrawal of the last British troops and complete the division of military assets. On 21 June he turned sixty-three and Tahirah, who had escaped the Delhi heat and gone up to Simla with the children, sent him a sweater she had knitted as a birthday present. 'I am looking forward to being able to wear it, but not at this moment in Delhi,' he said when he wrote to thank her, sending his love to Hassan and Shahnaz and his *adaab* – greetings – to 'the little one', my mother Shama. 'What a muddle we are getting into,' he added. 'I hope it will come all right in the end.'

By late June the tensions in Punjab's two key cities, Lahore and Amritsar, had boiled over, with devastating attacks on Muslims in Amritsar and on Hindus and Sikhs in Lahore. Arson had become commonplace as a terrifyingly easy way for one group to target another, requiring not a mob but fireballs thrown from roofs and through windows.[237] Nehru wrote to Mountbatten about Amritsar being in ruins and the perils facing Lahore. 'Fires are raging and consuming hundreds of houses ... At this rate the city of Lahore will be just a heap of ashes.'[238] He asked for martial law to be declared in Punjab, and Jinnah agreed. 'I don't care whether you shoot Muslims or not,' he said to the Viceroy. 'It has to be stopped.' But the Governor of Punjab feared the number of troops available were insufficient for the purpose: martial law was the highest card possible to play and it might fail.[239]

It was in this climate that legislators in Punjab and Bengal voted on the partition of their provinces, after their districts were nominally categorised on the basis of faith, majority Muslim or otherwise. If either set voted for separation, the other could not block it and the results came in as expected: the provinces were to be divided. Precisely where these dividing lines would be was yet to be decided, and would be revealed only *after* the moment of independence.[240]

❧❦❧

The Boundary Commission set to work on that task operated in two parts, in order to decide on Punjab and Bengal, and was chaired by barrister Sir Cyril Radcliffe, who arrived in India in July 1947. It was his first time in the country, which was considered an advantage, as he could not be influenced by prior connections, friendships or attachments, but it meant that he approached a complex exercise with no prior knowledge of the two provinces' history, geography, relationships between communities, trading routes, water supplies or infrastructure.

There was a nominal understanding of where the dividing lines were likely to be, based on the demographics of more Muslims living in the east of Bengal and the west of Punjab, and Radcliffe was to preside over work done by judges nominated in equal numbers by Congress and the Muslim League. He was also assigned a British assistant who did know the country, a young man called Christopher Beaumont who had previously been a civil servant in India. It was Beaumont's account of what he saw, revealed in the 1990s, that cast new light on how the Punjab border line was drawn and suggested that Mountbatten had pressurised Radcliffe to alter it, in India's favour.

Beaumont's involvement had begun with a letter informing him of his assignment and telling him to meet his new boss at London's Victoria station before they flew to Delhi. He was immediately impressed by Radcliffe's intellect and had plenty of time to observe it, as they would spend the next six weeks living as well as working together, initially staying with the Mountbattens at Viceroy's House. 'Mountbatten and Radcliffe did not get on well,' Beaumont said. 'They could not have been more different. Mountbatten was very good-looking and had a well-deserved history of personal bravery. But – to put it mildly – he had few literary tastes ... Lady Mountbatten, to her credit, adroitly kept conversations on an even keel.'

Once set up in their own house on the Viceregal estate, Beaumont noticed Radcliffe struggling. 'There was no air-conditioning in those days,' he remembered. 'It was a very hot summer, even by Indian standards. Sir Cyril suffered acutely. He had never before been, I think, east of Gibraltar.' At one point he sent Beaumont out into the bazaar to try and source some wine, preferably white. 'I succeeded and brought back some cases of Alsatian,' he said. 'Then work on the Partition began.'

※❧※

They travelled to Calcutta and to Lahore, capitals of the two provinces they were to divide, and it soon became clear that the politically appointed judges could not be relied upon to give an impartial view. 'They all took a communal line and had to be discarded,' Beaumont said, which meant the only people involved in drawing the lines were himself, Radcliffe and V. D. Iyer, the Assistant Private Secretary to the Commission, who was a Hindu. 'It was a serious mistake to appoint a Hindu – the same would have been true of a Muslim – to the confidential post,' Beaumont concluded later. 'I have not the slightest doubt Iyer kept Nehru and V. P. Menon informed of progress.'

The broad principle of Muslim-majority districts going to Pakistan was in line with the expectations of princely states in the same period, that they would accede to one country or the other on the basis of demographics. Radcliffe pored over maps and analysed population data, but his decisions had economic as well as community impact, as infrastructure and resources of all kinds would fall into either India or Pakistan. The secret that Beaumont kept for decades was over a change Radcliffe made on two Muslim-majority districts south-east of Lahore, originally assigned to Pakistan but moved into India in the final days before the border announcement in August.

The districts of Ferozepur and Zira were noteworthy because they contained two important facilities: an arsenal and a canal headworks relied upon for irrigation by places further south. Soon after Radcliffe had allocated them to Pakistan, Beaumont said there was a late-night knock on the door and V. P. Menon, the senior Indian on Mountbatten's staff, asked to speak to the chairman. 'I told him politely that he could not,' Beaumont wrote, explaining that the sensitivity of the border work meant that Radcliffe was supposed to be isolated from such contacts. 'He said that Mountbatten had sent him. I told him, less politely, that it made no difference. He departed with good grace.'

In the morning Beaumont told Radcliffe what had happened and then, a few hours later, Radcliffe informed him that he was going out to lunch, on his own. This was unusual – they usually went everywhere together – but Radcliffe explained that it was a lunch with Mountbatten, at the home of his Chief of Staff, where the table was not big enough to accommodate Beaumont. This could not be true, Beaumont knew; he had previously occupied that very house himself and knew exactly how big the table was. 'But my suspicions were not aroused, as they should have been,' he wrote. 'I was leaving India the next week, had many preoccupations and welcomed the chance to get on with my own affairs.'

That same evening, Radcliffe made the change that gave Ferozepur and Zira to India. Shortly after independence Pakistani officials discovered a map showing the original version, mistakenly left in Lahore by the pre-independence British Governor of Punjab. In 1948 Beaumont heard that this was part of a complaint Pakistan was taking to the United Nations, and the events of the previous year came back to him. The more he thought about the late-night visit, his exclusion from the lunch and the line being changed immediately afterwards, the more certain he became that the Viceroy had intervened. He went to see Radcliffe in his chambers in London. 'I was a most unwelcome visitor,' he recalled. 'He said he was very busy and shuffled off.'

Beaumont was prepared to acknowledge the extreme circumstances: Nehru and Menon might have told Mountbatten India was prepared to go to war over this, which the Viceroy then relayed to Radcliffe. But he thought the sequence of events as he remembered them should be recorded, and he gave an account to those working on the *Transfer of Power* series of official British government documents on India.[241] It did not make it into the published papers, he said, probably because it was thought too explosive: there had been fighting in Kashmir for months after independence and relations between India and Pakistan continued to be fraught.

In 1992, conscious that he was one of the few surviving witnesses to that period in Delhi, Beaumont gave a newspaper interview, which Shahid saw, and the two of them met, just once, that summer.[242] I know that my grandfather was encouraged to see that, by then, a greater range of views on 1947 was emerging in Britain: shortly before he died he showed Tahirah a letter he had received from the historian Andrew Roberts, asking to meet.[243] His own cuttings and handwritten notes for what might have been another book, on partition, are still there in his files, and when I went through them I wished he had lived to see the internet. He would have found it a magical resource, not only for research but to reconnect with the long-lost friends who were then still alive, across the border in India.

❧

In August 1947, despite the febrile conditions in some areas, my grandparents' Delhi social circles were scheduling farewell receptions and trying to part in an atmosphere of civility. I saw that for myself in the wording of the invitations Shahid kept, for gatherings to say goodbye to 'Brother Officers leaving for the Dominion of Pakistan'. At one event he attended on 6 August, gifts were exchanged and arms linked as they all sang 'Auld Lang Syne'. It was an 'au revoir', the senior Indian officer General Cariappa said, as he expressed hope that 'we shall meet each other frequently as the best of friends, in the same spirit of good comradeship that we have had the good fortune to enjoy all these years. We have worked together so long on the same team ... May this spirit continue even after we are separated.'

There was a reply from the senior Pakistani officer, calling all those present brothers-in-arms. Pakistan's new Army would continue to uphold the traditions it shared with the Indian armed forces, he said, 'not only in the interest of our own people, namely the inhabitants of the subcontinent, but also for universal security'.[244]

As he looked around the room that night Shahid realised that few of his fellow Pakistanis had any personal knowledge of Jinnah, the founder of their new country. Most had never seen him in person, let alone had the opportunity to speak to him. 'What do you suggest?' Jinnah said when Shahid mentioned this to him, and he proposed a reception, hosted by himself and Tahirah, at Willingdon Crescent.

Only a few days remained before Jinnah and his sister were to leave India, but time was made available and the gathering took place on the lawn behind the house. 'To my surprise the Quaid was in a talkative mood,' Shahid wrote, and he watched him answering many questions from servicemen. Only once did he appear annoyed, when someone asked about the chances of getting promoted in Pakistan, and Shahid saw him look the questioner up and down before replying. 'You Muslims, either you are up in the sky or down in the dumps,' he said. 'You cannot adopt a steady course. All the promotions will come in good time, but there will be no mad rush.' There was also a warning to those who might believe the new Pakistan Army was

a route to political power, as he emphasised that the elected government would be run by civilians: 'Anyone who thinks contrary to
democratic principles should not opt for Pakistan.'[245]

The pictures taken that night show Fatima Jinnah in white, wearing her customary *gharara*, the long divided skirt of Lucknow. Her
brother is also in traditional dress but to me his appearance is shock-
ing, his face little more than skin and bone. 'He looked frail,' Shahid
acknowledged, 'but otherwise he was on good form. For Tahirah
and I it was a great honour to have him at our house.' Jinnah met and
embraced the three Hamid children, and left with parting words to
all: 'Now it is for you to build Pakistan as the greatest Muslim state
in the world.'

It was one of his final engagements in India, as he flew to Karachi
three days later. 'We will miss him and his guidance,' Shahid wrote in
his diary, not knowing when he would be able to go to Pakistan himself: Auchinleck had said nothing about releasing him from service.

❧❧

At that point, exactly where Radcliffe would draw the borders was still unknown, but a mass transfer of population – precisely what Mountbatten had said would not happen – was already under way. Sometimes the spark was actual violence, at other times the fear of it, and people were also acting on the basis of their own judgements about whether they would find themselves on Indian or Pakistani territory on 15 August. Often, those from minority communities had not intended to leave, but were suddenly threatened. In Lahore Krishen Khanna described the experience of his Hindu family: 'You could see it from where we were, flames going up, houses being burned. *Allahu Akbar* on one side and on the other side *Har Har Mahadev.*'* His family's departure came after they were told a mob would be coming, but even then they thought they would be able to return, once the situation calmed. Instead, Khanna was soon living in temporary accommodation near Ambala in eastern Punjab and trying to assist people at the station. The scenes were awful: Hindu and Sikh women who had come east ahead of their husbands and were hoping to see them arrive safely, and fearful Muslim refugees trying to get on trains to Pakistan.[246]

Further up towards Simla a Sikh doctor saw how the local community became destabilised through the stories being told by arriving Hindu and Sikh refugees, of what they had faced at the hands of Muslims. When he urged people to adhere to 'the old traditions of communal harmony and brotherhood', he could tell from the expressions on their faces what was brewing instead: anger towards local Muslims. In the bazaar daggers were being sold, and guns were widely available, including those sold by British officers before they went home.[247]

On 11 August Shahid's cousin Hameeda, born and brought up in Aligarh, set off with her family for Pakistan. They were not refugees. Her husband Akhtar was a civil servant who had opted for Pakistan, and the train they boarded in Delhi with their four young sons

---

*'God is great' and a chant in honour of Lord Shiva.

would take them across the border. Overnight, as they travelled west through Punjab, it was attacked and brought to a standstill. 'The night was pitch dark and bullets began to rain down on both sides of the train,' she remembered. The family stayed where they were for half an hour, as the terrifying sound continued, but Hameeda had the presence of mind to grope through her luggage in the dark, finding disinfectant, scissors and cotton wool. She tore her *dupatta* scarf into strips for bandages and tied everything together in one of her baby's cloth nappies; if someone was wounded at least she would be able to respond.

As the gunfire subsided they heard voices, and then banging on the door of their compartment. Akhtar had a PhD and word had gone out that there was a doctor on board, but Hameeda told the stranger that she was a nurse and would come instead. 'Akhtar called out "What are you doing? You are not a nurse!" But I pretended not to hear,' she said. She was gone for two hours, tending to the wounded, and in the morning those who had died were buried. Part of the train continued on its way, and once in Pakistan, she saw throngs of strangers at every stop, trying to do what they could for the travellers. 'Lumps of brown sugar, wheat bread, maize bread, earthenware pots of yoghurt, corn, guavas, vegetables, fried food, sugar cane and boiled eggs,' Hameeda remembered of the food thrust towards them from the platforms. 'My eyes kept filling with tears at this flood of generosity.'[248]

Punjab's trains had become a route to safety and also a target; depending on the direction of travel any mob would know whether those on board were mainly Sikh and Hindu or mainly Muslim. Sometimes those going in opposite directions came face to face. 'We stared at each other silently,' a Hindu who fled east remembered of one such encounter. 'They had also come after being looted, leaving behind all their friends, relatives, houses, property, and our story was also the same, we had left everything. We kept looking at each other for quite some time, like a relationship of loss had developed, a relationship of sympathy, kinship.'[249]

꧁꧂

As 15 August approached there was still no announcement about the border. Radcliffe had completed his work but the decision on when to publish rested with the Viceroy. Doing so early would enable troops to be deployed to the most contentious areas, but Mountbatten was said to favour doing it later, so that the inevitable controversy did not mar the moment of independence.[250] Shahid heard other explanations: 'It is said that he is terrified to announce it before the Independence celebrations as disturbances may ensue on a large scale which would be his responsibility and that of His Majesty's Government to handle and control.'[251]

On 13 August Evan Jenkins wrote a hair-raising final report as Governor of Punjab, telling the Viceroy that raids and murders were now so common they could barely be tracked. 'Most of the rural casualties – and they have been very heavy – have been caused by Sikhs working in fairly large bands and raiding Muslim villages or Muslim pockets in mixed villages,' he said. There were repercussions in Lahore, where Muslims targeted Hindus and Sikhs and set their property on fire. Police forces could not be relied upon and troops assigned to the specially set up Punjab Boundary Force were trying to operate in over 17,000 towns and villages, with a population of fourteen million people.[252]

Auchinleck decided he must see Lahore for himself, and Shahid went with him. 'We flew over East Punjab and came in very low to watch the columns of refugees,' he wrote in his diary. 'Smoke covered the countryside. It presented a grim picture of a battleground.' At Lahore they were briefed by Jenkins and Pete Rees, the British general leading the Punjab Boundary Force, who had with him a Muslim officer Shahid had never seen before: Ayub Khan, later to be Pakistan's Army Chief and President. 'Poor Pete Rees is doing his level best under the circumstances,' Shahid said, and Auchinleck's own report said that but for the Army there would have been a 'complete holocaust' in the city.[253] The whole situation was bad and getting worse, he wrote, and the delay in revealing the border was having a 'most disturbing and harmful effect'.[254]

❦

They arrived in Karachi, where Pakistan's independence celebrations were due to take place, and Shahid, by now 'thoroughly depressed', went to brief Jinnah and Liaquat Ali Khan on what he had seen in Punjab.

That evening there was a banquet, for which Mountbatten had flown in from Delhi, and after Jinnah's speech and toast to the King, he responded. People often wondered, he said, why he had brought the date for the transfer of power forward from 1948. He smiled as he explained. The best way to teach a youngster to cycle, he said, was to take him to the top of a hill and push him down; by the time he reached the bottom he would be cycling. Amid the death and destruction in Punjab and elsewhere, this was not a parallel appreciated by many of those listening.[255]

Afterwards, Shahid saw Jinnah step away and stand to one side of the gathering. 'Physically he looked frail, tired and preoccupied. Somehow I could sense that he wanted the reception terminated as soon as possible'. Protocol demanded that no one could leave before Mountbatten, the King's representative, and eventually Shahid saw Jinnah beckon his aide over and heard the instruction: he was to tell Mountbatten to go home.

Jinnah was no doubt exhausted as well as ill by this stage, but relations with the Viceroy were also rock-bottom compared to ten weeks before, when he was willing to praise him publicly for his approach to the planned transfer of power. The next day the two men travelled together through the streets of Karachi and attended a short ceremony in Pakistan's brand-new Constituent Assembly, where Jinnah had made his key address a few days earlier. Speaking against bribery, corruption, nepotism and black-marketeering, he said Pakistanis had to work in the spirit of equality. They were free to go to mosques, temples or any other place of worship and to belong to any religion, he said: this had nothing to do with the business of the state.

Over time, he said he hoped the 'angularities' of different communities would vanish, and he asked people to reflect on the change that had taken place in Britain, from the days when Roman Catholics and Protestants used to persecute each other. 'I think we should keep that in front of us as our ideal and you will find that in course of time Hindus would cease to be Hindus and Muslims would cease to be Muslims, not in the religious sense, because that is the personal faith of each individual, but in the political sense as citizens of the State.'[256] In Pakistan's first government one of the ministers was a Hindu, and on the first Sunday after independence Jinnah attended a service of thanksgiving at the Anglican Cathedral in Karachi.[257]

Shahid flew back to Delhi, for the last time, on the afternoon of 14 August. Tahirah and the children were in Simla and he planned for them to stay there until he had gone ahead to Pakistan, sorted out a house and made arrangements to get them over.

That evening India's celebration of independence began, as astrologers had deemed the 15th inauspicious. In the streets Shahid heard conch shells being sounded, an important symbol in Hindu tradition, and the song 'Hindustan Hamara' – Our Hindustan – based on a poem written by Mohammed Iqbal in 1904. As he walked through the Mughal Gardens of the Viceroy's estate he stopped when he saw a familiar figure sitting alone on a bench: Nawab Ismail Khan, one of the Muslim League's most senior leaders, who often deputised for Jinnah and chaired party meetings on his behalf. When Shahid asked when he was leaving for Pakistan he replied that he wasn't; he did not feel he could abandon his native area of Meerut, near Delhi, where people had voted for him to represent their interests over many years. 'He felt that such people needed him more now than ever before,' Shahid recorded. 'He could not let them down.' He thought the decision selfless, as the nawab would have been assured of high office in Pakistan, but it also went to the heart of the dilemma faced by many who had supported the Muslim League, only to face a choice between their native areas and migration to unknown ones. In her tapes, Tahirah also mentions the nawab and how his choice deprived Pakistan of a man of stature and authority. 'It was a tragedy for the country', she says, 'that he decided not to come.'

At midnight, Nehru uttered his famous words on India waking to life and freedom, and the next morning Mountbatten was sworn in as the independent country's first Governor-General. He had just been created an earl. 'For some days every shop had been selling the new Indian Dominion flag which is the Congress tricolour,' Barbara Swinburn wrote in a letter home to England. 'There was much talk about the hauling down of the Union Jack from public buildings, and in most cases, to avoid any possible unpleasantness, the Jacks came down without ceremony at sunset on the 14th.' Unexpectedly, she said, the morning of the 15th was grey and drizzly as people gathered inside the Viceroy's House for the ceremony: 'The great majority were Indians as this was their day, the women as ever making a wonderfully colourful show in their very lovely saris.'

❧

On that day Mumtaz, Mary and their four children were still in Delhi. Mumtaz had received orders to report to the medical branch of the new Pakistan Air Force in Peshawar, close to the Afghan frontier, but it was difficult to know how to get there. 'With each passing day one heard gory tales of trains and busloads of Muslims arriving at their destinations with bodies butchered, and the same "compliment" being paid back with trains and buses the other way,' he wrote. 'The dilemma confronting all optees for Pakistan was how to get across.' Military aircraft were only for senior people and so he went to the station in Delhi to get a first-hand account of security on the westbound trains. The situation had improved, the station master told him, and he booked tickets for the six Husains on a train to Lahore and then Peshawar, on 16 August.

In his final days at Air Headquarters he took his leave of colleagues and found most of the encounters warm and heartfelt. There were exceptions: one Hindu officer spikily said it was not goodbye, but au revoir: 'We will see each other soon, maybe within six months. I would be surprised if your Pakistan even lasts that long.'

Amid the farewells Mumtaz came across one new face, a British RAF doctor based in Peshawar who was over in Delhi for meetings.[258] Realising they would soon be serving together, he and Mumtaz started to talk, and the officer looked aghast when Mumtaz said he and his family would be going to Peshawar by train. It was foolish, he said, to think of such a journey in the current turbulent times. 'I've come here by plane and the Dakota will be returning entirely empty,' he said. 'I advise you to change your mind and go by that aircraft.' He offered to look after the paperwork, and Shrinagesh, told Mumtaz he should take the option.

There were social farewells, too, in those final days, including a banquet for those going to Pakistan on 14 August and a small dinner at the Shrinageshes' home the following night. 'It was a rather sad affair,' Mumtaz remembered, with toasts, many drinks downed and considerable emotion. At the end Jaya wept as she hugged Mary and said she still hoped they would 'abandon this foolish course' and change their minds about Pakistan. Mumtaz found himself almost in tears as he said goodbye to Shrinagesh, who had believed in his abilities and helped make it possible for the family to be together in Delhi.

The plane was leaving on the 17th, which meant they were in Delhi throughout the independence festivities. Mumtaz struggled as he saw celebrations and fireworks, knowing that at the same time 'the blood of all communities was being spilled over the streets and the sands of the countryside'. When the Dakota took off and flew low over Punjab he and Mary spotted tell-tale signs of violence from the air. 'It was a depressing sight,' he said. 'Some cultivated fields but mostly burned ones, perpetrated by wild mobs a month or so before, when it must have been harvest time on land which was the granary of the subcontinent.' They could see people too, columns of men, women and children, trying to keep together for safety, on foot or in bullock carts. Most were travelling in the same direction as the plane, towards Pakistan, but there were also columns he could see in the distance moving in the opposite direction. Other military families were on board and all the adults remained at the windows, transfixed, for the duration of the flight: 'No one could snatch themselves away, despite the horrendous drama being enacted below.'

They learned later that the train they had been booked on became one of the notorious 'ghost trains' of that time, arriving at Lahore full of bodies. 'Not a living soul survived,' Mumtaz said, news which wore Mary's rosary thin as she flung herself into grateful prayers. 'Don't I keep telling you', she said, 'about the Virgin looking after us always?' He worried about the responsibility he had for her, not only as his wife but because of all she was leaving behind, and he hoped he had made the right decision. 'What kind of a country will it turn out to be? What happiness will we find in it?' he wondered. 'Once more we were launching into the unknown.'

❧⬧❧

Shahid remained in Delhi for another fortnight, working for Auchinleck and witnessing the atmosphere as the decision of Radcliffe's Boundary Commission was published and accounts of violence continued to flow in. He saw Nehru's despair, as he asked how massacres could take place on trains that had military escorts. 'He was told that the gangs got on to the train with their arms concealed,' Shahid said. 'Once on, they attacked suddenly. Sometimes, they put one man on the train to pull the communication cord at the spot where the rest of the gang was already waiting. The train escorts could do little.'[259]

The temporary Punjab Boundary Force led by General Rees was under unimaginable pressure: it was simply too small for what was unfolding. While the officers were mostly British, the men were all Indian – or now Indian and Pakistani – and, depending on where they came from, they were desperately worried for their own families' safety. At the same time the process of splitting up regiments, and soldiers peeling off for India or Pakistan, continued for several weeks. In one memo in the Auchinleck papers a British officer describes escorting groups of Muslim refugees towards the border with Pakistan, and the makeup of his men changing at the same time: two Muslim companies arrived, having been detached from their old regiment, while Hindu and Sikh troops departed in the opposite direction. 'It was a sad moment,' he said. 'We had a combined parade and a *bara khana* [feast] before they left, in the greatest friendship, and the senior Sikh wept in my office as he was about to go. In spite of this I think everyone felt it was time to part, for the compulsion of outside events was too great for the individual.'[260]

And yet, throughout those months, and despite coming face to face with the targeting of their own communities, troops like these overwhelmingly maintained discipline. For this, Shahid gave full credit to Auchinleck. 'If Auk had not been there to keep the Army intact there would have been a disaster and tragedy out of all proportion,' he said when his partition diary was published in 1986. 'Troops would have been firing at each other in the cruellest of civil wars. It was his personality alone, together with the respect in which he was held, which prevented this from happening.' Auchinleck's death in 1981 had finally enabled Shahid to publish his book about their time together, but he continued to feel injured on the ex-Chief's behalf: 'Somehow we still refuse to recognise the greatness of this man.'

The final order of the old Indian Army had been issued on 14 August, leaving Auchinleck with responsibility but little power. British troops equivalent to three divisions were still stationed in South Asia but could not be called out and were now mere spectators to events. Shahid's own designation had changed alongside the Chief's – he had become 'Private Secretary to the Supreme Commander' – and he realised Auchinleck intended to keep him on in Delhi until work on troop withdrawal and dividing assets was complete, which probably meant into 1948. This was unwise, he felt.

'I told the Auk it was advisable that I should give up the present job and go over to Pakistan, where I had volunteered to serve despite my home being in India,' he wrote in his diary. 'It was in his own interest that I relinquish the present assignment otherwise he would be censured by the Congress for keeping a Pakistani in such a key position.'[261]

Reluctantly, Auchinleck agreed, and Shahid packed up the Willingdon Crescent house. With the Punjab disorder spilling over into Delhi he felt a pang of guilt as this home, in its well-protected location, might have been used by friends as a place of safety. He felt bad, too, about leaving Auchinleck at a time of turmoil, and at a farewell dinner on his last night in Delhi, some of his Hindu 'brother officers' were still trying to persuade him to stay. He left on an Air Force plane for Rawalpindi on the morning of 27 August. 'The way things are shaping out, it may become difficult to travel between the two countries,' he wrote. 'I hope and pray this does not happen. I have too much at stake, with my mother and other relations still in Lucknow. There has been no communal friction in the city until now, and I hope there never will be.' He could not know that he wouldn't be returning to India for another thirty years, but he was deeply aware of the resonance of his flight that day: 'Now I go to Pakistan, to begin life as a Pakistani.'[262]

14

Crisis

At the moment of independent India's birth its founding father, Mahatma Gandhi, was not present at the celebrations in Delhi. He had planned to be in the eastern part of Bengal as it became Pakistani territory, hoping to calm tensions in a place where there had been violence against Hindus the previous year. But as he travelled through Calcutta a prominent Muslim League leader asked him to stay: trouble was brewing and Gandhi's moral stature might prevent it boiling over.[263]

Gandhi agreed, on condition that it was a joint approach. Together, they moved in to an abandoned Muslim-owned house in a largely Hindu neighbourhood, where local people were not at all happy to see them: by then Gandhi was being blamed, variously, for acquiescing in the division of the country or for being too accommodating of Muslims. At one point a group broke through the police cordon and entered the house, shouting at Gandhi to go.[264] Then, as word spread further that he was in Calcutta, living alongside a Muslim, the mood in the city changed and there was no repeat of the terrible scenes of August 1946.

When I filmed at that house in 2009 and saw the rooms that he had lived in, it brought home the conflicting emotions so many felt at

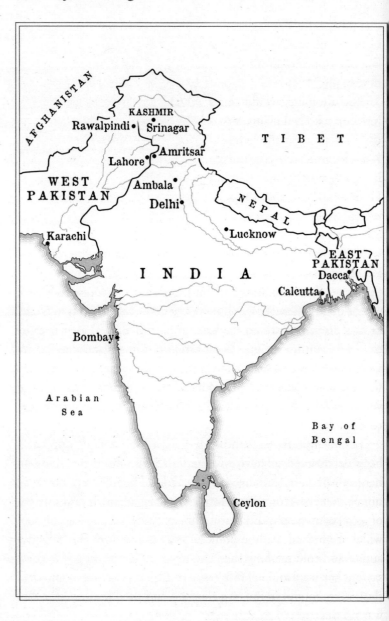

that time, as freedom came alongside separation, insecurity and fear. Gandhi, the world's best-known advocate of non-violence, had to face the opposite in his own country at what should have been a time of joy.[265]

The instability would continue for many months, causing some Muslims who had planned to remain in India, or Hindus and Sikhs who had thought the same in Pakistan, to change their minds. In Karachi, nineteen-year-old L. K. Advani, later a senior figure in India's Bharatiya Janata Party, was active in the local branch of the Hindu-nationalist RSS group. It had advised Hindus in the province of Sindh to stay where they were. 'Unlike Punjab where riots broke out even before Partition, in Sindh even after Partition there were no riots,' he remembered. The Hindu community watched Pakistan's independence celebrations with unease and did not accept the sweets that were being distributed, he said. But Karachi was still their home: 'We were living in our own place, and Pakistan was a kind of imposition on us.' During September 1947 their instincts changed: Muslim refugees began arriving, some from areas of India where violence had been perpetrated by Hindus and Sikhs, and it was possible that a cycle of violence might envelop them. Advani was among those who left, taking the first plane journey of his life, to Delhi.[266]

In Lucknow, Shahid's mother was also forced to rethink. Having been determined to stay in the city of her birth, the place where her husband and her daughter Jamila were buried, she began to feel unsafe. A key factor was a visit from the local police, possibly part of a crackdown on militia groups, but conducted in an atmosphere which frightened the household of women and children. My great-aunt Aziza told me how the policemen went from room to room, saying they were looking for weapons, and then sat down and made themselves comfortable as if sizing up the place, confident that there was no man to tell them not to. As they left, they warned Feroze they would be back, and she knew they might then find Hamid's old *shikaar* hunting rifles, which were locked in a cupboard.

That night, under cover of darkness, the guns were wrapped up and buried in a hole in the garden, with a few shrubs planted above to disguise the newly dug earth. The behaviour of the police left Feroze and her daughters badly shaken: even decades later Aziza's eyes widened in fear as she told me about it. Times felt too insecure to continue as they were. They packed a few suitcases and four generations of the family – from Feroze's elderly mother to Jamila's young children – boarded a train to Bombay and then a ship to Karachi. Pakistan would now be their country too.

❧❦❧

In India's capital, conditions deteriorated early in September 1947. 'We are having rather an awkward time here now as the Punjab troubles have spread to Delhi,' Barbara Swinburn told her mother. Graphic accounts of what was happening to Hindus and Sikhs across the border led to revenge targeting of Muslims, and despite a twenty-four-hour curfew, lawlessness spread from the old part of the city to the normally sedate surroundings of Lutyens' New Delhi.

'This morning, the police arrived and said all Muslim servants and their families were being collected into a huge camp for protection,' she wrote. 'Henry has just made four trips taking them all away.' The barbed wire around the improvised camp made her husband feel 'as if he was back in the old days', she said, meaning his prisoner-of-war camp in Germany. There was no doubt, though, that the measure was required: she knew people whose Muslim staff had been dragged out of their houses and slain, and the nearby shopping area had been looted. 'Nehru went down to break up the mob in Connaught Circus himself yesterday ... It's all so pointless and the numbers killed are appalling. Far more than one reads in the papers.'

Delhi then came to a virtual standstill: no post, no shops open, no trains running. 'The station is deserted,' Barbara said. 'All Muslim drivers and other railway personnel have gone away to hide.' She had some tinned food in the house but the lack of supplies was deeply worrying: 'No vegetables or eggs have come in and no *aata* [flour] or food grains for the Indian people. Delhi has been within two days of starvation.'

The camp where Muslims were taken was in the Purana Qila, the Old Fort, and when Barbara went there she found her staff and their families among thousands of others, including people who had worked for her friends. 'They'd had no food and heaps of them came up and asked me to tell their sahibs where they were and bring them food ... There are crowds all living on the floor inside the thick walls. There is one tap of filtered water and the queue for it is endless. They're very pathetic and all long to get to Pakistan. Our nice cook cried this morning and said he didn't want to leave us but he was too frightened to stay in Delhi so he and all his family will go when transport is possible,' she wrote. 'It's awful to think that within three weeks of freedom all the Punjab and Delhi provinces should be slaughtering each other like maniacs.'

❧❧❧

Soon Simla, where Tahirah was with the children, was also affected. They had initially been in a rented summer house, where Shahnaz's fifth birthday had been celebrated earlier that summer, but as law and order deteriorated Auchinleck had insisted on a move into Snowdon, his official residence in the hills. 'You may be sure of all my help and protection should it be needed, which I hope it will not,' he wrote to Tahirah on 3 September. 'I pray that this madness may pass soon and people will be sane again.'

By the 5th, Shahid was worried enough to write to Auchinleck from Pakistan. 'My own Chief,' his note on a small piece of writing paper begins, 'I miss you. I miss working for you. I do hope that you are well. I feel that Tahirah and the children should be got down from Simla. They are not safe up there.' He continued regretfully: 'You have so many things on your hands that I feel guilty in asking you to make arrangements to get Tahirah down. You may like to send someone up to Simla ... I am a little worried. Very sorry for this disjointed letter.'

Phone. "Northern 132"
Army HQ
Rawalpindi
How goes your plan? OK
Sep 5.
My own Chief.
I miss you, I miss working for you. I do hope that you are well.

I feel that Tehirch + the children should be got down from Simla. They are not safe up there I do know that you have been most kind to them & they are in Snowden but the sooner they come up here the better.

I feel that they should be brought back under an escort.

You have so many things on your hands that I feel guilty in asking you to get Tehirch down. You may like to send some one up to Simla. But you would know the best.

I am a little worried. Very sorry for this disjointed letter.

Yours ever
Shahid

Auchinleck seems to have been thinking along similar lines already, probably conscious that in the face of a mob even an Army residence could be compromised. In red pen he wrote a note to his ADC Govind Singh on Shahid's letter: 'Gom – How goes your plan?'

'Gom' was the nickname they all used for Govind, who knew the Hamids well and was often the one who walked the children from Willingdon Crescent up to Auchinleck's Delhi house and back. Within four days of the letter, he arrived in Simla with a platoon of infantry, and Tahirah told me about their subsequent journey together: it was only at this moment, she said, that she understood the full extent of the rage unleashed in the country. As they drove in convoy groups of men were lining the road and their expressions were terrifying, she said, almost crazed with anger, as if they might move forward and attack the vehicles at any point.

She could tell Govind was tense, even though he had come with an armed escort, but the gravity of their situation was only fully apparent when she heard him turn and speak to the two older children, Hassan and Shahnaz. If anything happened to the car and anyone asked who they were, he said, they should give their nicknames, Hassu and Guria, and Chotu, the little one, for their sister.

It was Govind's way of preparing for the worst: if the adults were not there to protect the children, then masking their Muslim names might, perhaps, give them a chance. Hassan, who was then six, remembers something more. 'We were told if we were stopped and someone asked our name, not to give it, and to say that we were Govind Singh's children. Govind said this directly to me.' The children picked up on the adults' apprehension as they travelled, in a family group that included Tahirah's sister Amina and her three children, who had been with them in Simla. Later two Muslim officers joined the convoy with their own families, for there was safety in numbers.[267]

They left the hills behind them and Auchinleck's plane was waiting further down, at Ambala, where Hassan remembers leaving the vehicles and crossing a bridge. It stuck in his mind because that was where he lost his toy cars, when they fell into the stream beneath. 'And then we got to the aircraft,' he said. 'And there was no more fear.'

❧❦❧

For Tahirah though there was anguish: as they flew over Delhi she could see that parts of the city she loved had been set alight. Once they had landed Govind took them straight to Flagstaff House, and they arrived to see Auchinleck standing outside, waiting. 'Thank God you have arrived safely,' he said, looking graver than Tahirah had ever seen him, and for the next two weeks she and the children stayed with him. Hassan remembers he and Shahnaz having the run of the mansion, with its stuffed animal heads on the walls, but also the distress of the adults when, every morning, reports would arrive of the latest incidents in the riot-torn city and the locations where bodies had been found.

By then many of Delhi's Muslims were being protected inside the Old Fort. 'The refugee camp in the Purana Qila gets worse and worse and fuller and fuller,' Barbara Swinburn wrote to her mother on 21 September. 'There must be about 60 or 70,000 people, with no sanitation of any kind,' she said. 'I go and help in the improvised hospital where babies are born all the time ... and hundreds of sick babies and children and injured people come in. Only voluntary doctors and helpers are there and only candles from 7pm till daylight. I go and take food to the cook and his family. There are others who have joined, like the *darzi* [tailor]. Their future is grim. They dare not stay in Delhi.'

Among those in the Fort in those days was thirteen-year-old Eqbal Ahmed, whose elder brothers had ordered him to go to Pakistan with them. He arrived in Delhi on foot, having walked hundreds of miles west from his village in Bihar, and with a significant journey to the border still ahead. 'I was one of the refugee children inside,' he said on camera as he saw the Fort again with a TV crew in 1996. 'I have many memories attached to this place, almost every inch of it. Conditions were very harsh but children managed to play.' He remembered the shortage of water, as there was only one well in the Fort, and two visits from Nehru. 'He asked the refugees how things were and what their needs were. He heard complaints that we were very cold at night. A few hours later some blankets arrived.' Then came the day when the refugees gathered at the Lahore Gate of Delhi's Red Fort, to set off together for Pakistan. Eqbal became separated from his brothers and trudged along among strangers, on a journey challenged by hunger and disease, fear and fatigue.[268]

⁂

In newborn Pakistan, the British civil servant Edward Penderel Moon was an eyewitness to the fate of Hindus in an area called Hasilpur, which, when I looked it up, turned out to be close to Mumtaz's home city of Multan.

Penderel Moon had come to check on the situation there soon after independence, but found Hasilpur's streets silent and the bazaar eerily shuttered. He asked where the Hindus were and was told they had all gone to the old village of the same name, two miles away. As he drove on, he saw what looked like heaps of manure on a stretch of sand further ahead. It soon became clear that they were people, and for a brief moment he wondered why they were lying on the ground, until the sickening realisation that he was looking at corpses. 'In twos and threes and sixes and tens, more and more came into view as we rounded the curve of the village ... I was forcibly reminded of pictures that I had seen as a child of Napoleonic battlefields.' In the village itself he found women and children, 'whose sobbing and whimpering swelled to a deafening crescendo of mingled grief and resentment as soon as they caught sight of us. It was hard to endure.' Outside, there were a few men still alive, but badly wounded, one almost naked and covered in blood, a woman fanning his face but unable to do more for him.[269]

In the days that followed, the survivors of Hasilpur, and other Hindus and Sikhs in fear of their lives, had to get to India, just as Muslims such as Eqbal Ahmed were travelling the other way. Even if the distances were small, as was often the case within Punjab, refugees had to be accommodated and kept safe until transport could be arranged. At a station right on the new border, Penderel Moon saw evacuees from one country catch sight of those who had moved in the opposite direction. 'As those standing in the trucks looked down at those sitting by the track an expression of half-dawning comprehension crept into their gloomy, bewildered eyes,' he wrote. 'All alike had been driven from their homes by the exigencies not of war but of freedom. It did not make sense, but it had to be endured.'[270]

❧❦❧

In Delhi that September, Auchinleck decided that the safest way for Tahirah and the children to get to Pakistan was to take them himself, by plane, which meant waiting for his next trip across the border as Supreme Commander. He did not appreciate one of his generals questioning if this was really necessary and suggesting that the trains were now much improved. 'Do you know what you're

Auchinleck and Tahirah

saying?' Auchinleck responded fiercely. 'People get slaughtered on those trains. I gave my word to Shahid that I would see them safely to Pakistan and that is what I will do.'

Departure was set for 23 September, and in the final days Tahirah had an extraordinary gesture from Govind. 'He came and presented her with a box,' Hassan told me. 'He said it was a gift, something for the children. It was large, about 8 inches long and 3 inches wide and when she opened it she found it was filled with jewels.' Govind was related to the royal family of Jaipur and such a treasure had to be part of his inheritance, Tahirah thought. 'The children will grow up,' he said. 'There will be marriages. And you are not rich people, you will need this.'

She was floored. Their lives had been intertwined for the past eighteen months through the bond of Auchinleck's circle, but the extent of Govind's love and generosity, on the brink of their departure, was now at a different level. 'Gomji, I can't accept this,' she said.

For a while he persisted, telling her the jewels were his own, not the property of the state of Jaipur: 'These are my personal items and I am giving them to you for the children.'

She did not take the box and from the early 1950s it was no longer possible to keep in touch, even by letter: such contact between military families was suspect on either side of the border. But when Govind heard of Shahid's death in 1993 he wrote to Tahirah in Rawalpindi, and I remember the letter being passed to each one of us to read; we knew how much it meant to her. Forty years had passed but they had not forgotten each other.

❦

'Can I have a receipt for goods delivered?' Auchinleck said to Shahid, smiling, as he brought the family to Rawalpindi in late September 1947. It had been nearly a month since they had parted in Delhi and they sat and talked for some time in the hotel where, in the absence of family accommodation, Shahid had taken some rooms.

He discovered that Auchinleck felt his position as Supreme Commander, taken up on 15 August, was already becoming untenable: his relationship with Indian ministers was deteriorating amid the contentious task of dividing military assets. Far from being a source of support, Mountbatten was part of the problem. He was supposed to be the impartial chair of the Joint Defence Council involving representatives of the two countries, but he was also by then India's Governor-General. It was an impossible situation, Shahid wrote in his diary, concluding that Auchinleck had become 'a very sad man carrying within him a deep sense of failure'.[271]

Matters then moved faster than either had thought possible: three days after the conversation in Rawalpindi Auchinleck received a letter from Mountbatten, asking him to resign. Indian leaders regarded the Supreme Commander's office as a drag on their sovereignty, he said, but their criticism was also personal. 'I should be a poor friend if I did not admit that this resentment, which was initially directed against your position, has inevitably turned against yourself,' Mountbatten wrote. He said he had argued on Auchinleck's behalf but had failed to convince the ministers, who were on the brink of seeking the abolition of the Headquarters. The way to head this off, he suggested, was for Auchinleck himself to propose an early shutdown and, in that case, a peerage could be announced alongside his resignation.[272]

'So the Congress has succeeded in getting rid of the Auk,' Shahid concluded when he heard. 'In a nutshell the Indian leaders have decided not to honour their pledge of dividing the assets and stores. They were finding the Auk a stumbling block in their designs.'[273]

There was no room for discussion or negotiation as Mountbatten's letter made clear he had already sought – and received – Attlee's support. Auchinleck then wrote himself to the Prime Minister and to the military Chiefs in London. 'I have no hesitation whatever in affirming that the present Indian Cabinet are implacably determined to do all in their power to prevent the establishment of the Dominion of Pakistan on a firm basis,' he said. 'I and my officers have been continuously and virulently accused of being pro-Pakistan and partial, whereas the truth is we have merely tried to do our duty impartially and without fear, favour or affection.' The work of dividing assets was not complete, he said, and India was determined to prevent Pakistan receiving 'her just share, or indeed anything of the large stocks of reserve arms, equipment stores, etc, held in the arsenals and depots of India'.[274]

While angry, he also recognised that his departure had to be carefully handled: relations between the new states were so strained that there was a real risk of open war. The truth was therefore kept from Pakistan. At the next meeting of the two governments, Mountbatten said that riots and massacres in Delhi had brought about a charged atmosphere which made it very difficult for the Supreme Commander's Headquarters to function. Not unreasonably, Liaquat Ali Khan proposed a move to Pakistan's capital, Karachi, where there was no such trouble. This was, of course, never going to wash and excuses were made, but India's representatives said they would ensure Pakistan received its share of the pre-partition assets.[275]

In 1951 Shahid became Pakistan's Master-General of Ordnance, a role which gave him oversight of military supplies of many kinds. When he went through the inventories he concluded that Pakistan had got seventy-four of the 17,000 Indian Army vehicles it had been allocated, and 23,000 rather than 160,000 tonnes of items from the stores. 'Many boxes contained canvas shoes meant for Gurkha troops with small feet,' he wrote. 'Some boxes contained building bricks to make up the tonnage due to us.' No ammunition was included.[276]

❧❀❧

Before he left Delhi towards the end of 1947, Auchinleck had one more crisis to deal with. It was over Jammu and Kashmir, one of the most important princely states, whose status was still unresolved that October when almost all other rulers had made decisions to join either India or Pakistan.

Its significance lay both in its size and its strategic location, as the state stretched across a large expanse of British India's northern frontier, nestled against what was already Indian and Pakistani territory. It was prized for the beauty of its landscape, and it had great personal resonance for Nehru, who was of Kashmiri heritage. The makeup of its population led to the presumption that it would accede to Pakistan: in the Kashmir Valley in 1947 some 92 per cent of people were Muslim and the state as a whole was three-quarters Muslim.[277] And yet, from the early summer of that year there were rumours that its Hindu Maharaja was trying to find a way to avoid joining Pakistan.[278]

In June 1947, as Mountbatten prepared to holiday in Kashmir. he asked Nehru to send him a briefing note on the state. That document is preserved in the official British records for the period, setting out the demographics of Kashmir while also telling Mountbatten that both the Maharaja and a popular Muslim leader then in detention wanted to join India: 'If any attempt is made to push Kashmir into the Pakistan Constituent Assembly, there is likely to be much trouble.'[279]

Independence came and went without a decision. The Maharaja suggested to the governments of both India and Pakistan that he needed more time, and he told Mountbatten he was thinking about a referendum.[280] Uncertainty continued and Kashmir became destabilised: the Maharaja was not popular and Muslims in the Poonch area began agitating over the possibility of being taken into India. In late October a crisis point was reached when Muslim tribesmen from Pakistan's North-West Frontier Province crossed into the western part of the princely state and advanced on Srinagar.[281] The Maharaja and his family abandoned their palace in the capital and fled to Jammu, in the more Hindu part of the state.[282]

After that events moved at pace. The Maharaja had already asked for armed help from India, but he had not as yet acceded to the country. That changed in the following days, as an accession agreement was signed and Indian troops flew into Srinagar.[283] When the journalist Ian Stephens dined with the Mountbattens in Delhi in this period, he was amazed by the atmosphere and the way they talked: they had become, he felt, 'wholly pro-Hindu'. Mountbatten then confided that Kashmir's accession to India, subject to a plebiscite, was being finalised. 'I was flabbergasted,' Stephens wrote. Kashmir was a place of resonance and importance and dealing with it this way seemed counter to the principles of majority population that had been at the heart of the transfer of power. 'At a Hindu Maharaja's choice, but with a British Governor-General's backing, three million Muslims, in a region always considered to be vital to Pakistan if she were created, were legally to be made Indian citizens.'[284]

Jinnah reacted with fury. India and Mountbatten had been underhand all along, he believed, and he told his own – British – Chief of the Pakistan Army to deploy troops to Kashmir.[285] This Auchinleck could not allow: it would mean two British generals going to war with each other, as the post-independence Indian Army also had a British Chief. He flew to Lahore to meet Jinnah, telling him that the orders violated what was now Indian territory. As Supreme Commander, he would respond by instructing all British officers to 'stand down', which would have paralysed a Pakistan Army that relied on them across senior positions. Reluctantly, Jinnah rescinded his orders and agreed to Auchinleck's suggestion of a conference, bringing him together with Indian leaders, Mountbatten and the Maharaja.[286]

The gathering never took place, and nor did a plebiscite. India maintained that the tribesmen who marched on Srinagar were commanded by Pakistani officers, and battles continued in Kashmir throughout 1948. The issue remains unresolved: to this day there is no recognised international border through Kashmir, only a 'line of control' corresponding to the ceasefire agreed in January 1949.[287]

In December 1947 Auchinleck left India. 'We all got up early and went to the airport to say a last goodbye to the Chief,' Barbara Swinburn wrote of that morning. 'For the last three months they've been trying to get rid of him from this side. Pakistan would have wanted him to stay.' There was no guard of honour or ceremonial farewell, as Auchinleck had refused them. 'He just shook us all by the hand and stepped into the plane and away he flew,' Barbara said. 'We all felt miserable. He had been so let down by the high up Indians and he has devoted his whole life to this country, the army in particular.'

❧❧

In Rawalpindi, Shahid had arrived at Pakistan Army headquarters with no idea what job he would be assigned. He was given the serial number PA-27, meaning he was the twenty-seventh most senior person in the force at its inception, and he was told to 'complete the order of battle'.[288] This involved tracking down and accounting for all units that were supposed to be part of the new Army. Some, he discovered, were still in India, and arrangements had to be made to get them across; others were serving with British forces overseas. 'There was not much trouble in locating major units,' he said. 'But tracing small ones was a headache. Some took months to locate.'[289]

It was not a high-profile assignment, not that Tahirah had expected otherwise, after Auchinleck warned her that Shahid's prominent role in Delhi for the previous eighteen months would count against him in Pakistan: 'Jobs like he has done with me do not win you friends.' The family of five settled into their temporary hotel accommodation and Shahid and Tahirah saw a changed Rawalpindi: the Hindus and Sikhs who had played an important role in building up the garrison town had gone. Among the most striking Sikh-owned properties was one they knew well, a mansion full of precious art and antiquities that belonged to Sardar Mohan Singh, a well-known businessman who knew Shahid and had asked him and Tahirah to come and stay when they were first married and posted to Rawalpindi. 'He and his wife did not feel a bride should be running a home,' Tahirah remembered of those days in 1940, and thus the newlyweds had stayed in a wing of the house.

By the summer of 1947 Mohan Singh had fled to India, but when he heard that Shahid and Tahirah were back in Rawalpindi he wrote to offer them the use of the house. Shahid declined: in such insecure times it was too much to be responsible for such a home, he told Tahirah. But Mohan Singh's staff came to see them at the hotel, she remembered, asking them to reconsider and – if they really weren't going to come across – offering to bring furnishings, or food, to make them more comfortable.

Shahid was right to be worried about the house: it was looted that autumn, even though he had asked the Rawalpindi police to guard it. My aunt Shahnaz was at school close by when it happened and she remembers hearing the sound of destruction as Pathan tribesmen on their way to Kashmir rampaged through the museum-like rooms and ran off with priceless artefacts, from carpets to statues and rare books to illuminated manuscripts. Shahid was away, but Tahirah heard the noise and ran to the house to try and stop it. By then the damage had been done and the street was littered with torn pages and fragments of objects. More treasures disappeared later, and Shahid suspected the officials who were supposedly safeguarding the building of being responsible.[290]

❦

In those early days after independence some of the refugees crossing the border had relatives they could go to. They were the lucky ones. Hundreds of thousands of others found themselves in unfamiliar places, hearing languages they could not understand, homeless, destitute and often in a precarious physical state. In and around Rawalpindi, Tahirah soon became involved with working to support these arrivals. 'I was so conscious it was my country,' she said. 'It seemed the most natural thing to do: to receive the refugees, to find hospital beds for them and ultimately, when Rawalpindi city overflowed, to find other places where they could go.'

Her children remember the Army truck that would arrive every morning to pick her up, and how the prevalence of disease meant they were not allowed to touch her when she returned, until she had showered and changed her clothes. While the Army provided resources, the people who worked alongside Tahirah and whose contribution she never forgot were the nuns of Rawalpindi. 'They were a fantastically dedicated group and ran the biggest hospital, the Holy Family,' she said. 'Without any discrimination they had patients inside and outside, even on the roof, and when there was no more space then the college across the road and other buildings were given over to them.' One nun, Sister Julia, was a master organiser and supervised the construction of more hospital facilities, brick by brick, before finally withdrawing from the world and taking a vow of silence. Later, the Holy Family hospital was nationalised and Tahirah hated seeing it taken away from the women she so admired. 'They said the nuns were converting people but they were doing nothing of the sort,' she says on tape. 'They may have converted a few but they were doing it by setting an example from their lives.'

Shahid, too, found purpose in his work in those early days of Pakistan. 'I discovered a world which was full of enthusiasm, spirit and optimism,' he said. 'A new country was being created and all were keen to do their best.' There was feverish activity everywhere, albeit with few resources, but the contrast with what happened later was painful. 'Patriotic exuberance and fervour were soon replaced by regionalism and this had many repercussions,' he wrote. 'The all-important task of moulding individuals into a nation and persuading them to think collectively for the well-being of the country as a whole was forgotten, and replaced by materialism.'

Both he and Tahirah felt the death of their leader, Jinnah, was a turning point of the worst kind, barely a year after independence. 'He was the only man who had the stature, personality and charisma to lead the nation,' Shahid said. 'He was determined to get the Constitution framed at the earliest possible opportunity but alas, it was not to be and he soon died. The struggle for power began.'

❦

Mary and Mumtaz's first home in Pakistan was Peshawar, close to the Afghan border. They had landed there in August 1947 with no idea of what facilities would be available or where they would live, but found a group of officers and their wives waiting on the tarmac. Each couple had been assigned to look after a particular arriving family and one stepped forward to greet the Husains, embracing the four children. 'They explained that we were to stay with them until accommodation was sorted out,' Mumtaz said. 'The warmth of this reception was immediately captivating, coming as it did from total strangers.'

He found the Peshawar base where he would work much more rudimentary than Air HQ in Delhi. The newcomers were addressed on their first day by the British officer who was the first Chief of the Pakistan Air Force and who offered a sobering assessment of its assets: a few Dakotas and Spitfires and some ageing Furies. More aircraft would soon arrive from India, he assured them. 'We all came away quite depressed,' Mumtaz said.

As he wandered around the base in search of an office he bumped once again into David Sheehan, the man but for whom he and Mary would have travelled from Delhi by train. Sheehan was about to leave Pakistan, with other RAF staff, and said the rooms that they were using would soon become available. Mumtaz thought it best to stake a claim: locating a table and two chairs and marshalling the services of a clerk, he set himself up on the verandah outside and called it the medical branch.

His friend Abid arrived later from Delhi, with a tale that made Mumtaz and Mary realise afresh how lucky they had been. Abid had thought he would take his time winding up his family's affairs before heading to Pakistan, and that meant he was still there when rioting broke out in September. Even after Muslim homes in Old Delhi had been set alight, the family believed they would be secure in their more affluent neighbourhood. But before long they heard that their house, too, had been identified as a Muslim one and that people were coming for them.

Abid tried to reach Shrinagesh but telephone lines were down, and when a mob turned up that night – shouting anti-Muslim slogans and trying to force entry – the family took to the roof, from where Abid and a cousin fired warning shots. After the third such night Shrinagesh managed to send a Jeep to evacuate them to a refugee camp at the airport and from there Abid, his wife Helen and their children were flown to Peshawar. Mary and Mumtaz were shocked to see their tattered state on arrival, carrying nothing with them. 'We made them as comfortable as we could,' he said, 'and listened to the awful time they had been through.'

What was Mary thinking in this period, I wondered, far away from her mother, sisters and brother and in a new, unfamiliar region where the main language was no longer Urdu or Punjabi but Pashto. Peshawar was also insecure, given the local Pathans' fondness for firearms and the ongoing looting of supposedly sealed Hindu- and Sikh-owned shops. Even in the relatively sedate residential environment of the cantonment, Mumtaz wrote, dead bodies lay uncollected for days and locals would be seen 'running away with whatever "enemy" property they could lay their hands on'.

I suspect my grandmother had little time to think of her loved ones across the border, for her hands were very full. Even after they had been assigned a flat there was no sign of their Delhi luggage, which meant no furniture and no pots and pans. Nor was there any help available, with cooking or with the four children. 'I was desperate to get some competent help for Mary,' Mumtaz said of this time. 'Being stoic and devoted is one thing but there is a limit to human endurance and I was apprehensive that if she were to break down, we would really be up the creek.'

As ever, Mary sought comfort in her faith and in Peshawar, as elsewhere, she looked for a new place of worship. 'We located the Cathedral on the Mall,' said Mumtaz, 'found out the timings for the various services and went to one in the morning, the following Sunday.'

That day he knelt in the pew next to her but found himself wondering if Jaya was right about bigotry and whether this new homeland for Muslims would truly be a place where people were free to go to temples and churches, as Jinnah had promised. 'I started stealing glances around to see if there were any familiar faces,' he said, and there were; a Muslim officer he knew from the base was in a pew further forward, alongside his own Christian wife. 'I nudged Mary to look,' he said. 'We finished the Mass with complete reassurance that if another very senior officer could "declare" himself so openly, I too should have no worries about any untoward consequences.'

15

New Beginnings

In Pakistan, both families put down new roots, and grew: Mary and Mumtaz had a fifth son, Arshad, in 1948, and Tahirah and Shahid a fourth child, Ali, in 1949. They would not meet until 1957, when the Husains were posted to Rawalpindi and assigned a house on Steward Road, next door to where the Hamids were living. My mother became friends with my father Tazi and his brothers, and after he went away to England in 1967 they wrote to each other. By 1970 Tazi had told Mary and Mumtaz that Shama was the only possible wife for him, and they married in 1972.

After independence, both my grandmothers faced the difficulty of keeping in touch with parents and siblings across the border in India. When Tahirah left Delhi in 1947 she had been comforted by the thought of Aligarh's strong sense of community, and by an assurance she had from the Indian general K. M. Cariappa, who was a friend. 'Tahirah, as long as I am there,' meaning while he remained in service, 'I promise you there will be no trouble in Aligarh.' Then, as months went by with little news of Ataullah and Ameerunissa, she became worried. 'I told Shahid I was frantic about my parents,' she says on tape, but it was not easy to know how to arrange a trip: instability continued and passport and visa rules were still being established.

Shahid had the idea of approaching the British general commanding the Pakistan Army, who did go back and forth to Delhi, and Tahirah was allowed on the plane for his next trip over.

She doesn't record the exact date but it must have been in the first half of 1948. Auchinleck had left India, but both Cariappa and Govind came to meet her at the airport, and she planned to go from Delhi on to Aligarh by train, a journey she had made countless times before.

Cariappa refused to let her, saying that the climate was still too insecure, and she was to go by car instead, with his driver and an armed guard. But when the car broke down en route Tahirah ended up finding the nearest railway station and getting on an Aligarh-bound service, which meant she arrived in her home town in the old, familiar way. 'It was the middle of the night when we got to Aligarh, 2 or 3 a.m., but at the station were the same old *tonga wallahs* I knew,' she said. 'They recognised me. "Bitiya" [daughter], they called out. "Where have you come from? How long you have been away!" And so, with the gunman still next to me, I reached the house.'

After this she had at least one more trip to Aligarh with similar arrangements made for her in Delhi by the old 'brother officer' friends. But then the atmosphere changed. After one of her visits India's Home Minister Sardar Patel came to see Cariappa and told him that this friendship with a Pakistani officer and his wife was unwise. In Pakistan Ayub Khan, who became Army Chief, said something similar to Shahid, that Tahirah's India trips didn't look good. 'Sorry, sir,' Shahid responded. 'I would never stop her seeing her parents.'

Tahirah did keep going, every year, but no longer let the Delhi friends know she was coming. 'I told Shahid that things are changing,' she said. 'People here don't like us mingling and over there it's the same for them.' Instead, she and the children would board the Amritsar-bound train from a fenced-off high-security part of Lahore station and transit through Delhi with 'third-class' visas, reporting to the police in Aligarh on arrival and before departure. Shahid was never able to come with them, but the trips meant my mother and her siblings remained close not only to their grandparents but to uncles, aunts and cousins in India.

As the years went by life became harder for Ataullah and Ameerunissa; the house started to look run down and they rented some rooms out. Then, in 1965 – after Shahid had left the Army – war broke out between Pakistan and India, again over Kashmir, after which Tahirah felt her trips to Aligarh would become impossible.[291] 'I went to Aligarh to bring them away,' she says on tape. 'I told them "My darlings, the time has come for you to leave with me, because

I cannot guarantee I will be able to return."' Her parents understood. 'With great forbearance and dignity they made their preparations,' Tahirah said. 'They told me what to pack and I did it. And, placing our faith in God, I told them they were still fortunate; they were leaving their house but their son was there in India and he would use it. And thus the third stage of their lives began, in Pakistan.'

Before she and Shahid lost touch with their old friends in India, there had been one occasion a couple of years after independence that brought some of them to Karachi. It was an Inter-Dominion conference attended by three contemporaries who all became generals and, in turn, Chiefs of the Indian Army: Sam Manekshaw, Kodandera Thimayya and Satyawant Shrinagesh, the brother of Mumtaz's old boss. 'For nearly two years they had been in and out of our house in Delhi,' Tahirah said. 'We were very close.' At the time, Shahid had been given the task of setting up Pakistan's intelligence service, not a job he could talk about, but when the Indians came for dinner it was obvious they knew exactly what he was doing. 'Well, Shahid, the best ISI [Inter-Services Intelligence] man in the Indian subcontinent now is you,' Shrinagesh said teasingly.[292] They kept away from tricky topics such as Kashmir, apart from when Tahirah couldn't resist it. 'What a mess you've made,' she said to the guests, tongue in cheek. 'Left us with one hill station and taken all of the Himalayas.'

Soon, contact faded away. 'This was such a huge break in my life,' she says on tape, with a sigh. 'We never saw them again.' And yet even in the worst of times, the wars of 1965 and 1971 – when East Pakistan broke away and became Bangladesh – threads of the former bonds remained. In the first of those wars Cariappa's son, an Indian Air Force pilot, was taken prisoner after being shot down over Pakistan. 'I had known him as a boy, from when I stayed in their house in Delhi,' Tahirah said, and her heart went out to him when she heard he had been injured and was being treated in a military hospital. It was her great wish to go and see him, to be of some assistance, but it was impossible to ask to see a prisoner of war privately.[293]

In 1971, Tahirah and Shahid's son-in-law Jafar, husband of my aunt Shahnaz, became a captive of the Indian Army, one of more than 90,000 taken prisoner when Pakistani forces surrendered.[294] Jafar was held for two years, first in a jail in Agra, where conditions were especially hard, and then at a camp in Ranchi in Bihar, where he was told one day that there was a message for him. It was Cariappa, by then a long-retired Indian Army Chief, who had discovered

Auchinleck with the Hamids during a trip to Pakistan

Shahid and Tahirah had a son-in-law among the POWs and tracked him down. General Cariappa would like to know how he was, Jafar was told, and whether he needed anything. He did not, but when Shahid and Tahirah heard of the gesture they were deeply touched.

Auchinleck remained part of the Hamids' lives, as he came to Pakistan several times in the years after independence and they visited him at his home in Suffolk too, where he would raise the Pakistan flag to greet them. 'The house was full of books and often he had corresponded with the author,' my uncle says of those visits to the former Chief. 'He placed the correspondence inside the book and it made it so much more interesting to read.'

In 1974 Auchinleck had a ninetieth-birthday party in London, and Shahid and Tahirah made a surprise appearance: 'Even now an ex-Commander-in-Chief must have his ex-Private Secretary,' Shahid said as they greeted him. Seven years later he died, in Morocco, and Shahid travelled to London for the memorial service at Westminster Abbey. 'It was the last gathering of people connected with the British Raj,' he wrote. 'There were faces we had not seen since the partition of the subcontinent.' Some he managed to speak to, briefly, in the Abbey, but there was no organised opportunity to gather afterwards and he was saddened by that. 'The old guard is fading out,' he said. 'It would have been a marvellous opportunity to revive old friendships and associations.'

Mumtaz's memoir continues to detail his and Mary's life in Pakistan for a few years after independence but then tails off abruptly, almost mid-sentence, around 1954. By the time he was writing he was in his seventies, but I suspect it was not age or health that affected him, rather that later events were more painful to recall, and he lost heart.

Like Shahid and Tahirah, he thought Jinnah's death thirteen months into Pakistan's existence was a crushing blow. He saw him in the flesh twice: once in Delhi in July 1947 and then in Peshawar in 1948, when the Governor-General and his sister Fatima were guests at the Air Force Mess. Mumtaz was the one to ask what Jinnah would like to drink – the answer was a dry sherry – and he was shocked by the Quaid's appearance. 'I was amazed to see the heavy toll that time and the exhaustive negotiations had taken on him,' he wrote. 'Even though one did not know the actual state at that time, it was obvious that he was a spent man and, perhaps, not to last for much longer.'

Jinnah's death in September 1948 was followed in 1951 by the assassination of the country's first Prime Minister, Liaquat Ali Khan. Through most of that decade, Shahid remained in the Army and witnessed the development of a culture he found nauseating: obsequious flattery in the interests of advancement or financial gain, as contracts linked to development of the new nation were awarded. He saw it happen around Ayub Khan after he became Chief. 'It was disgusting to see a certain general appearing in his drawing room and instead of sitting on a chair, squatting on the floor,' he wrote. 'When Ayub Khan told him not to do so, he said he preferred to sit near the feet of the great man.'

In mid-1958, while serving as Adjutant-General, he became aware of a changed atmosphere in GHQ as groups of officers huddled together whispering to each other, and there were rumours of troop movements disguised as military exercises. That October, he heard on the radio that martial law had been declared. 'The great Quaid's words rang in my ears,' he wrote, remembering Jinnah: '"Soldiers must take their orders from a duly elected government."' Instead, he saw generals 'bragging that they would "fix" the politicians and eradicate all evils in the country' and he was sure the Army's involvement in government would be harmful to Pakistan.[295]

His own relationship with Ayub Khan was characterised by the formality required before a senior officer, but the two couples did socialise together, and one evening in that fraught period the Chief asked for his view on the situation. 'I suppose that he must have had enough of his sycophants,' Shahid wrote. 'I said his recent actions had done great harm to the country. His colour changed and I could see he did not relish my remarks. Still, he listened. I said that the worst thing that had happened was the abrogation of the constitution, and that too the first constitution of Pakistan, which had taken so long to draft.'[296]

Martial law needed to end as soon as possible, Shahid continued, telling Ayub Khan that if he sought political power he should set a date for elections, resign from the Army and run for office: he was popular enough to be successful. 'We talked on and on,' Shahid said, 'but I felt my views were not acceptable to him.'*

---

*In 1965 Jinnah's sister Fatima challenged Ayub Khan in presidential elections, as the candidate of the combined opposition parties. She came close to winning, and died two years later.

❦

Through conversations with my great-aunt Anne, I did learn a little of what Mary's mother felt about her departure for Pakistan. Understandably, Mariamma was concerned, and in 1949 she travelled to Pakistan to see Mary, Mumtaz and the five children. It must have been quite a journey from Anakapalle, all the way west across India and on to Karachi in the south of Pakistan, where the family were by then living. She seems to have been not entirely reassured, for on her return she asked Anne to take a break from her nursing work in Calcutta and travel to Pakistan too. 'I'm very worried about Mary,' she said. 'I'd like you to go and stay with her for a while.'

Anne agreed, and what was supposed to be a brief holiday changed her life: in Karachi she met her husband Michael, the son of an RAF officer who had stayed on after independence. She found

Tazi on the far right with his parents, brothers and grandmother

Mary and Anne in Karachi with the five boys

a new nursing position and lived, initially, with Mary and Mumtaz. 'It was not a smooth marriage,' she said, describing how Mary would sit just inside the front door until late into the night, waiting for Mumtaz to return from 'stag' nights out with friends. I thought then how alone Mary was in Pakistan, and understood afresh why she formed such strong bonds with Catholic priests and nuns wherever they lived; this was one network and set of relationships she could call her own. I know, too, that she was insecure about Rahima: even in the 1970s she told my mother that she believed her in-laws were still hoping the original, arranged, marriage would take place.

In his memoir, Mumtaz portrays everyone as fully reconciled within a few years. Initially, he had refused his parents' invitations to Multan, as they asked him to come with the children but not Mary, but then there was an unexpected breakthrough. His father Mohammed Ali went on the Hajj pilgrimage to Saudi Arabia, then a huge undertaking involving a sea voyage and a journey overland, carrying all your own food. On his return to Karachi three months later Mumtaz, Mary and the boys were all at the docks to receive him, witnessing his exhausted and frail appearance. 'I was astounded', Mumtaz wrote, 'that apart from hugging and kissing the children, this time he responded to Mary's greeting by putting his hand on her head.' He accompanied his father back to Multan and before he left again, his parents asked him to return soon, bringing the children 'and daughter' – meaning Mary. 'How do I describe my feelings and relief?' Mumtaz wrote. 'We had lost so many precious years in acrimony and denial.'

There were still tricky moments. When the seven of them went to Multan together for the first time, Mumtaz's parents joined the train en route and handed Mary a small parcel. It was a burqa, for her to wear on arrival. 'Mary, despite the shock she must have felt, received it with her usual aplomb,' Mumtaz remembered, grateful for his wife's tact. She was assured that she only had to wear it from Multan station to the house, and despite her obvious discomfort, she did so. 'We were a complete family from there on,' he said, 'because Mary was prepared to give all to the cause, except of course conversion from her faith, which was never directly asked of her.'

In 1955, Mumtaz moved from the Pakistan Air Force to the Army Medical Corps, and two years later Mary made a rare post-independence visit to India, taking the two youngest boys with her. I think she made only one further trip to Anakapalle in her lifetime, though from the album preserved by my uncle Mickey I can see how carefully she kept the photographs she received of her siblings' growing families, each one pasted in with names, dates and places. Alongside her own letters home she made her sons write regularly to their

Mary in Anakapalle with Saleem and Arshad, 1957

grandmother Mariamma, whom they barely knew. In Anakapalle, these letters were stored safely in a drawer, where other grandchildren would read them and wonder about these faraway cousins with Muslim rather than Christian names.

Once the boys grew up and started to go in different directions they, too, kept in touch with each other by letter. Saleem, who left Pakistan to train as a chartered accountant in Manchester in 1963, kept all the early letters he received from home, and when he showed them to me I discovered how my father Tazi came to move to England himself, in 1967. He had studied medicine at King Edward Medical College in Lahore, just like his father, even living in the same accommodation at Broome Hostel. And, in a further echo of Mumtaz, he also graduated at a time of war, in 1965, and was immediately drafted into military service as a medic.

I remember him talking about this period, and the experience of going from student life to field units outside Lahore, but the letters told me much more. In March 1966, six months into his emergency short-service commission, he was already looking forward to being released. 'I like the Army, but still I want to see the world and to finish whatever postgraduate study I must do,' he wrote to Saleem. Aged twenty-three, and in a country where people married young, he was also starting to feel family friends were a little too interested in his personal life. 'Apparently I've reached the dangerous age when everybody wants me married off,' he said. 'Thank God the disease hasn't struck Mummy and Daddy yet.'

In another letter, he broke sad news to Saleem about the family's beloved springer spaniel. 'Spooky died yesterday,' he wrote, with rage as well as grief, because he felt the vet had been incompetent. 'He saw us all grow up and leave for other places. For me he was the symbol of a childhood. Say a prayer for him.'

Tazi on the right with Spooky

That summer, after a series of run-ins with senior officers, he began to seriously explore alternatives to the Army Medical Corps. 'I'm almost considered a trouble-maker in my unit,' he said. 'Nobody has any guts in the A.M.C.: no traditions, no discipline, no pride of service. The old Army has gone, I'm afraid. That is why I'd rather concentrate on my profession.' He considered the United States, a move that would require appearing for the American MD exam, but in England Anne was also exploring opportunities at her hospital, Oldham Royal Infirmary. One of her surgeon colleagues was immediately interested in her doctor nephew in Pakistan, but Tazi worried that his experience was insufficient. 'I am reluctant to start there,' he said to Saleem, conscious that his year of experience as a doctor had been spent entirely with soldiers in the field. 'I feel Aunty Anne is obliged to put in a good word for me and the hospital may be disappointed.'

He was, in time, persuaded and arrived in Oldham in January 1967, on a salary of £600 per year. Training as a surgeon would involve short stints in different hospitals and by the following January he was in Blackburn, Lancashire. 'Had a very busy Christmas and New Year – was on call throughout and admissions just poured in,' he told Saleem, as they continued to write to each other. 'England now has an "Asian flu epidemic" and this, with the Foot & Mouth epidemic, is keeping me occupied and very worried. We have nothing but "chesty" people in the wards, simply pouring in, and creating absolute Hell!' By the time my parents married he was based in Northampton, where I was born, and later assignments included Great Ormond Street in London, where we lived in a prefab on the edge of the long-since-disappeared hospital tennis court.

❦

Mary never completed her nurse training, but in the late 1950s she began a new career, teaching in the Catholic schools attended by her sons. It must have been a welcome source of income, given the difficulty of raising five children on an Army salary, and Mumtaz

continuing to send money to Multan every month. It was not until 1971 that their circumstances improved, when he retired and joined the World Health Organisation.

Around the time I was born in 1973, Mary was diagnosed with breast cancer, of a type that I am sure she would have survived today. She had treatment which was, for a time, successful, but in 1984 my parents, my brother Haider and I were all in Rawalpindi when she left for what turned out to be the last time, to see her doctor in London. It was obvious how sick she was, and as Haider and I lined up with the other grandchildren to kiss her goodbye at the airport, I think all of us knew that we would not see her again. She and Mumtaz had only just completed work on their house and the garden she had planted was coming into bloom for the first time that spring: it was clear that she would have preferred to stay at home and gaze out on her flowers in those final days.

Mumtaz was sixty-four when she died and the vision of old age he had imagined they would share was shattered. He took up short assignments with the UN in order to be useful again and later led public health projects in Karachi, still influenced by the hygiene, sanitation and infection-control miracle he had seen during the Second World War.

Some time later my father, who was a keen, and good, painter of faces, decided to embark on a portrait of his parents. He wanted to work from a photograph but struggled to find the right one and in

the end created a composite, seating my mother in a chair and asking Mumtaz to perch on the armrest. Once Shama's image had been
replaced with an old one of Mary he had what he wanted, and the
result hangs in my hallway in London. I often think there is a time-
travelling aspect to it: Mary is as she was in the 1970s while Mumtaz
is not only older, but his face is worn and his expression sombre.
Here, it is as if she has come back from the grave to sit beside him.

Shahid and Tahirah did grow old together, and lived in Pakistan from independence until the end of their days. In his final years he chaired the board of governors at a school in Rawalpindi named after Sir Syed, through which, he told Tahirah, he hoped to give back a little of what he had received in Aligarh. 'We have to draw inspiration from the deeds of the old and pass it to the younger generation,' he said, 'who must know that Pakistan was established as a result of great sacrifices.'

In the 1980s Tahirah felt that the character of Rawalpindi was changing, as people moved away to the new Pakistani capital of Islamabad, and she tried to persuade Shahid to do the same. 'I do believe that in the last few years we have been too far from people,' she said to him in one letter found by my mother. 'It has been an insular life. Pindi is not the city that it was and we are refusing to accept the fact that almost all our friends that are living are residing in Islamabad.' He would not agree, unable to contemplate uprooting himself, while she had taken a different lesson from partition and leaving old homes behind. 'Bricks and mortar don't matter,' she used to say. 'People do.'

She was seventy-three when he died, and afterwards I saw a new side to her: in the place of her usual stoicism she mourned, agonised over the right lines of Urdu poetry for his grave and composed her own for him. It was in this period that she pressed record and play on her tape recorder and started talking into it, her tone light and free as she spoke of Delhi and Aligarh and more laboured as she reached the 1950s and beyond, her voice becoming inaudible at times and her sentences tailing off. Confronting realities was painful: deficiencies in Pakistan's leadership, the intolerance that came with Islamisation and greater religiosity, corruption and the trampling of democracy. 'My generation can take the blame,' she said. 'We should have started to protest.' She remembered her mother Ameerunissa's disapproval of the greed and excesses she observed after she moved to Rawalpindi. 'She used to sit and watch Pakistan, having seen the trials and tribulations of India's Muslims, which had left a mark on her life,' Tahirah said. 'She kept thinking

of the sacrifices they had made for the country in which Pakistanis were living.'

Tahirah's memory faded in her final years, but her influence is there in the way I lay a table, or look at a garden, or tie a sari, although my fingers will never scissor through fabric and flick it to create swift, sharp folds the way hers did. 'Maybe I'll try and recapture our life, the fabulous happy life that we had, five decades of it,' she said on tape, after she was widowed, though she shied away from the idea of writing history. 'Partition was a sad, sad era,' she concluded. 'I will not hesitate to say it here – even though this is not meant to be a political book – but it need not have happened, had the majority in India accepted ordinary demands from a minority. But it happened, and the way it happened was tragic. And to the eternal shame of the people of India and Pakistan, that big tragedy has been followed by others.'

I know that she and Shahid felt let down by those in power in Britain at the time of the 'big tragedy'; she once told me that she could never forgive Labour for its handling of partition. And as I looked through the official papers from the time – and what the key players said later – it was hard not to conclude that decision-making was coloured by personal impressions in a way that was not fitting for a colonial power in the midst of a task with historic and generational implications. Attlee had a low opinion of Jinnah, failing to even reply to one letter he wrote, asking for more action to curb communal violence. Once he had appointed Mountbatten he largely left him to it, and the implications of the former Viceroy being Governor-General of one country and not the other – the reality through the Kashmir crisis – seem not to have been thought through.[297]

As for Mountbatten, there is no doubt he inherited a very difficult situation. But he was also a man in a hurry, keen to return to his naval career, mindful of protecting his reputation and image, and with extreme opinions of Jinnah that were in stark contrast to his closeness to Nehru. As early as April 1947 he described the Muslim

League leader in an official despatch as 'psychopathic' and even thirty years later his expression soured at the mention of Jinnah's name in a conversation with his biographer, as he questioned why he would want to write about someone so humourless.[298]

Publicly, Mountbatten would always say he believed his actions in 1947 were right in the circumstances. Privately, though, there is one occasion when he is known to have acknowledged shortcomings. It was in 1965, at a lunch where he was seated next to a BBC correspondent who had recently returned from covering the India–Pakistan War and whose reports he had heard. When the conversation turned to 1947 and partition, Mountbatten blamed himself and spoke in the baldest terms about how he had 'got things wrong' and, ultimately, messed up the assignment.[299]

I was looking back from an even longer-term vantage point, conscious of what would continue to cause Mumtaz, Mary, Shahid and Tahirah pain if they were alive today, including the Pakistan Army's continuing involvement in politics and the battles of minority communities on both sides of the border. There is also the lost potential in trade and contact between these two countries, and what they might have done together over these past decades, in different circumstances.

Today, only a small fraction of Pakistanis and Indians get the opportunity to visit the other country and even fewer would have emotional attachments similar to those of my grandparents. For the most part, they simply don't know anyone across the border. The state of relations affects diaspora communities too, when those with Pakistani links try to visit India, and vice versa. And yet when contact is possible there is often an appreciation of shared heritage, or simply an unspoken understanding, because independence and partition are still – just – within living memory. When I travelled to India with my mother in 2005 the immigration officer in Delhi looked up at us and said, 'First time?' I gave a quick yes but from my mother there was a pause, before she said slowly, 'We used to come here.' Nothing more was asked and we both felt, in that instant, that the rest was obvious, the tangle of relationships, emotions and history behind the few words. On that trip, the Hindu family who had bought my mother's family home in Aligarh welcomed her when she knocked at the door and said who she was, and I have heard similar tales from those visiting former homes in Pakistan. Perhaps, then, the threads are more frayed than broken, because stories have been handed down in countless families, creating an oral link with the past. Today those tales connect people like me with those who went before, but taken together they also reveal bonds across borders, which one day might be more than memories.

ACKNOWLEDGEMENTS

In the process of drawing the threads of my family story together I had to go much deeper into the politics of South Asia and further back into its history than I had imagined. My primary hope is that Shahid, Tahirah, Mumtaz and Mary would feel I have been true to their life experiences. And, as millions of others lived through the same tumultuous period, I also hope that those of similar heritage find something in this that helps illuminate their own ancestors' times.

I have dedicated this to my mother Shama, but I also owe a great deal to her siblings Hassan Hamid, Shahnaz Jafar and Ali Hamid, all of whom shared memories and observations. Ali's professional life as a soldier and his subsequent research and writing also made him an invaluable source of information and context about Shahid's experiences.

My father Tazi was much missed during my research and writing, though I was able to dip into his blogs, photograph albums and letters and was helped by my uncles Ejaz, Niaz and Saleem Husain, especially through the questions they answered via WhatsApp. Mumtaz and Mary's story would have been impossible without Ejaz (Mickey) retrieving the memoir from Mumtaz's computer when he died, and saving his papers and documents, as well as Mary's photograph album. It is also thanks to him that I have Tazi's portrait of Mumtaz and Mary in London, after he hand-carried it over from Karachi a few years ago.

Several of Tahirah and Shahid's nieces and nephews shared insights: Sultana Al Qu'aiti, Zeenut Ziad, Fareed Malik, Sameen

Rushdie, Qazi Azmat Isa, Naveed Henderson, Nada Hasan and Yamina Qadri. I would have loved Shahid's niece Shahmeen to still be alive to see this project: she was not only the one who gave me the sari-shawl wedding present but also the prime keeper of Hamid family history in her lifetime. Among the next generation are my cousins Junaid Jafar, Unver Shafi Khan and Ali Dayan Hasan – as well as his wife Sahr Ataullah – and Hasan Jafar and his wife Amena. They are the rock of the family in Islamabad, custodians of Tahirah's last home there, and the ones who found Shahid's 1932 passport.

Mary's nieces and nephews also gave of their time and helped in different ways, especially Lesley Todd, Cymbeline D'Souza, Rose Goubert, Bernadine Peluri, Christine Filatriau and her husband Coco, and my great-aunt Louisa's son Jake Leith, who shared her letters and was the first to suggest to me that our Anglo-Indian heritage was worth exploring. I still think there is more to say about this unique community, now scattered across the world.

My great-aunt Anne Frost has been a very special figure in all of this: without her, many threads would have been impossible to explore. I continue to marvel at all she has seen in her life, from Anakapalle to Calcutta to Pakistan and then England. 'I am the last one left,' she said to me recently, but she is undimmed, and I am deeply grateful for the love she has shown me over many years, and to her sons Tom and Mike Frost for their help.

The excerpt from Faiz Ahmed Faiz's poem 'Freedom's Morning' is used with the kind permission of the Faiz Foundation. It was written in the middle of August 1947 as the 36-year-old poet travelled from Lahore to Srinagar in Kashmir and witnessed mass displacement and insecurity. The translation is my own.

Excerpts from the Auchinleck papers are courtesy of the University of Manchester. The use of Barbara Swinburn's letters is thanks to her daughter-in-law Gillian, who responded to my query about any old diaries or correspondence by painstakingly going through the files carefully kept by her late husband David. Christopher Beaumont's full testimony was made available to me by his son Robert, after I made contact via Twitter. Although perplexed, he replied! My thanks also go to All Souls College, Oxford, for safeguarding his father's original, private account.

Mahmood Masood took the time to talk to me about his grandfather Sir Ross Masood and great-grandfather Sir Syed Ahmad Khan, while from India, Inder Vijai Singh confirmed details about his father Thakur Govind Singh. Najma Ataullah-Jan told me more about her father Syed Abid Hasnain and found a photograph of Mumtaz in his student days which was new to me, and my father's dear friend Mansoor Ishani talked to me about their time as students in Lahore in the 1960s. In Islamabad, Parveen Qadir Agha gave me an insight into the INA through the story of her father Colonel Ehsan Qadir: again, there is so much more to delve into there, including the prisoners' interrogation records in the British Library.

I am indebted to those who read drafts of the manuscript or answered specific queries: Yasmin Khan, Victoria Schofield, Ian Talbot, William Dalrymple, Eugene Rogan, Margaret MacMillan, Andrew Whitehead and Anuradha Awasthi. Anu and I worked together on my first trip to India, in 2005, and perhaps we will one day, inshallah, go together to her home city of Lucknow.

I would also like to thank the staff of the Asian and African Studies Reading Room at the British Library, especially John Chignoli who looked up the Quinn family in the registers for me; Glyn Prosor at the National Army Museum in London; Anthony Morton at the Royal Military Academy, Sandhurst; Ghee Bowman; Iqbal Ahmed of the BBC in Delhi, with whom I went to Aligarh in 2014; Syed Talha Ali for research assistance in Aligarh; and Phil Goodwin and David Page who spotted the recording of Shahid in the BBC Urdu Service archive.

Philip Watson, Haroon Shirwani and my late and much missed friend Zishan Afzal Khan all gave me early encouragement for this project, and I am fortunate to have an ever-wise writer neighbour in Francesca Segal. Sanjana Puri answered questions about Hindu terminology and practice, Professor Rafey Habib helped with the references to marriage in the Qur'an, and Dominik Treeck and Waltraud Schönhofer both helped with the German in Ataullah's *Lebenslauf*. August Courtauld was my researcher in the final stages, and my eldest son Rafael pitched in too.

Elly James and the HHB team and Louise Haines and the Fourth Estate team: thank you for believing in this book. Louise saw it morph from the original idea and bore with me through periods when the scale seemed almost overwhelming, guiding me on narrative and structure and stopping me from going down too many rabbit-holes. My agent Elly kept me going through what could have been difficult junctions, and I know she always has my back. I am also deeply grateful to Peter James, Alex Gingell and Richard Marston for the thoughtful way they went through the manuscript and to others who looked after different aspects of the book: Victoria Pullen, Patrick Hargadon, Liv Marsden, Ola Galewicz, and Martin Brown, who did the maps and family trees.

To my brother Haider: this is your story too. Heartfelt thanks to you and Dawn for your love and support.

To the next generation, Rafa, Zaki, Musa and my nephew Albert: I hope this helps you to know your heritage and the long links between peoples and continents.

And finally to Meekal, whose reserves of patience and goodwill I have severely tested but found to be infinite: you are companion, counsel and love of my life. Thank you.

NOTES

The Auchinleck Papers are held in the University of Manchester Library and the Transfer of Power series in the British Library.

CHAPTER 1 *Mary*

1 William Dalrymple, *The Anarchy: The Relentless Rise of the East India Company*, Bloomsbury, 2019, pp. 75–6; William Dalrymple, *White Mughals: Love and Betrayal in Eighteenth-Century India*, Viking, 2003, pp. 34 and 50–1.

2 Alison Blunt, *Domicile and Diaspora: Anglo-Indian Women and the Spatial Politics of Home*, Blackwell, 2005, pp. 1–3.

3 Jill C. Bender, *The 1857 Indian Uprising and the British Empire*, Cambridge University Press, 2016, p. 61.

4 The Sisters of St Joseph of Annecy http://stjosephofannecyvsp.org

CHAPTER 2 *Mumtaz*

5 Michael Wood, *In the Footsteps of Alexander the Great: A Journey from Greece to India*, BBC Worldwide, 1997, pp. 188–90.

6 The history and operations of the Indian Medical Service as it stood in 1925 are set out in a House of Lords debate recorded in Hansard: 29 July 1925.

7 The mosque's name came from it being built by a man who travelled from Lahore to Australia and liked the country very much.

8 Mumtaz lost touch with Jimmy at independence. His brother Sam Manekshaw was a famed post-independence Chief of the Indian Army.

CHAPTER 3   *Shahid*

9   My uncle Ali has traced this story: Syed Ali Hamid, 'Three Swords of Subedar Meer Jaffir', Parts 1 & 2, *The Friday Times*, 27 March and 3 April 2020.

10 S. Shahid Hamid, *Autobiography of a General*, Ferozsons, 1988, Preface.

11 Ibid., Appendix B, p. 155.

12 John Keay, *India: A History*, HarperCollins, 2000, p. 435.

13 Rosie Llewellyn-Jones, *The Last King in India: Wajid Ali Shah*, Hirst, 2014, pp. 11–41 and 114–25. This is a comprehensive account of Wajid's life, his court in Lucknow and his exile in Calcutta.

14 One example is a petition presented to Parliament in 1813 by William Wilberforce, arguing that it should be lawful to impart the benefits of Christianity to natives 'in a state of deplorable ignorance': Hansard, 19 February 1813.

15 Rudrangshu Mukherjee and Pramod Kapoor, *Dateline 1857: Revolt against the Raj*, Lustre Press, 2008, pp. 15–28.

16 J. A. B. Palmer, *The Mutiny Outbreak in Meerut in 1857*, Cambridge University Press, 1966, pp. 60–70. This detailed account has been widely relied on.

17 Mahmood Farooqui, *Besieged: Voices from Delhi, 1857*, Viking, 2010, p. 21.

18 William Dalrymple, *The Last Mughal: The Fall of a Dynasty, Delhi, 1857*, Bloomsbury, 2006, p. 398. Zafar died in exile in Rangoon in 1862.

19 Jawaharlal Nehru wrote: 'The Revolt of 1857 was a joint affair, but in its suppression Muslims felt strongly, and to some extent rightly, that they were the greater sufferers.' Jawaharlal Nehru, *The Discovery of India*, John Day, 1946, p. 375.

20 Some knighthoods were given to Indians but there was also an India-specific honours system with titles varied by faith, e.g. 'Khan Bahadur' for Muslims, 'Rai Bahadur' for Hindus and 'Sardar Bahadur' for Sikhs.

21 Syed Rafiq Hussain was a writer of short stories in Urdu. Eight have been translated into English and published in India, with an introduction that includes an 'autobiographical sketch' originally published in an Urdu literary journal. Syed Rafique Hussain, *The Mirror of Wonders and Other Tales*, trans. Saleem Kidwai, Yoda Press, 2013.

22 Colvin Taluqdars' College.

CHAPTER 4 *Tahirah*

23 Both forms of response are explored in Barbara D. Metcalf, *Islamic Revival in British India: Deoband, 1860–1900*, Princeton University Press, 1982.

24 G. F. I. Graham, *The Life and Work of Syed Ahmed Khan*, Blackwood, 1885, p. 28; Rajmohan Gandhi, *Understanding the Muslim Mind*, Penguin, 2000, pp. 22–3.

25 Translation from the original Urdu by two of Syed Ahmad's friends, George Graham and Auckland Colvin: *The Causes of the Indian Revolt*, Medical Hall Press, 1873, pp. 11–13.

26 From an Urdu biography of Sir Syed by Altaf Hussain Hali, quoted in the introduction to Sir Syed Ahmed Khan, *The Causes of the Indian Revolt: Three Essays*, ed. Salim Qureshi, Sang-e-Meel Publications, 1997.

27 He lodged in London's Mecklenburgh Square, where a blue plaque at Number 21 commemorates him as a 'Muslim reformer and scholar'.

28 Syed Ahmed, *Strictures on the Present State of English Education in India*, n.p., 1869. The issue of language had exercised Syed Ahmad for some time as he saw the replacement of Urdu and Persian by English and Hindi as a serious threat to the ability of Muslims to hold official positions and advance under the Raj.

29 David Lelyveld, *Aligarh's First Generation: Muslim Solidarity in British India*, Princeton University Press, 2020, pp. 105–7 and 74–5.

30 Graham, *The Life and Work of Syed Ahmed Khan*, p. 1.

31 Victoria Schofield, *Kashmir in Conflict: India, Pakistan and the Unending War*, I.B. Tauris, 2010, pp. 6–9.

32 Sialkot is today a major industrial centre of Pakistan, with World Cup footballs among its products.

33 One brother, Khalifa Abdul Hakim, obtained a doctorate from Heidelberg University in the 1920s and became an accomplished academic and writer in Hyderabad, India, and in Lahore after independence. www.khalifaabdulhakim.com

34 Hameeda's brother was Shaukat Omar, and his friend was K. M. Ashraf, later a leader of the Communist Party of India. Hameeda Akhtar Husain Raipuri, *My Fellow Traveller*, trans. Amina Azfar, Oxford University Press, 2006, pp. 1–3.

35 Sheikh Abdullah and his wife Waheed Jahan were the founders of Tahirah's school.

36 Ajmal Khan Tibbiya College, affiliated with Aligarh Muslim University.

37 Syed Mahmood, Ross Masood's father, became the first Indian judge at the Allahabad High Court in 1882 and was known for dissenting judgments. See Mohammad Nasir and Samreen Ahmed, *Syed Mahmood: Colonial India's Dissenting Judge*, Bloomsbury, 2022.

38 'Syed Ross Masood', in E. M. Forster, *Two Cheers for Democracy*, ed. Oliver Stallybrass, Penguin, 1965, p. 296.

39 Wendy Moffat, *E. M. Forster: A New Life*, Bloomsbury, 2010, pp. 90 and 110.

40 P. N. Furbank, *E. M. Forster: A Life*, Sphere Books, 1977, pp. 144 and 226–77.

41 Syed Ross Masood, Presidential Address Delivered at the 42nd Session of the All-India Muslim Educational Conference, Held at Benares in 1930, Muslim University Press, Aligarh.

42 Forster, ibid., p. 298.

43 Amina Majeed Malik was later a prominent educator of Karachi and founder of the PECHS Girls School.

44 British India's capital had previously been Calcutta, and the plan to build New Delhi was announced by George V in 1911.

45 The college is named after Lady Hardinge, wife of a former viceroy, who had come up with the idea and envisaged it being named for Queen Mary, to commemorate her 1911 visit to India. When she died during the construction phase it was named in her memory instead.

46 Shaukat Omar was an engineer. After Jamila's death in 1947 he married again in 1956, but died soon afterwards. His widow founded a hospital in Karachi in his memory.

CHAPTER 5 *Jinnah and Gandhi*

47 These details come from Jinnah's sister Fatima, who was working on a biography of her brother at the time of her death in 1967. The three chapters discovered were later published. Fatima Jinnah, *My Brother*, Peace Publications, 2021, pp. 54–61.

48 Hector Bolitho, *Jinnah: Creator of Pakistan*, John Murray, 1954, p. 9.

49 Petition of 25 April 1893, held by the Honourable Society of Lincoln's Inn. Jinnah was called to the Bar on 28 April 1896.

50 Jinnah, *My Brother*, pp. 83–5.

51 Stanley Wolpert, *Jinnah of Pakistan*, Oxford University Press, 1984, p. 21.

52 Account of the meeting of the Central Legislative Council in January 1910 in Calcutta, Bolitho, *Jinnah*, p. 48.

53 M. H. Saiyid, *Mohammad Ali Jinnah (A Political Study)*, Sh. Muhammad Ashraf, 1945, pp. 66–8; G. Allana (ed.), *Pakistan Movement: Historic Documents*, Islamic Book Service, 1977, pp. 25–48.

54 Jinnah was among those keen to meet Gandhi on his return in 1915. Ramachandra Guha, *Gandhi: The Years that Changed the World, 1915–1948*, Penguin, 2018, p. 11.

55 Jawaharlal Nehru, *An Autobiography*, John Lane, 1936, p. 35.

56 William Dalrymple, *The Anarchy: The Relentless Rise of the East India Company*, Bloomsbury, 2019, pp. 13–14; Victoria and Albert Museum, https://www.vam.ac.uk/articles/indian-textiles.

57 Shrabani Basu, *For King and Another Country: Indian Soldiers on the Western Front, 1914–18*, Bloomsbury, 2015; Santanu Das, *India, Empire, and First World War Culture: Writings, Images, and Songs*, Cambridge University Press, 2018. Punjab, Nepal and the North-West Frontier provided some of the most sought-after soldiers.

58 Edwin S. Montagu, *An Indian Diary*, ed. Venetia Montagu, Heinemann, 1930, pp. 57–8.

59 Wolpert, *Jinnah of Pakistan*, p. 55; Guha, *Gandhi*, pp. 59–60.

60 The franchise, based on property and income as well as sex, excluded much of the population. Guha, *Gandhi*, pp. 70–1.

61 Saiyid, *Mohammad Ali Jinnah*, pp. 114–16.

62 Guha, *Gandhi*, pp. 76–7; Saiyid, *Mohammad Ali Jinnah*, p. 117; Rajmohan Gandhi, *Gandhi: The Man, His People and the Empire*, Haus Books, 2007, p. 207.

63 Gandhi, *Gandhi*, pp. 209–10.

64 Details from Kim A. Wagner, *Amritsar 1919: An Empire of Fear and the Making of a Massacre*, Yale University Press, 2019.

65 Shaista Suhrawardy Ikramullah, *From Purdah to Parliament*, Cresset Press, 1963, (Oxford University Press 1998 edition), pp. 36–8.

66 Wolpert, *Jinnah of Pakistan*, pp. 63–7.

67 Lloyd George spoke in London in January 1918 of not depriving Turkey of 'the rich lands of Asia Minor and Thrace, which are predominantly Turkish'.

68 Speeches in London and Paris in March 1920, in Afzal Iqbal (ed.), *Select Writings and Speeches of Maulana Mohamed Ali*, Sh. Muhammad Ashraf, 1944, pp. 4–9 and 14–19.

69 Saiyid, *Mohammad Ali Jinnah*, p. 125.

70 David Lelyveld, *Aligarh's First Generation: Muslim Solidarity in British India*, Princeton University Press, 2020, pp. 336 and 330–40; Tariq Hasan, *The Aligarh Movement and the Making of the Indian Muslim Mind, 1857–2002*, Rupa, 2006, pp. 160–5.

71 Aijaz Ahmad, *Aligarh Muslim University (An Educational and Political History, 1920–47)*, Lata Sahitya Sadan, 2005, p. 31.

72 Jamia Millia Islamia, where Mohammed Ali Jauhar was the first Vice-Chancellor. Sultan Jahan, Aligarh's first Chancellor, was one of several female rulers of Bhopal. See Shahryar M. Khan, *The Begums of Bhopal, A Dynasty of Women Rulers in Raj India*, I.B. Tauris, 2000.

73 Saiyid, *Mohammad Ali Jinnah*, pp. 127–30; Ayesha Jalal, *The Sole Spokesman: Jinnah, the Muslim League and the Demand for Pakistan*, Cambridge University Press, 1985, pp. 8–9.

74 Nehru, *An Autobiography*, p. 69 and 72. The story of Lord Ram is told in the ancient Sanskrit epic the *Ramayana*. Gandhi wrote in his publication *Young India* in September 1929 that in referring to Ramarajya he meant not a Hindu Raj but a Divine Raj or Kingdom of God: 'The ancient ideal of Ramarajya is undoubtedly one of true democracy.'

75 Saiyid, *Mohammad Ali Jinnah*, p. 134

76 Ikramullah, *From Purdah to Parliament*, pp. 38–9.

77 Guha, *Gandhi*, pp. 155–6.

78 Afzal Iqbal, *The Life and Times of Mohamed Ali: An Analysis of the Hopes, Fears and Aspirations of Muslim India from 1778 to 1931*, Institute of Islamic Culture, 1974.

79 Gandhi, *Understanding the Muslim Mind*, p. 121.

CHAPTER 6   *A Passage to England*

80 Hazratganj in Lucknow, from Yasmin Khan, *The Raj at War*, Penguin Random House, 2015, p. 3.

81 General Sir Archibald Galloway, 12 December 1849, at the Company's military academy at Addiscombe; quoted in John Connell, *Auchinleck*, Cassell, 1959, p. 21.

82 From the essay 'Passing It On' (held in the National Army Museum in London) published in S. Shahid Hamid, *Courage Is a Weapon*, Karachi, Sani Communications, 1980.

83 Translation of interview on BBC Urdu Service, 3 July 1984. The book is S. Shahid Hamid, *So They Rode and Fought*, Midas Books, 1983.

84 Arising out of the Government of India Act 1935, which also provided for a future federation of provinces and princely states.

85 Jawaharlal Nehru, *An Autobiography*, John Lane, 1936, p. 602; John Keay, *India: A History*, HarperCollins, 2000, p. 490.

86 Ian Talbot and Gurharpal Singh, *The Partition of India*, Cambridge University Press, 2009, p. 32.

87 The poet Iqbal was an important influence on Jinnah in this period: Akbar S. Ahmed, *Jinnah, Pakistan and Islamic identity: The Search for Saladin*, Routledge, 1997, pp. 74–6.

88 Guha, *Gandhi*, pp. 535–6. Abul Kalam Azad, Congress's most prominent Muslim leader, said the allegations were false. He did criticise some of his party's decisions and attitudes towards non-Hindus in a part of his memoir only released decades after his death. Maulana Abul Kalam Azad, *India Wins Freedom: The Complete Version*, Orient Longman, 1988, pp. 16–18 and 24–5

89 Shaista Suhrawardy Ikramullah, *From Purdah to Parliament*, p. 128.

90 Nehru, *An Autobiography*, p. 605; Stanley Wolpert, *Jinnah of Pakistan*, Oxford University Press, 1984, pp. 168–9.

91 M. S. Golwalkar, *We or Our Nationhood Defined*, Bharat Publications, 1939, pp. 35, 41 & 47–8. The text is now difficult to obtain but is reproduced in Shamsul Islam, *Golwalkar's We Or Our Nationhood Defined*, Pharos Media & Publishing, Delhi, 2006. In 1948 Gandhi was assassinated by a Hindu nationalist, Nathuram Godse.

CHAPTER 7 *Burma's Descent*

92 Abul Kalam Azad, *India Wins Freedom*, p. 28. In the biography of Linlithgow written by his son, he says 'India's constitutional position was clear. With Britain at war India was at war automatically. No declaration by the Viceroy could initiate this, or gainsay it. It was a fact.' John Glendevon, *The Viceroy at Bay: Lord Linlithgow in India, 1936–43*, Collins, 1971, p. 135.

93 Yasmin Khan, *The Raj at War*, Penguin Random House, 2015, pp. 7–11; Glendevon, *The Viceroy at Bay*, p. 138. The Nizam of Hyderabad issued an appeal to the Muslims of India to support the war effort, and several princes made substantial financial contributions.

94 See Ghee Bowman, *The Indian Contingent: The Forgotten Muslim Soldiers of Dunkirk*, History Press, 2020. pp. 71–3

95 The US aircraft belonged to the AVG or American Volunteer Group,

manned by ex-service personnel as President Roosevelt could not be
seen to be directly helping China against Japan at that time.

96 Victoria Schofield, *Wavell: Soldier and Statesman*, John Murray, 2006,
p. 239.

97 Winston Churchill, *The Second World War*, vol. IV: *The Hinge of Fate*,
Cassell, 1954, p. 87.

98 Schofield, *Wavell*, pp. 245–6.

99 Fergal Keane, *Road of Bones: The Epic Siege of Kohima, 1944*, Harper
Press, 2010, pp. 20–1.

100 Ibid., pp. 15–16.

101 Field Marshal Viscount Slim, *Defeat into Victory*, Cassell, 1956, p. 14.

102 Clare Boothe, 'Burma Mission', *Life* magazine, 27 April 1942.

103 The last soldiers crossed the border into India in May 1942.

CHAPTER 8   *Mary and Mumtaz*

104 Josephine Thomas, *When The Japs Came to Vizag, India*, contributed to
the BBC's 'WW2 People's War' on 7 July 2005.

105 Yasmin Khan, *The Raj at War*, p. 97.

106 Sir Stafford Cripps (1889–1952) was Ambassador to Moscow 1940–2
and later Chancellor of the Exchequer under Clement Attlee.

107 Gandhi, *Gandhi: The Man, His People and the Empire*, pp. 448–9.

108 Guha, *Gandhi*, p. 648. Cripps' main Congress interlocutor was Abul
Kalam Azad, who set out his assessment of the failure to agree in *India
Wins Freedom*, pp. 57–64.

109 Azad, ibid., p. 75.

110 Guha, *Gandhi*, p. 671.

111 Field Marshal Viscount Slim, *Defeat into Victory*, Cassell, 1956, pp. 202–
6; John Connell, *Auchinleck*, Cassell, 1959, p. 773; Fergal Keane, *Road of
Bones: The Epic Siege of Kohima, 1944*, HarperPress, 2010, p. 82; Khan,
The Raj at War, p. 252.

112 Keane, *Road of Bones*, pp. 83–4; Khan, *The Raj at War*, pp. 162–3.

113 The Qur'an, Chapter 4, 'The Women', verse 3. Later in the same
chapter (verse 129) the Qur'an says it is impossible to be fair and just
between wives, however much that may be the desire. See translation
and commentary in Abdullah Yusuf Ali, *The Holy Qur'an*, Khalil Al-
Rawaf, 1946, p. 179 and p. 221.

CHAPTER 9: *Auchinleck*

114 My uncle Ali managed to piece together Mahmood Butt's wartime service after investigating a photograph of him meeting Louis Mountbatten in 1943: Syed Ali Hamid, 'Searching For My Uncle, the Hawker Pilot', *The Friday Times*, 10 January 2020.

115 Rosie Llewelyn-Jones, *The Last King in India: Wajid Ali Shah*, pp. 165–71.

116 Ian Stephens, *Monsoon Morning*, Ernest Benn, 1966, pp. 174 and 177.

117 Ibid., p. 170.

118 Ibid., pp. 178, 181–3 and Appendix IX.

119 Amartya Sen, *Home in the World*, Allen Lane, 2021, p. 121.

120 Ibid., p. 117.

121 '1943 Bengal Famine', *Witness History*, BBC World Service, 1 April 2015.

122 John Connell, *Auchinleck*, Cassell, 1959, pp. 758–9; Yasmin Khan, *The Raj at War*, Penguin Random House, 2015, pp. 212–13.

123 On 1 and 2 July 1942. The vote was comfortably won.

124 Telegram of 1 August 1942, after which Churchill flew to Cairo and to Auchinleck's headquarters in the field, to see the situation for himself. Winston Churchill, *The Second World War*, vol. IV: *The Hinge of Fate*, Cassell, 1951, p. 411.

125 *The Auk at 90: David Dimbleby Interviews Field-Marshal Sir Claude Auchinleck*, BBC TV, 1974.

126 Philip Warner, *Auchinleck: The Lonely Soldier*, Buchan & Enright, 1981, pp. 168–9; Connell, *Auchinleck*, p. 716. Auchinleck wrote to the *Sunday Times* in 1958 to say Montgomery's assertion about a withdrawal plan was 'incorrect and absurd'.

127 Field Marshal Viscount Slim, *Defeat into Victory*, Cassell, 1956, p. 201.

128 Roger Parkinson, *The Auk: Auchinleck, Victor at El Alamein*, Granada Publishing, 1977, p. 248.

129 C in C's Victory Broadcast, 10 June 1945, Auchinleck Papers AUC /1089.

130 Shahid had heard accounts of returning POWs first hand, including Mahmood Khan Durrani who received the George Cross and wrote a book about his experiences (*The Sixth Column*, Cassel & Co., 1955). After 1947, former INA men were widely seen in India as part of the liberation struggle. This was not the case in Pakistan. See Ahmad Salim, *A Lost Page of History*, Sanjh, (Lahore) 2015. The foreword is by Parveen Qadir Agha, whose father Colonel Ehsan Qadir, from a

prominent Muslim family of Lahore, joined the INA and was imprisoned in the Red Fort 1945–46

131 Mateen Ahmed Ansari's grave is at Stanley Military Cemetery, Hong Kong, looked after by the Commonwealth War Graves Commission.

132 Khan, *The Raj at War*, pp. 294–5.

133 Correspondence of 6 and 14 July 1945, Auchinleck Papers AUC/1092 and AUC/1094.

134 Auchinleck to Viceroy, 24 November 1945 and 26 November 1945, Auchinleck Papers AUC/1121, and summary of military reactions to the INA recorded in the Punjab, 29 December 1945, Auchinleck Papers AUC/1125.

135 The charge was 'abetment to murder'.

136 1 January 1946, Auchinleck Papers AUC/1127.

137 Letter to commanders, 11 February 1946, Auchinleck Papers AUC/1137.

138 Jawaharlal Nehru letter to Auchinleck, 4 May 1946, Auchinleck Papers AUC/1149.

139 Exchange of letters between Edwina Mountbatten and Auchinleck, 8 and 9 July 1947, Auchinleck Papers AUC/1231 and AUC/1232.

CHAPTER 10 *To Delhi*

140 After independence Flagstaff House became Jawaharlal Nehru's home as India's Prime Minister and was renamed Teen Murthi Bhavan or 'Three Statues House', after the figures in the First World War memorial at its gate.

141 Shahid later asked Auchinleck if he might keep copies of some of the documents that passed his desk, recording his response as follows: 'He has no objection but said that if I ever intended to publish them it should not be in his lifetime.'

142 When I was in Delhi making the Gandhi series for the BBC in 2009 I tried to see the house, but it proved complicated: it remains government property and has been occupied by many ministers over the years, including Indira Gandhi. The then occupants were not keen on letting in a journalist with links to Pakistan, I was told.

143 Akbar S. Ahmed, *Jinnah, Pakistan and Islamic Identity: The Search for Saladin*, Routledge, 1997, pp. 112–13. In Punjab the Unionist party of Khizar Hayat Tiwana formed a government, with Congress and Sikh support.

144 Yasmin Khan, *The Great Partition*, Yale University Press, 2007, pp. 33–7.

145 'Cabinet Mission to India', Statement by Secretary of State for India in the House of Lords, 19 February 1946, Hansard.

146 Statement in House of Lords, 16 May 1946 and by Sir Stafford Cripps in the House of Commons on 18 July 1946, Hansard.

147 Victoria Schofield, *Wavell: Soldier and Statesman*, pp. 350–2.

148 Stanley Wolpert, *Jinnah of Pakistan*, 1984, p. 273.

149 Guha, *Gandhi*, p. 779; Maulana Abul Kalam Azad, *India Wins Freedom*, p. 158.

150 Gandhi, *Gandhi: The Man, His People and the Empire*, p. 521.

151 Azad, *India Wins Freedom*, pp. 164–5; Gandhi, *Gandhi*, p. 532.

152 Stanley Wolpert, *Shameful Flight: The Last Years of the British Empire in India*, Oxford University Press, 2006, p. 115; Schofield, *Wavell*, p. 354; Ayesha Jalal, *The Sole Spokesman: Jinnah, the Muslim League and the Demand for Pakistan*, Cambridge University Press, 1985, pp. 204–7.

153 *Meeting Dina Wadia on Madison Avenue*, 2002 interview by Andrew Whitehead, published after her death in 2017: http://www.andrew-whitehead.net.

154 English text of the broadcast of 17 May 1946, Auchinleck Papers AUC/1154.

155 Shaista Suhrawardy Ikramullah, *From Purdah to Parliament*, pp. 84–5.

156 Ibid., p. 131.

157 https://www.youtube.com/watch?v=VpT7AkECf8A.

158 A brother was part of Shahid and Tahirah's circle: S. M. Shrinagesh, who became India's Army Chief in 1955.

CHAPTER 11 *Dividing Lines*

159 Gandhi was also unhappy with the way Nehru had expressed himself, and wrote to tell him so (Gandhi, *Gandhi: The Man, His People and the Empire*, pp. 532–3).

160 Minutes of All India Muslim League Council meeting, Bombay, 27–29 July 1946, S. Sharifuddin Pirzada (ed.), *Foundations of Pakistan*, vol. II: *1924–1947*, National Publishing House, 1970. Jinnah's comments were in a letter to Attlee: Stanley Wolpert, *Shameful Flight: The Last Years of the British Empire in India*, Oxford University Press, 2006, p. 115.

161 Shaista Suhrawardy Ikramullah, *From Purdah to Parliament*, p. 133.

162 Francis Tuker, *While Memory Serves*, Cassell, 1950, pp. 156–61.

163 Gopal Patha speaking to Andrew Whitehead, *India: A People Partitioned*, BBC World Service, 5 June 1997.

164 Tuker, *While Memory Serves*, Appendix V (accounts of Major Livermore and Major Dorney).

165 Ikramullah, *From Purdah to Parliament*, pp. 136–7.

166 Sir Hugh Dow, November 1946, quoted in Wolpert, *Shameful Flight*, p. 125.

167 Shahid Hamid, *Disastrous Twilight: A Personal Record of the Partition of India*, Leo Cooper, 1986, p. 114.

168 King's diary entry for 5 December 1946, recorded in the official biography; John W. Wheeler-Bennett, *King George VI: His Life and Reign*, Macmillan, 1958, p. 706.

169 Victoria Schofield, *Wavell: Soldier and Statesman*, John Murray, 2006, pp. 364–5.

170 Francis Williams, *A Prime Minister Remembers: The War and Post-war Memoirs of the Rt Hon. Earl Attlee*, Heinemann, 1961, pp. 209–10.

171 King's diary entry for 17 December 1946, in Wheeler-Bennett, *King George VI*, pp. 709–11.

172 King's diary entry for 28 July 1942, in ibid., p. 703.

173 King's diary entry for 21/25 April 1943, in ibid., p. 700.

174 King's diary entry for 17 December 1946, in ibid., p. 711.

175 Wavell's messages to Attlee of 17 January and 5 February 1947, Prime Minister's Office records, The National Archives PREM 8/554.

176 Hamid, *Disastrous Twilight*, p. 133.

177 Nicklaus Thomas-Symonds, *Attlee: A Life in Politics*, I.B. Tauris, 2010, pp. 169 and 175.

178 Nicholas Mansergh et al. (eds), *The Transfer of Power* 1942–7, 12 vols, HMSO, 1970–83, vol. IX, pp. 773–5.

179 Evan Jenkins' top-secret note of 16 February 1947, ibid., pp. 728–31.

180 Auchinleck to Sir Geoffrey Scoones, staff officer to the Secretary of State for India, 2 March 1947, Auchinleck Papers AUC/1215.

181 Hamid, *Disastrous Twilight*, p. 142.

182 Schofield, *Wavell*, p. 376.

183 Gandhi, *Gandhi*, pp. 577–8; Guha, *Gandhi*, pp. 830–1.

184 Eqbal Ahmad, *Confronting Empire: Interviews with David Barsamian*, Haymarket Books, 2017, p. 100.

185 *Stories My Country Told Me – with Eqbal Ahmad on the Grand Trunk Road*, BBC1, 1996, https://vimeo.com/76753842; Ahmad, *Confronting Empire*, p. 2.

CHAPTER 12 *Mountbatten*

186 1941 census. See Gopal Krishan, 'Demography of the Punjab (1849–1947)', *Journal of Punjab Studies*, 11, no. 1 (2004), pp. 77–89.

187 Including Nankana Sahib, where Guru Nanak was born, and Gurdwara Sahib Kartarpur.

188 Ian Talbot and Gurharpal Singh, *The Partition of India*, Cambridge University Press, 2009, pp. 75–6.

189 As told to Andrew Whitehead, *India: A People Partitioned*, BBC World Service, 7 June 1997.

190 Abul Kalam Azad, *India Wins Freedom*, p. 198; Yasmin Khan, *The Great Partition*, Yale University Press, 2007, p. 86.

191 Saul David's *After Dunkirk: Churchill's Sacrifice of the Highland Division*, Brassey's, 1994, tells the story of Henry Swinburn's cohort of POWs.

192 The letters were carefully kept by Barbara and Henry's son David and then by David's widow Gillian.

193 Philip Ziegler, *Mountbatten: The Official Biography*, Phoenix Press, 2001 edn (first published 1985), p. 575.

194 Clement Attlee, *As It Happened*, Heinemann, 1954, p. 183; Alan Campbell-Johnson, *Mission with Mountbatten*, Robert Hale, 1951, p. 19. Campbell-Johnson had worked on Mountbatten's diaries while he was Supreme Commander in South-East Asia and came to Delhi as Press Attaché.

195 Transcript of BBC1's *Tonight*, on which Earl Mountbatten was interviewed by Dennis Tuohy, *Listener*, 30 October 1975; Nicklaus Thomas-Symonds, *Attlee*, p. 175.

196 Attlee, *As It Happened*, Heinemann, 1954, p. 183; Campbell-Johnson, *Mission with Mountbatten*, p. 19 ; *Transfer of Power* vol IX, pp 972–4.

197 Shahid Hamid, *Disastrous Twilight: A Personal Record of the Partition of India*, Leo Cooper, 1986, pp. 151–2.

198 Ibid., p. 155.

199 Ziegler, *Mountbatten*, p. 701.

200 Both meetings are described by Alan Campbell-Johnson in *Mission with Mountbatten*, pp. 45 and 56.

201 Gandhi, *Gandhi: The Man, His People and the Empire*, pp. 582–5.

202 Campbell-Johnson, *Mission with Mountbatten*, p. 55. Shahid records in his diary that Mountbatten told Auchinleck on 19 April 1947 that the emergence of Pakistan could not be avoided. Hamid, *Disastrous Twilight*, p. 163.

203   Ziegler, *Mountbatten*, p. 378.

204   Hastings Ismay, *The Memoirs of Lord Ismay*, Heinemann, 1960, p. 420.

205   Azad, *India Wins Freedom*, pp. 206–7.

206   Hamid, *Disastrous Twilight*, p. 167.

207   Ibid., pp. 167 and 152.

208   East Pakistan became Bangladesh in 1971.

209   20 April 1947, Auchinleck Papers AUC/1223, and 24 April 1947, Auchinleck Papers AUC/1224.

210   Ismay, *Memoirs*, p. 421.

211   Nehru to Mountbatten, letter of 11 May 1947, *Transfer of Power*, vol. X, p. 756.

212   Top-secret note of a meeting in Simla on 11 May 1947, ibid., pp. 762–6.

213   Ziegler, *Mountbatten*, pp. 378–9; Stanley Wolpert, *Shameful Flight: The Last Years of the British Empire in India*, Oxford University Press, 2006, p. 147; meeting of India committee of Cabinet, 19 May 1947, *Transfer of Power*, vol. X, pp. 896–7.

214   Cabinet minutes, *Transfer of Power*, vol. X, pp. 967–8.

215   Mountbatten's account of his meeting with Churchill, *Listener* interview transcript.

216   Hamid, *Disastrous Twilight*, p. 175.

217   Note sent by Jinnah to Mountbatten, with his views on the Draft Announcement, received on 17 May 1947, *Transfer of Power*, vol. X, p. 852.

218   Jinnah statement of 4 May 1947, National Archives FO 371/63533. Mountbatten recorded that Liaquat Ali Khan had told him in relation to Bengal and Punjab: 'You may make us bow to the inevitable.' 15 May 1947, *Transfer of Power*, vol. X, p. 825.

219   *Listener* interview transcript.

220   Prime Minister's statement and debate on India, Hansard, 3 June 1947.

221   Edward Penderel Moon, *Divide and Quit*, Chatto & Windus, 1961, p. 93.

222   Ziegler, *Mountbatten*, p. 388. Alan Campbell-Johnson does not explain what happened but writes that the first informal indication of the 15 August transfer of power came at the press conference: Campbell-Johnson, *Mission with Mountbatten*, p. 109.

CHAPTER 13   *Freedom and Farewells*

223   Sahibzada Aftab Ahmad Khan, Anis's father, was one of Aligarh's first generation of students and a key figure in its journey to become a

university in 1920. He was also a founding member of the Muslim League and led a delegation to plead Turkey's case to Woodrow Wilson in 1919.

224 Fatima Jinnah, *My Brother*, 2021, pp. 10 and 27.

225 Barbara Swinburn letter, 8 June 1947.

226 Ibid., 15 July 1947.

227 Barney White-Spunner, *Partition*, Simon & Schuster, 2017, p. 173.

228 Shahid's diary entry for 11 June 1947, Hamid, *Disastrous Twilight*, p. 186.

229 Auchinleck to Ismay, Chief of Staff to the Viceroy, 11 June 1947, Auchinleck Papers AUC/1229.

230 Alan Campbell-Johnson, *Mission with Mountbatten*, p. 112.

231 Related by Mountbatten in Viceroy's Personal Report No. 10, 27 June 1947, *Transfer of Power*, vol. XI, p. 682.

232 Yasmin Khan, *The Great Partition*, Yale University Press, 2007, pp. 118–19.

233 Hastings Ismay, *The Memoirs of Lord Ismay*, Heinemann, 1960, p. 431; Campbell-Johnson, *Mission with Mountbatten*, p. 118.

234 Hamid, *Disastrous Twilight*, p. 186.

235 Viceroy's Personal Report No. 11, 4 July 1947, *Transfer of Power*, vol. XI, pp. 899–900.

236 Hamid, *Disastrous Twilight*, p. 200; Ziegler, *Mountbatten*, pp. 398–99.

237 Governor of Punjab Evan Jenkins' description recorded in Alan Campbell-Johnson's diary for 1 July 1947, *Mission with Mountbatten*, p. 126.

238 Nehru to Mountbatten, 22 June 1947, *Transfer of Power*, vol. XI, pp. 561–2.

239 Stanley Wolpert, *Shameful Flight: The Last Years of the British Empire in India*, Oxford University Press, 2006, p. 160.

240 For the format and outcome of the votes in the provinces, see Ayesha Jalal, *The Sole Spokesman: Jinnah, the Muslim League and the Demand for Pakistan*, Cambridge University Press, 1994. p. 287 and p. 290.

241 Beaumont and George Abell spoke to Edward Penderel Moon, former civil servant, who was working on the papers.

242 Simon Scott Plummer, 'How Mountbatten Bent the Rules and the Indian Border', *Daily Telegraph*, 24 February 1992.

243 Andrew Roberts, *Eminent Churchillians*, Weidenfeld & Nicolson, 1994, contains an essay on Mountbatten.

244 Hamid, *Disastrous Twilight*, pp. 220–1. Brigadier A. M. Raza was the responding Pakistani.

245 Shahid Hamid, *Early Years of Pakistan: Including the Period from August 1947 to 1959*, Ferozsons, 1993, p. 11.

246 Krishen Khanna became a prominent artist of India. Mallika Ahluwalia, *Divided by Partition, United by Resilience: 21 Inspirational Stories from 1947*, Rupa, 2018, pp. 87–90.

247 Khushdeva Singh, in Mushirul Hasan (ed.), *India Partitioned: The Other Face of Freedom*, vol. II, Roli Books, 1997, pp. 89–95.

248 Hameeda Akhtar Husain Raipuri, *My Fellow Traveller*, pp. 296–8.

249 Kuldip Nayar in Ahluwalia, *Divided by Partition, United by Resilience*, p. 103.

250 Campbell-Johnson, *Mission with Mountbatten*, pp. 151–2.

251 Hamid, *Disastrous Twilight*, p. 222.

252 Evan Jenkins' note to Mountbatten from Government House, Lahore, 13 August 1947, *Transfer of Power*, vol. XII, pp. 700–2.

253 Peter Rees and Reginald Savory, also a general on Auchinleck's staff, are both in the group pictured with Shahid and Tahirah in Simla in July 1947, at Shahnaz's fifth birthday.

254 Auchinleck's Note on Situation in Punjab Boundary Force Area, for Joint Defence Council, 15 August 1947, *Transfer of Power*, vol. XII, pp. 734–6.

255 Hamid, *Disastrous Twilight*, p. 228.

256 National Archives of Pakistan, Address of 11 August 1947.

257 Wilfrid Russell, *Indian Summer*, Thacker, 1951, p. 127. The minister was Jogendra Nath Mandal, who also chaired inaugural sessions of the Constituent Assembly in Pakistan. After Jinnah's death he was sidelined, faced discrimination and left Pakistan for India.

258 Flight Lieutenant David Sheehan, whose daughter contacted me after I initially wrote about this in the *Sunday Times* in 2014.

259 Hamid, *Disastrous Twilight*, p. 234.

260 Lt Col. J. C. Bell, 18 October 1947, Auchinleck Papers AUC/1268.

261 Hamid, *Disastrous Twilight*, pp. 236–7.

262 Ibid., p. 240.

CHAPTER 14 *Crisis*

263 The Muslim League leader was Hussain Shaheed Suhrawardy.

264 Eyewitness Soroj Mukherjee, https://www.youtube.com/watch?v= kxA4uW3mWp4.

265 The house in Calcutta was Hyderi Manzil: *Gandhi: The Road to Freedom*, BBC TV, 2009.

266 *Partition Voices: L.K. Advani*, transcript and audio of interview by Andrew Whitehead in 1997 www.andrewwhitehead.net.

267 The full convoy included Ayub Khan, future Pakistani leader, who was evacuating his family.

268 Eqbal Ahmad, *Confronting Empire: Interviews with David Barsamian*, Haymarket Books, 2017, pp. 101–2; *Stories My Country Told Me – with Eqbal Ahmad on the Grand Trunk Road*, BBC1, 1996, https://vimeo.com/76753842.

269 Penderel Moon, *Divide and Quit*, Chatto & Windus, 1961, pp. 134–5.

270 Ibid., pp. 259–60.

271 Shahid Hamid, *Disastrous Twilight: A Personal Record of the Partition of India*, p. 253.

272 Mountbatten to Auchinleck, 26 September 1947, Auchinleck Papers AUC/1260.

273 Hamid, *Disastrous Twilight*, p. 258.

274 Auchinleck report on Situation in India and Pakistan, 28 September 1947, Auchinleck Papers AUC/1262.

275 Minutes of the Joint Defence Council meeting, Lahore, 16 October 1947, Auchinleck Papers AUC/1267.

276 Shahid Hamid, *Early Years of Pakistan: Including the Period from August 1947 to 1959*, Ferozsons, 1993, p. 84.

277 From Nehru's note of 17 June 1947, *Transfer of Power*, vol. XI, p. 442.

278 Wilfrid Russell, *Indian Summer*, Thacker, 1951, p. 101.

279 *Transfer of Power*, vol. XI, pp. 442–8. The jailed leader was Sheikh Abdullah, who became Indian-administered Kashmir's Prime Minister and later Chief Minister.

280 Viceroy's Personal Report, 16 August 1947, *Transfer of Power*, vol. XII, p. 769. A 'Standstill Agreement' understanding was reached with Pakistan in August 1947, continuing existing arrangements pending a settlement.

281 Victoria Schofield, *Kashmir in Conflict*, pp. 41, 46–7.

282 Andrew Whitehead, *India: A People Partitioned*, BBC World Service, 8 August 1997.

283 The precise sequence of events remains contested. See Victoria Schofield, *Kashmir in Conflict*, ibid., pp. 52–4.

284 Ian Stephens, *Horned Moon*, Ernest Benn, 1966, pp. 109–10.

285 Hastings Ismay, *The Memoirs of Lord Ismay*, Heinemann, 1960, p. 444.

286 Telegram from Supreme Commander to London, 28 October 1947, Auchinleck Papers AUC/1275.

287 India blames Pakistan for years of unrest and insurgency in Indian-administered Kashmir.

288 PA-1 was General Akbar Khan, veteran of the First World War, who had been with Shahid's brother-in-law Anis when they landed at Marseille in 1939

289 Hamid, *Early Years of Pakistan*, p. 36.

290 Ibid. The house, Bachan Niwas, still stands and is now Fatima Jinnah Women's University. Shahnaz recalls members of Mohan Singh's family returning in the 1980s and being given permission to break into a wall in the house, where some treasures had been hidden in 1947.

CHAPTER 15 *New Beginnings*

291 Emboldened by a clash in the Rann of Kutch coastal border in April 1965, which resulted in mediation and the gaining of territory, Pakistan sent troops and irregular fighters across the Kashmir ceasefire line. It underestimated both Indian capability and response. Indian troops crossed the international border in Punjab and advanced on Lahore. In late September Pakistan accepted a UN Security Council ceasefire resolution and was promised by the US and the UK that they would help settle the Kashmir dispute. See Victoria Schofield, *Kashmir in Conflict: India, Pakistan and the Unending War*, I.B. Tauris, 2010, pp. 107–11.

292 Shahid was happy to leave ISI and get back to commanding troops in 1950, as he said intelligence jobs had the effect of making you suspect everyone and believe no one. Hamid, *Early Years of Pakistan*, p. 69.

293 Kodandera 'Nanda' Cariappa: *When I Was a Prisoner of War in Pakistan*, *Outlook India*, 10 August 2015. He was held for four months and repatriated in 1966.

294 The 1971 India–Pakistan War came after the constitutional deadlock arising from parliamentary elections in 1970 and a military crackdown in East Pakistan. A civil war began and India intervened on the side of the Bangladeshi liberation movement. See Ian Talbot, *Pakistan: A New History*, Hurst & Company, London, (2015 edition), pp. 94–6.

295 Shahid Hamid, *Early Years of Pakistan*, pp. 133–4. In the mid-1950s the process of Constitution-making intensified political differences

between the two wings of the country and President Iskander Mirza's favouring of increased centralisation stoked unrest in East Pakistan. In October 1958 Mirza abrogated the Constitution and made the Army Chief, Ayub Khan, the Chief Martial Law Administrator. Within three weeks Ayub deposed Mirza, who was forced into exile.

296 Ayub Khan later introduced 'Basic Democracy', a system that included 80,000 'Basic Democrats' electing the President. Ian Talbot, *Pakistan: A New History,* Hurst & Company, London, (2015 edition), p. 76

297 'Not a man I ever thought very highly of' was Attlee's view of Jinnah: Francis Williams, *A Prime Minister Remembers: The War and Post-war Memoirs of the Rt Hon. Earl Attlee,* Heinemann, 1961, p. 211. Attlee's 'hands off' approach and lack of reply to Jinnah, as well as Mountbatten's concerns over his own position during the Kashmir crisis, are detailed in Nicklaus Thomas-Symonds, *Attlee: A Life in Politics,* I.B. Tauris, 2010, pp. 180–3.

298 Viceroy's Personal Report No. 3, April 1947, *Transfer of Power,* vol. X, p. 300. The conversation with Jinnah's biographer Stanley Wolpert took place in 1979: 'From the sourness of his face at every mention of Jinnah's name, I could see how negatively Mountbatten felt about the Muslim leader.' Stanley Wolpert, *Shameful Flight,* 2006, p. 10.

299 John Osman related this in a letter to the *Spectator* in 2004: 'To this day his own judgment on how he had performed in India rings in my ears and in my memory. As one who dislikes the tasteless use in writing of the dictionary's "vulgar slang" word, I shall permit myself an exception this time because it is the only honest way of reporting accurately what the last Viceroy of India thought about the way he had done his job: fucked it up.' *Spectator,* Letters, 4 September 2004.

S. Shahid Hamid

R. S. S. East

Muslim University

Aligarh

Shahid Hamid Esq.

Student, First After,

Minto Circle, A

Muslim University.

Aligarh.

For some years now I have felt the
Black Wisdom Paper to an minute the
on paper. In years to come, those who
apprehensive and objective account of e...
feed our destiny and brought to the
... we may be for the brink of desaster
... I know powerful was the feeling that
... it is Hes will that prevails and
... or obeying them ...
... a jury only ...
... he had ...